INTERNATIONAL ORGANIZATION AND THE
CONSERVATION OF NATURE

# INTERNATIONAL ORGANIZATION AND THE CONSERVATION OF NATURE

Robert Boardman

INDIANA UNIVERSITY PRESS
Bloomington

Manufactured in Hong Kong

**Library of Congress Cataloging in Publication Data**

Boardman, Robert.
    International organization and the conservation of
nature.

    Bibliography: p.
    1.  Nature conservation – History.  2.  Nature
conservation – Societies, etc. – History.  3.  Nature
conservation – International cooperation – History.
I.  Title.
QH75.B6     333.78     80-8638
ISBN 0-253-16474-5    1 2 3 4 5 85 84 83 82 81

For Christine

# Contents

# Preface

It has been my aim in this book to make a provisional assessment of the work of international organisations dealing with the conservation of nature. This activity dates back more than a century. Governments, as opposed to scattered groups of scientists or naturalists joined in non-governmental associations, took part in conferences and signed conventions on the subject before the First World War. However, history is easy to forget: there is a niche for the chronicler. Within the field of international wildlife conservation, a mild form of amnesia can, perhaps, be functional. It is useful to be able to stress the newness of current strategies, the greater effectiveness of professionals over pioneers in coping with touchy governmental egos, or the advances in scientific knowledge that have made possible wiser policy recommendations than were available to past generations. But for those outside the field (and, it must be said, for many in it), the problem is simply that the historical record is little known. At the Stockholm conference on the human environment in 1972, Jean-Paul Harroy has observed, everybody had completely forgotten Lake Success[1] — the conference of 1949 that played a major part in putting endangered species of wildlife on the international agenda.

This is not to deny that there have been changes over the last century or so. Stockholm embraced concerns larger than the preservation of the marsupial banded anteater. But the past has a way of poking its way through even the best laid novelties of the present. In relation to wild fauna and flora, conservation has taken the place of protection in the lexicon. The distinction is not merely semantic. Older approaches looked at dwindling numbers of some species — particularly birds and the larger mammals — or at the encroachments of man on landscapes of great natural beauty, and identified needs such as the passing or tightening (or better enforcement) of laws on hunting, poaching, or the trade in animal parts and products, and for the setting aside of wilderness areas to be accorded special protection. Contemporary approaches, emphasising a more dynamic, ecologically grounded picture in which the intelligent use of the resources of nature was as much a priority as their preservation for ethical or aesthetic reasons, have added a fresh layer to this melange; but they have not taken its place.

Similarly, the hitching of wildlife to the various engines of political radicalism was largely a phenomenon of the 1970s, but the linking by way of ecological reasoning of the survival of wild nature with the survival of man was made much earlier, by Frank Fraser Darling and Fairfield Osborn in the 1940s, for example, or by the Swiss conservationist Paul Sarasin, who in the early 1900s took the leading role in the establishment on the eve of the First World War of the first intergovernmental organisation with responsibilities for nature preservation. It is a premise of this study, then, that there is value in tracing back the preoccupations of the present day to their largely forgotten origins or earlier counterparts — in watching the emergence of attempts to protect threatened species through the regulation of international trade, for example, from the inclusion of one such provision in the convention of 1900 on the preservation of African fauna, to the construction of a full treaty on the subject, the Convention on International Trade in Endangered Species (CITES), in 1973.

Book-length studies by political scientists or international lawyers of the more general subject of international co-operation on these matters have been rather rare. They include Sherman Hayden's *The International Protection of Wild Life* (1941),[2] and, more recently, *Okhrana Prirody i Mezhdunarodnye Otnosheniia* by V. A. Chichvarin (1970).[3] Several general histories were written in the pre-1914 and interwar years. The proposition that there are questions here that could usefully be tackled in greater depth by political scientists has been put forward in the technical literature.[4] My reservations about entering such a specialised area, in which experts from a variety of fields of the biological sciences abound, have also been quietened by the hunch that an outsider might be better able to approach it with a certain detachment. This is a subject, after all, in which passions are easily aroused, man is easily upper-cased, and differences of opinion are easily magnified into grounds for political divorce. At the same time, I am no plumber. The image of the political scientist as a person who knows how to bend pipes, pull levers, and give things the odd kick so that they work better is not one that has shaped either the research or its conclusions. Nor have I attempted a comprehensive history and survey of the whole field. Even for those questions on which the book concentrates I am all too aware of gaps and compressions. There is here a rich seam to be mined by a future historian of international organisation.

*Chester Basin*                                                                                    R. B.
*November 1979*

# Acknowledgments

Research for this book was begun in 1974. It is a pleasure to be able at last to thank the many individuals who have helped me in this task, although limitations of space prohibit a full account of my indebtedness. I should particularly like to thank officials of IUCN and WWF, then in Morges. David Munro, as Director-General, made the documentary resources of IUCN available to me, while Arnold Koenen was invaluable in guiding me through the union's library holdings. Sir Peter Scott, Chairman of WWF, and Lee Talbot took time out from busy schedules to discuss at some length various points in the history of international conservation. At the London offices of ICBP, Phyllis Barclay-Smith could not have been more helpful in giving me the opportunity to study the Council's past and present work.

During the course of the research I was fortunate in being able to visit a number of centres of conservation activity, including the Council of Europe, Strasbourg; IWRB, Slimbridge; LIPU, Florence; WHO, Geneva; UNEP, EAWLS, AWLF, the UNESCO Africa office, and WWF-Kenya, in Nairobi; FAO, Rome; and the Nature Conservancy Council, FPS and the TPC, London. I should like to thank those officials who helped to make these visits so rewarding. In addition to using documentary collections at several of these places, I also made use of other libraries and must extend a general note of thanks to the staffs of the Scott Polar Research Institute, and the Manuscripts Room of the University Library, Cambridge; the Science Library, and the Libraries of Imperial College, the British Museum (Natural History), and the Royal Institute of International Affairs, London; the McMillan Memorial Library and the Libraries of the University of Nairobi and the East African Natural History Society, Nairobi; and the interlibrary loan staff of Dalhousie University's Killam Library. Special thanks are due to Duncan Poore, Sir Hugh Elliott, Mona Bjorklund, Jean-Pierre Ribaut, Peter Sand, Colin Holloway, Peter Jackson, Gilbert Child, Moira Warland, Hugh Lamprey, Theresa Sexton, Nicholas Polunin and Gren Lucas. Others who assisted by correspondence included Gerardo Budowski, Jean-Paul Harroy, Sir Frank Fraser Darling, Harold J. Coolidge, Jr., Raymond Dasmann, Charles Jonkel and Norman Myers. I am also grateful for information on the histories and work of various organisations to Jeremy

Mallinson, Jersey Wildlife Preservation Trust; Richard Faust, Zoologische Gesellschaft von 1858, Frankfurt a.M.; William Conway, NYZS; A. A. Inozemtsev, All-Russian Society for Conservation of Nature; and Victor Sebek, Advisory Committee on Oil Pollution of the Sea, London.

Two former colleagues, Michael Schatzberg and Kwasi Nyamekye, respectively brought to my attention some useful African and UNCHE materials. Joseph Needham kindly gave permission for me to use his UNESCO documents deposited at the University of Cambridge. Aleksandra Kurowska translated for me the article by Zbigniew Kawecki cited in Chapter 3.

Finally, but certainly not least, John Goormaghtigh made office facilities available at the Centre de Recherches sur les Institutions Internationales in Geneva during the autumn term, 1977–8, and Georgette Dustour helped in numerous ways during my stay at the Centre. I am grateful to the Office of the President, Republic of Kenya, for permission to carry out research while in Nairobi, and to officials of the Department of Tourism and Wildlife for agreeing to meet with me. I should like to thank the Social Sciences and Humanities Research Council for financial assistance towards research during 1977–8.

My family bore the brunt of my absences of spirit while writing after our return from the travels of that year. Without their love and support it is doubtful that I could have stayed the course.

R. B.

# List of acronyms

| | |
|---|---|
| ACIWLP | American Committee for International Wild Life Protection |
| ASP | African Special Project |
| AWLF | African Wildlife Leadership Foundation |
| CCTA | Commission for Technical Co-operation in Africa |
| CEQ | Council on Environmental Quality |
| CIC | Conseil International de la Chasse |
| CITES | Convention on International Trade in Endangered Species |
| EAWLS | East African Wild Life Society |
| ECG | Ecosystem Conservation Group |
| ECOSOC | Economic and Social Council (UN) |
| FAO | Food and Agriculture Organisation |
| FPS | Fauna Preservation Society |
| FZS | Frankfurt Zoological Society |
| GATT | General Agreement on Tariffs and Trade |
| IBP | International Biological Programme |
| IBP/CT | IBP section on conservation of terrestrial biological communities |
| IBRD | International Bank for Reconstruction and Development |
| ICBP | International Council for Bird Preservation |
| ICSU | International Council of Scientific Unions |
| IFAN | Institut Français d'Afrique Noire |
| IOPN | International Office for the Protection of Nature |
| IUBS | International Union of Biological Sciences |
| IUCN | International Union for Conservation of Nature and Natural Resources |
| IUPN | International Union for the Protection of Nature |
| IWC | International Whaling Commission |
| IWRB | International Waterfowl Research Bureau |
| LIPU | Lega Italiana per la Protezione degli Uccelli |
| MAB | Man and the Biosphere Programme |
| NIEO | New International Economic Order |

| | |
|---|---|
| NYZS | New York Zoological Society |
| OAS | Organisation of American States |
| OAU | Organisation of African Unity |
| OURS | Orang Utan Recovery Service |
| RSPB | Royal Society for the Protection of Birds |
| SCAR | Scientific Committee on Antarctic Research |
| SCAR/WGB | SCAR Working Group on Biology |
| SPFE | Society for the Preservation of the Fauna of the Empire |
| SSC | Survival Service Commission |
| TPC | Threatened Plants Committee |
| UNCHE | UN Conference on the Human Environment (1972) |
| UNEP | UN Environment Programme |
| UNESCO | UN Educational, Scientific and Cultural Organisation |
| UNSCCUR | UN Scientific Conference on the Conservation and Utilisation of Resources (1949) |
| WCS | World Conservation Strategy |
| WHO | World Health Organisation |
| WWF | World Wildlife Fund |

# Part I

# Introduction: International organisation and the conservation of nature

# 1 The changing character of international organisation

> All nature is marvellous
> Aristotle, *On the parts of animals*

The relation between nature and politics has for long been a close one. The rulers of Indian and Chinese states gave protection to wild species in antiquity. Wildlife preservation officers earned high salaries under the later Han dynasty in China. One Northern Wei emperor ordered tributary states not to make any more offerings of live birds and mammals because of the serious reduction in their numbers that this practice had entailed.[1] The modern practice of nature conservation, not now dependent upon the whims of monarchs, has more diverse origins. National parks in the United States have from their inception been tied to definitions of nationhood that have allowed their supporters to gain political leverage by laying stress on their apolitical character; those in Canada emerged initially as a way of resolving the dispute which had arisen over rival claims to discovery of mineral hot springs near Banff railway station in 1885.[2] During the course of the present century, the natural environment has become a more intrusive subject of political debate. The millinery trade was a major target for attack by bird protection organisations in Britain in the early 1900s. And in 1978, in an episode the more bizarre aspects of which lost United States conservationists a measure of public goodwill, the Supreme Court upheld a decision to halt work on the almost completed Tellico dam on the grounds that this would destroy the habitat of the snail darter, a small and obscure member of the perch family.

Animals, often to their cost, pay no attention to lines drawn on maps. Conservation of wildlife has not only become more firmly implanted in the laws and domestic politics of states, it has also taken its place as a peculiarly tenacious topic of international discourse. Unless coincidentally, as with ocean coasts, rivers or mountains, the boundaries of states were not marked out on the basis of ecological processes. Species that do not migrate across borders may nonetheless form part of the international trade in trophies, products and specimens. Still others may, typically, live in some kind of threatened status in a country other than that of the would-be conserver. A nation's reputation can be tarnished by its government's treatment of a species which, justifiably or not, happens to have become a focal point of attention outside. The requirement of more thorough and effective international regulation has therefore been, not surprisingly, a refrain frequently taken up by national as well as by international conservation bodies. It is with the latter that this study is particularly concerned.

*Functions, networks and change*

However, the large number of organisations that could potentially be held to fit this description makes some pruning necessary. National groups, especially in richer countries or in those with traditional overseas interests, have occasionally taken an active external role in providing funds for ecological research into local problems, education and training, the maintenance of protected areas or the design of management plans in developing states. Some government agencies have also been innovative pursuers of broader international conservation regimes. In this they have been assisted by the growing complexity and specialisation of modern government, which in some settings can enhance the degree of autonomy of technical low-priority departments. But the most characteristic actor on global environmental affairs is the non-governmental organisation (NGO). Taxonomies are elusive here. The International Union for Conservation of Nature and Natural Resources (IUCN), for example, the central non-governmental actor in this area, has a large state and state agency membership. The fact produces intriguing policy dilemmas. Some organisations, that is, have the option of acting chiefly either as quasi-intergovernmental monitoring bodies in conjunction with other regulatory agencies, or as collaborators with other NGOs in displays of verbal (and sometimes physical) protest against whalers, hunters or corporate developers. Both strategies can, of course, be attempted; but the success of either can also depend in part on the degree to which a hankering for the other can be suppressed. As Huxley once suggested for the slippery term species, we should perhaps rather be thinking in terms of a gradation — in this case of organisations of varying governmental complexions. Several intergovernmental institutions have in addition incorporated at least some aspects of wildlife conservation into their range of tasks. Within the United Nations system, the Food and Agriculture Organisation (FAO) and the UN

Educational, Scientific and Cultural Organisation (UNESCO) are old hands at this game. They have been joined since 1973 by the UN Environment Programme (UNEP). At the regional level, both the Council of Europe and the European Community have been among the institutions that have extended their competence into such areas.

This diversity is paralleled in areas other than environmental conservation. Three trends can be discerned: first, an increase in the sheer numbers of organisations that can with justification be described as international; second, the emergence of new kinds of actors different from the classical intergovernmental organisations that first made their appearance in nineteenth-century Europe; and third, an expansion of the inventory of functions performed by international organisations of these various types, and the adoption by different ones of activities stretching from the military defence of groups of states to the setting of quotas for fisheries.[3]

In this more complex milieu, the questions that the observer can most appropriately ask have altered. The traditionally germane one, though, is still pertinent. It can be couched in this way: to what extent, if at all, can such organisations be viewed as agents of change in the international system? The answer clearly depends partly on the type of organisation being investigated. For the major intergovernmental institutions, the debates of the 1970s on the capacity of such bodies to deal effectively, if incrementally, with global problems of food, resources, population or the environment mirrored those of the 1930s between realists and idealists.[4] At that time, such bodies could be seen on the one hand as political entities, as more than the sum of their constituent member-state parts, capable of initiating change, of diminishing the incidence of international conflict, and of ushering in a new order resting on the progressively greater involvement of international institutions in economic and social matters. On the other hand, sceptics have always had ample ammunition: the rhetoric and repetitiveness of assemblies, the exploiting or ignoring by nation-states of international organisations depending on their own definitions of their national interests, and the evident failure of these clubs to curb unruly behaviour or to eke out the communal spirit of the pliant. Security, economic or social goals could better be sought in the ordered anarchy of an international system free of the expectations raised in the gullible by ersatz world governments. One difference in the later period, however, was the locus of the idealist point. In the 1930s it tended to move within a clearly defined, and confined, space: idealism was synonymous with support for the institutions of the day; the League of Nations had withered through neglect. By the 1970s, idealism, though the word itself had lost something of its earlier respectability, was associated more with the search for alternative forms. From this perspective, established international organisations fared badly. Many — UNESCO in particular — seemed to have succumbed to political squabbling and bureaucratic sclerosis. Others — such as UNEP — had teething problems that gave way not to a vigorous youth but rather to a cranky and timid adolescence.

Views like these may be characteristic of some NGOs, but the variety of organisations covered by this term — even excluding multinational corporations — can make generalising a hazardous sport. Some have established working connections with state agencies. The relationships thus created make for further difficulties of definition. 'We should think of "international organisation" ', Raymond Hopkins has suggested in a study of United States bureaucracy, 'as including those officials who are part of the organisational networks that perform international functions, whether they are formally in international or domestic bureaucracies, within governments or the private sector.'[5] Others have a quasi-supranational authority. The International Committee of the Red Cross has this, the author of a recent study has pointed out, in the form of a right of automatic access to certain detainees in international armed conflict.[6] Organisations less securely established, with roles less clearly legitimised, have made use of the international arena to extend the limits of domestic posturing. Several unofficial institutions, by gaining acceptance as centres of information gathering or for the harvesting of expertise, have assumed a less tangible but nonetheless significant position in relation to certain sets of issues: among these are the Club of Rome, Amnesty International, or, on arms control and disarmament affairs, the Stockholm International Peace Research Institute.[7] The roots of change in such instances may lie not so much in direct attempts to influence other actors, as in the ricochetting process whereby problems come to be defined, issues dissected and possible courses of action by the international community evaluated.

There is a further consequence of the proliferation of international organisations. The single-actor case study is still needed, but requires supplementing with investigations of the relations between organisations. In an area like environmental conservation, NGOs do not act simply as undifferentiated mouthpieces for the articulation of demands and the expression of common concerns. They are as often competitors: for prestige, territory or leadership roles. They may collaborate on longer term projects, and coalesce on an *ad hoc* basis when immediate questions erupt. Communications may break down completely and be difficult and painful to restore. The existence of state and semi-official bodies, and of full-fledged intergovernmental institutions, adds a further dimension of complexity.

Especially since many of the organisations at the non-governmental level are small, certain individuals may be crucial to the workings of the system. Research on such networks is beginning to make headway in the study of international organisation.[8] It follows too, probably, that no institution such as a world government is likely to be set up in any given functional area, though agencies with supranational powers may emerge in some. The jealous protection of hard-won niches is not a trait of which sovereign states have a monopoly. Differing forms of governing — considered as a process — can be expected, however, to be a growing feature of international organisation during the next two decades, to judge by the experimentalism that marked the 1970s. Non-governmental bodies are already adept at at least three kinds of activity: prodding states and intergovernmental organisations into taking action; probing for information; and reinterpreting the policies of these more authoritative institutions to wider and potentially critical publics. The three functions, it should be added, were adapted from a list given in a recent essay not on NGOs but on the changing role of parliamentary opposition parties in western democracies.[9]

*Scope of the study*

The main body of the research takes up three central questions that have now been touched on in more general terms. These are, first, the efforts by organisations to define problems more precisely, and their approaches to the task of establishing a basis of data and ideas on which the policies of states and other actors can be built — of cultivating, in other words, wider acceptance of the expertise which is the core of their legitimacy (Chapter 4); second, attempts to influence the behaviour of states, whether directly through advances and pressures, or more indirectly through means such as the promotion of international conventions covering particular aspects of the subject of nature conservation, or propaganda, education and the spread of information (Chapter 5); and third, the ways in which the broader network of interactor relations has evolved and has been structured, and the patterns of relationships that have emerged between the various conservation bodies at the non-governmental and governmental levels (Chapter 6). The study focuses primarily on a central nucleus of actors. The historical background to the establishment in 1948 of IUCN is the subject of Chapter 3. Three case studies deal with particular sets of conservation problems and examine the manner in which international organisations have tackled them: the circumpolar regions, east African wildlife, and the protection of migratory birds in Europe (Chapters 7–9).

Imposing a sense of order on the facts can be risky and costly. From the point of view of the actors themselves, a sense of disorder and fragmentation can be uppermost. An orderly progression of events may be glimpsed by some but, as was noted in the Preface, past developments may be more often ignored, forgotten or just not known. Uncertainty about the future, confusion about the present, despair sometimes, frustration more frequently, bitterness about the tactics of enemies or a resigned acceptance of the foibles of friends — these are all part of the basic data of the international politics of the wild. A fundamental problem stems from the difficulty of persuading sceptical outsiders of the importance of conservation issues. The next chapter looks at the character and at the political and environmental contexts of these questions.

# 2 Conserving nature: issues and perspectives

> Once, where detected worldlings now
> Do penitential jobs,
> Exterminated species played
> Who had not read their Hobbes.
> W. H. Auden, *Islands*[1]

The impulse to conserve wild nature is a distinctively western and urban one. It has flourished in diverse political environments. Marxist attacks on the destructive effect on nature of capitalism have found a niche here, as have conservative defences of the wildlife and ways of life of the countryside against encroachments from the city. Scientific approaches live side by side with more traditional outlooks criticised for their alleged emotionalism and anthropomorphism. Conservation of species and their habitats is seen on the one hand as integral to the survival of the human species, and on the other as having a profound irrelevance to human needs in developing countries. This diversity has its origins in the changing conceptions of nature to be found in western Europe from the late eighteenth century, in their turn a consequence of urban and industrial pressure on wild spaces, and of reaction to the casual ease with which rural landowners could tame their landscape for aesthetic effect. Variety is reflected in political organisation. There is here no one group for all seasons, but rather a continuous process of change, of fragmentation and consolidation, birth and extinction, harmony and rivalry. When conservation of nature has entered the agendas of interstate relations, or of intergovernmental organisations, it has often been difficult even to define the scope of the subject satisfactorily, let alone assure a degree of co-ordination among political actors.

## Traditional uses and attitudes

The promotion or hindrance of conservation goals, whether inadvertently or on a planned basis, is an inextricable part of traditional agricultural practice. At the simplest level, animals could be domesticated; some used for destroying pests, carrying loads, clearing forest, transporting produce, sending messages, ploughing fields, or hunting for food or by-products; and others kept at bay, controlled or eliminated. Some practices draw on an understanding of the more complex relations between species of flora and fauna. Preservation of the wildlife of hedgerows in England was a part of good land use. Fishermen's traditional authorities on the central Niger forbade access to certain parts of the river at fixed times so as to let wild animals wait there for the floodwaters, and prohibited the use of nets with too fine a mesh.[2]

Responses to wild or domestic animals and plants have also been an adjunct of social organisation. The conventions by which these have been used by primitive peoples as symbols of categories of men are not really any more eccentric than our own, Edmund Leach has maintained, but are simply more noticeable in a technologically restricted environment.[3] The history of the portrayal of nature and of different species in the arts provides clues to this symbolism, and to the evolution of attitudes.

In Greek literature in the Homeric and later periods, for example, no firm distinction exists between wild and tamed nature. The same word was often used indiscriminately to refer to any fertile spot, usually associated with deity.[4] Nature and landscape could be employed as stage sets for actions by men, as in the famous (though ecologically dubious) account of trees, birds and flowers that opens the fifth book of the *Odyssey*, or in the descriptions of forests to be found in the Indian *Mahábhárata* and *Rámáyana* epics. The 'wondrously wild wood' through which Sir Gawain rode achieves a similar effect, while the 'abrupt promontories riddled with kraken-caves' of the *Beowulf* seascape serve to define more sharply the menace of the unknown.[5] Medieval animal symbolism, as in the bestiaries of the twelfth to fourteenth centuries, blurred the boundaries between the human and the divine, or the real and the fabulous. The chimaera, sphinx, lamia, triton, unicorn, griffin or dragon each had distinctive characters; while the apparently bewildering variety of strange forms present in nature — glimpsed in such events as the presentation to the King of England in the thirteenth century of an elephant brought back from the Crusades — lent support to the view of the natural world as a manifestation of divine truth. The visual portrayal of Christian concepts was, accordingly, an important function of the representation in art of different species.[6] In other traditions, as in Nepali painting,[7] exotic animals could be depicted in order simply to satisfy an audience's taste for the novel. But in neither approach was concern for realism or for recreation of the moods of nature uppermost in the minds of artists. Animals have been good material for didactic use by writers, as, more recently, in Orwell's *Animal Farm* or Adams' *The Plague Dogs*; but here too the degree of attention to naturalistic detail has varied considerably. In the children's tales of Grahame or Potter, one critic has written, the animals are really 'Englishmen in funny zippered suits, often with a layer of human clothing added on top'.[8]

In the eighteenth century the balance began to be tipped in the other direction, away from man as the centre. In particular, mountains, once considered best avoided, became objects of fascination. The changing outlook contrasted with that of the previous two centuries. Then, as W. G. Hoskins has observed of England, people 'took their own wild places for granted. There are no contemporary descriptions of the woods, the heaths and the moors as scenery. The taste for "scenery" had yet to develop, and the few travellers who mention the wild places do so only in terms of distaste, for such country produced nothing useful and was inclined to be dangerous for strangers'.[9] Good nature was suitably tamed nature. A taste for wilderness was, according to Trevelyan, 'an inevitable reaction on the part of a society growing over-civilised'.[10] Nature took on at times almost mystical attributes: a source of replenishment, or a base from which to criticise the shortcomings and artificialities of contemporary society. This distinction between the human world and the natural world was essentially an urban one, a product of the pressures of city living and the availability of leisure time. From it also arose changes of attitude towards particular species of wild animals. These were no longer simply either useful, a nuisance, or irrelevant to man: some could be fascinating, subjects to inspire and excite the imagination of writers and artists.

As early as 1795 the new approach was censured by Schiller in an essay which contrasted what he claimed to be the simple good sense of the Greek approach to nature with that of the poets of his day. 'We find very few traces in Greek poetry of the sentimental interest with which the modern world looks upon scenes of nature and natural characters.... [The Greeks] do not cling to nature with the emotion, spirituality or gentle melancholy of the moderns.'[11] The force of this clinging has led some writers to suspect hidden motives. Raymond Williams has argued that in Europe in the eighteenth and nineteenth centuries wild regions of forest or mountain became, like the landscaped parks before them, for the most part objects of conspicuous aesthetic consumption on the part of members of fashionable society. The 'false conservationist and reactionary emphasis' that arose, he suggests, represented not an alteration of sensibility but strictly an addition of taste.[12]

It was, at least, an emphasis which did not always reward the search for greater understanding of the relations between species in the wild. This second source of more recent approaches to the problems of conservation of nature — the practice of direct observation of the behaviour of animals in their natural surroundings — can also be traced to the eighteenth century. Further, Gilbert White, in his meticulous notes on the natural history of the village of Selborne, periodically comments with regret on the disappearance locally, or diminution in numbers, of a species. Wood-pigeons, for example, were relatively absent in 1780 compared to fifty or sixty years earlier.[13] The tradition was kept up in the work of amateur naturalists and scientists in the following century. (Mr Pickwick's paper on tittlebats was read to his Club in May 1827.[14]) It was out of this activity, particularly by ornithologists, that there emerged in Germany in the 1840s the first moves aimed at the preservation of wildlife by international conventions signed by governments. On the other hand, a scientific interest in nature did not necessarily go hand in hand with concern for the protection of vulnerable species and habitats. Warming's early text on the *Oecology of Plants* (1909) identifies only three reasons for the rarity of a plant — lack of a suitable habitat, or the species as an immigrant or relic — and the author adds that such rarities are of interest to the botanical collector.[15] By way of contrast, it became common later for the compilers of *Floras* of different regions or countries to refrain from revealing too precisely the location and distribution of rarer species for just this reason.[16]

Traditional uses and attitudes have thus played an important part in the evolution of conservation politics at the national and international levels. Established practices generated a large stock of issues: the trade in feathers for the use of the millinery trade in Britain in the nineteenth century, the culinary use of small migratory birds in some Mediterranean countries, or threats of environmental deterioration from overgrazing, deforestation or burning. Older outlooks as well as those of the eighteenth and nineteenth centuries have persisted. A conservationist emphasis on those large mammals most attractive to humans has its limitations, but has sometimes been an obligatory consequence of the pursuit by organisations of active voluntarism and adequate financing. The species in question are not difficult to identify.[17] Conservation of wolves suffered for a long time from the bad image which the species had built up in centuries of real and imagined encounters with man. Adoption by the romantic movement of moors, lakes and mountains as its emblems made more difficult the task of promoting the conservation of marshes, bogs and other wetlands in the 1960s and 1970s. Confusion of the conservationist with the sentimentalist has weakened the ability of wildlife advocates to compete effectively with other claimants to political or budgetary priorities.

*Approaching the problem*

Other things being equal, intersection of the supply and demand curves should put little value on an abundant species, considerably more on one threatened with extinction. Until the nineteenth century, though, the disappearance of species went largely unnoticed. Extinction of the dodo or Steller's sea cow, both within a few years of their respective discoveries, was a matter of academic interest to some scientists. When the wolf vanished from England around 1500, or from Scotland in 1743, the absence of public regret was understandably conspicuous. Two spectacular declines in the following century, however, had a powerful impact on conservation politics, particularly in the United States. Reduction of the American bison from over sixty million to eighty-five individuals within the span of a few decades, and total elimination of the passenger pigeon after flocks numbering in the millions had been a common sight a few years earlier, threw assumptions of a natural and lasting abundance in the new world into disarray.

Only a relatively few species have entered the domain of extensive public debate in this way in various countries: the African elephant in the late 1920s and early 1930s, for example, the polar bear in the early 1970s, or the different species of whale a few years later. These represent a small part of a larger process. According to figures arrived at by James Fisher in 1968, and revised in 1973, a total of 117 species or subspecies of mammals have become extinct or — given difficulties of obtaining accurate data — possibly extinct since 1600, the biggest groups being Rodentia and Carnivora (27 each), Artiodactyla (23), Marsupiala (17) and Insectivora (11).[18] The rate of extinction, moreover, has shown some signs of increasing. One estimate in the 1940s was of 106 species or subspecies of mammals thought to have become extinct in the last two thousand years: but 31 of these were noted for the period 1851–1900, and 40 during the years 1901–45.[19] With growing human encroachment on habitats in the wild, the number of species of flora and fauna approaching various escalators to extinction has risen sharply. This has been shown most dramatically in relation to plants. Between 20–25,000 species of vascular plants have been estimated as falling within one or other of the categories conventionally used to measure degree of threat from rarity to extinction.[20]

It has never been easy, however, to state with confidence either what is happening or why it is happening. The efforts of international organisations to improve this situation, and to assure a firmer foundation of knowledge on which actions and policies can be erected, are discussed in a later chapter. There are major technical problems involved in making inferences from data produced by the various methods used to monitor animal populations from aircraft;[21] there are more human problems of 'count weariness' connected with attempts to assess numbers of bird species on a year-by-year basis using large numbers of volunteer observers. Lack of funds, or absence of official permission, may bar access to investigators trying to gauge the status of a species whose survival is thought to be precarious. One underlying factor has been the slowness of development, first, of ecology as a scientific discipline, and, second, of applied ecology, and more particularly of the application of ecological knowledge to problems of conservation, as one of its subfields. Some of the elementary principles involved were well known before the nineteenth century, but greater attention to problems of the evolution of species gave added impetus to their more specialised study. Darwin, for example, used his observation of the link between cats and flowers (more cats in a district led to more mice being killed, and, since these were not then able to destroy bee combs and nests with anything like their previous tenacity, more flowers got fertilised) to note 'how plants and animals, remote in the scale of nature, are bound together by a web of complex relations'.[22] Popularisation of the term 'ecology' to designate the study of such webs by the German biologist Ernst Haeckel from 1866 attracted wider scientific interest in the area.[23] But progress came slowly. When the Survival Service of the International Union for the Protection of Nature (IUPN) met in 1950 shortly after its founding, it was thus faced with data problems: threatened species had never really been a subject of ecological study, rarer species often being neglected by researchers because of their inaccessibility.[24]

The more specific development, of an applied science of conservation grounded on ecological knowledge, has been one largely of the period since the Second World War, and one that is still under way. As a result, identification of those causal factors operative in the declines of certain species has been at times a hit-and-miss affair. Some general categories are easily listed. Extinction is, first, a natural process. Man played no part in the disappearance of the dinosaurs. Human activities do, however, have consequences for plant and animal populations, most obviously because of the need for food and products, or the trade in live animals, trophies and souvenirs. More indirect effects are frequently of greater importance: destruction of natural vegetation, drainage of wetlands, air or water pollution, the introduction of species.[25] A report of 1969 put forward four major threats to species of mammals in Europe: loss of habitat, degeneration of the environment, disturbance of biological balance, and pursuit by man.[26] Growing pressure on threatened plant species has been attributed to human population, technology and affluence: by increasing the requirement for food production; increasing the rate of exploitation of existing plant resources; decreasing the areas available for the growth of plants; increasing man's capacity for destruction of plant communities; impairing the conditions for plant growth through pollution and other factors; and promoting conditions for the spread of plant disease.[27]

Many of the changes affecting species can be attributed simply to changes in their habitat brought about by human developments. Indeed, in the steady evolution of international conservation thinking since the Second World War a shift of emphasis can be discerned away from a focus on particular species and their problems, and towards questions of changes in habitats and ecosystems. Wetlands were of interest, that is, rather than simply the migratory bird species that made use of them. Similar changes have occurred in investigations of the status of individual species. International polar bear conservation activity began in the 1960s with a focus on hunting pressures affecting the animal, but turned in the following decade increasingly to problems of habitat loss related to Arctic industrial and mineral resource development. Different kinds of developments affect nature in different ways. Marshland drainage has a major impact, which can be traced in a number of ways: its effect on species of spiders for example.[28] Increases on the demand side for plants, animals and their various products have constituted an important threat to some, such as a taste for the meat of large carnivores, for the furs of the spotted cats, or for ivory trophies and souvenirs. This was identified as being among the decisive factors bringing about a decline in turtle populations in Indonesia in the mid-1960s. Many were killed by modern types of net and submarine hunting, particularly by the Japanese; the holding of a large naval exercise on the main approach route for turtles coming in to lay did not assist the process of restoration of numbers.[29] In 1963 Nicholson and Colling produced a useful list of the effects of different kinds of human activity on habitats in Britain, including land reclamation, forestry and silviculture, various types of agriculture, fisheries, coal and mineral extraction, fuel supply, manufacturing, distribution, sewage disposal, defence, tele-communications, tourism, recreation, and others — including conservation activity by various organisations.[30]

Given that scientific studies of particular problems cannot be adequately summarised here, these few examples do nonetheless serve to highlight a central dilemma of international conservation. To argue for the conservation of nature has often seemed to imply neglect of issues affecting human welfare; or worse, where more fundamental and complex questions are in fact addressed, to imply that the latter should stand lower in the scale of national or global priorities than the former. This at least is how outsiders have sometimes tended to perceive both the case for conservation and those making it. The fact that the perception is held has real political consequences, but it is not at bottom an accurate one. From the 1940s, if not before, international conservation organisations have been at pains to emphasise the close relation which exists between the state of human welfare — materially as well as spiritually — and the state of man's natural environment. However, the argument is not an easy one to make persuasively, particularly where it has been inserted into the context of developments already planned or in progress, such as major transportation or hydroelectric schemes. And because of the diverse character of the support generated by conservation questions, the more traditionalist defence of nature does continue to jostle for attention amid more recent rationales that focus either on human needs in the developing countries or on the survival of man as a species. It is to these kinds of arguments that we must now turn.

*Conservation as a political issue*

Why, in other words, does it matter if certain species are threatened with extinction? Are some species of flora or fauna more worth saving than others? Is there a calculus which can resolve conflicts between human needs and those of other species?

In tackling such questions, we cannot turn for much assistance to the past works of political philosophers. Occasionally, concerns surface in unexpected ways. In 1864 John Stuart Mill protested to the Royal Horticultural Society about its plans to hold a contest to determine the two best herbaria in each county in England. This would be an event, he said, that would make that year the last that many already rare species of wild flora would exist.[31] His more considered writings, however, reveal more of an interest in amending for human benefit the world of nature. Hegel, similarly, expressed a preference in his *Aesthetik* for uniformity and symmetry in gardens, on the grounds that only thus could human beings dominate the landscape.[32] The concept of rights was first extended to other animals than man by Jeremy Bentham who, in the context of a discussion in the *Introduction to the Principles of Morals and Legislation* (1780) of the plight of negro slaves in America, looked forward to the day when 'the rest of the animal creation may acquire those rights which never could have been withholden from them but by the hand of tyranny'.[33] Where this topic has been taken up in later writings by philosophers, most recently by Peter Singer in *Animal Liberation*,[34] the emphasis has been on the ethical questions raised by man's direct use of different species for food, raw materials, laboratory experimentation, transport or recreation; broader questions such as rights to wild spaces, or the ethics of reintroduction, tend to be ignored. But even so, treatment of the subject does not form a substantial part of the history of ideas. The neglect has been attributed to an inherent anthropocentrism of Christian belief, even of the apparently less self-centred Franciscan tradition; other traditions, though, including that tied to the Jainist interpretation of the doctrine of *ahimsa*, or non-violence towards members of any species, have not in practice been noticeably more productive.[35]

Lack of a sure intellectual foundation has given conservation a certain ambivalence as a political issue, a malleability that permits its espousal by adherents of a variety of political faiths. Appreciation of the pleasures afforded by wild nature has a long history as a virtue of conservatives, to be contrasted at times with an allegedly impoverished mass culture of the urban working classes. In the 1960s, the evidence of survey research in the United States and elsewhere appeared to show that the conservation movement was essentially an upper-middle-class phenomenon.[36] In the 1970s, though, the values of conservation of nature were increasingly a concomitant of a political radicalism. Approaches were accordingly different. The Newfoundland and Scottish seal culls were physically disrupted by protesters; in Bologna, members of wildlife preservation groups invaded zoos to liberate monkeys and launched a campaign of bombings aimed against hunters' associations.[37] Clearly an interest in conservation was not, as one zoologist surprisingly suggested in 1977, a function of senility.[38] The more established social democratic left tended to remain aloof from these concerns on its left and its right. In Britain, for example, there were periodic complaints from environmentalists of the failure of the Labour Party to treat such issues as anything more than an affectation of the privileged; the overlapping question of animal rights did surface prominently in the party during the 1979 General Election campaign, but the way the issues were couched indicated their descent from more traditional grassroots targets such as fox hunting, factory farming or vivisection.

There is a further complication. Conservation of nature and wildlife has also traditionally enjoyed impeccable marxist-leninist credentials. Engels and Marx both expressed strong criticism of the destruction of nature by the unchecked advance of capitalism. Lenin stressed the importance of the rational exploitation of natural resources according to scientific principles; soon after the 1917 revolution the new Soviet authorities issued a series of decrees and regulations aimed at the protection of forests, parks and important natural sites and objects.[39] More recently, conservation of nature and natural resources has been described, by L. K. Shaposhnikov, as one of the most important problems facing mankind;[40] and, in the People's Republic of China, the importance of official encouragement of amateur and professional ornithology has been acknowledged.[41] The complaints of western ecologists about conditions in their own countries have also been harnessed to this task. In 1977, one Polish analysis of the deterioration of the natural environment of the United States drew on writers such as Fairfield Osborn to identify American consumer habits, the practices of the early settlers, and hunting pressure on wild species, as forces in American history and society running counter to such developments as the establishment of national parks and wilderness areas.[42]

Conservation of nature is thus an issue, or set of issues, that can nestle comfortably within very different political or ideological environments. The rationales for conservation have displayed a similar variety of defences and appeals.

First, and with greatest urgency, the need for conservation has been linked to the survival of the human species. While this case assumed greater public prominence in the late 1960s and 1970s, it is not fundamentally a new one. One United States preparatory document for a major United Nations conference on the conservation and utilisation of the earth's natural resources held in 1949 cited statistics on the decline and extinction of various species, and added: 'The most important of the many reasons for preserving wildlife is that it may contain the key to the survival of man himself'.[43] As the argument was expressed by one student of threats to birds posed by pollution in 1978: 'Despite his development of civilisation, man is and remains part of the biosphere. The roots of his physiological existence are therefore endangered by damage to the natural milieu of human life.'[44] Second, there is the argument of utility. Wildlife conservation serves immediate and longer term human needs for food, clothing or medicine. The practical value to man of conserving nature and natural resources is central to Soviet and Chinese rationales. A. G. Bannikov and B. N. Bogdanov, in a 1972 paper, wrote that in Soviet policy wildlife is considered as a necessary component of the natural environment, requiring conservation and rational utilisation; protection was withheld only from animals which were causative agents of communicable diseases, carriers and vectors of infections, or pests of agriculture and forestry.[45] Third, and more traditionally, the taking of measures to ensure the survival of wild species of fauna and flora can be supported on a mixture of ethical, religious and aesthetic grounds. Here, the criterion of utility to man begins to evaporate. The need to plant potatoes is not denied, to use the example of

Count Lippens, merely the suggestion that cathedrals need be pulled down in order to provide space for them. Finally, the development of scientific knowledge is held to justify conservation. Certain species, such as the aye-aye, or the marine iguana of the Galapagos, have a particular importance in this regard. The requirements of scientific research played a large part in the concerted efforts of the 1960s and 1970s to secure the establishment and international protection of a worldwide network of areas representative of the earth's different ecosystems.

These kinds of answers raise other questions in turn. Some dilemmas are left unresolved. The pragmatist at least has fewer boundary problems of the sort that could perturb those arguing from ethical or scientific first principles: would a rare species of bed bug merit devoted attention?[46] Do *all* of the species continually being discovered — a bird-flea left over from a 1937 expedition to Peru and found forty years later, or a new species of mite collected in a Tokyo street in 1974[47] — have an equal claim to be conserved? (More speculatively, and more difficult: what would be our response, Edward Wilson has asked, to an inferior species of australopithecine man-ape, half-way between chimpanzees and human beings, if this had survived into the present time?[48]) While some conservation issues are plainly connected with questions of survival of the biosphere — further destruction of the Brazilian rain-forest is one — others may not be. The disappearance of some species may have a marginal or, in policy terms, negligible impact even within a small area. Mauritius survived the passing of the dodo. Is there therefore a point at which economic development to serve human needs might be compelled to tolerate the controlled — not merely the accidental — extinction of other species? Further, if the flaw in the scientific lens can lead to hypertechnicality and neglect of broader questions, discarding it altogether can promote a selectivity of concentration at times overwhelming in its arbitrariness: on mammals (or birds) rather than reptiles; on big mammals rather than little ones; on the ostensibly more intelligent ones; on those regularly and visibly harvested or culled rather than those facing deterioration of habitat; on species in isolation rather than communities or ecosystems.

In the last analysis, the one major political cleavage that the issue of nature conservation has failed to bridge adequately is that between the industrialised and the developing countries. Despite their efforts, advocates of conversation can remain a suspect group in the eyes of third world leaders or officials, tolerated if they are seen as precursors of economic aid, but otherwise to be safest ignored. 'How can we urge preservation of animals?' the Prime Minister of India asked at the UN Conference on the Human Environment in 1972; 'How can we speak to those who live in the villages and in the slums about keeping the oceans, the rivers and the air clean when their own lives are contaminated at the source?'[49] Another speaker at the same conference drily suggested that a connection might exist between western calls for protection of tigers on the one hand, and for tighter controls over human population growth in Asia on the other. The character of the divide has changed in the intervening decade, but it remains a central one that will be taken up in later chapters.

*Conservation as an environmental issue*

International conservation is not, then, an apolitical issue. It is in some senses: it has not in general been tied to the particular objectives of any one state, or of any one political creed; international organisations promoting conservation goals have not, like some others, been battlegrounds for the waging of cold wars or hot conflicts; their policies and practices have for the most part been based on the findings of scientific research. In other ways, though, it is reasonable, and also more useful, to view international conservation activity as constituting, and as being undertaken within, a political arena. Internally, in the relations between the various actors in the conservation network, issues can divide activists from gradualists, amateurs from professionals, traditionalists from modernists. Questions can generate fierce arguments about values, approaches and methods, and mobilise competing factions and groups within, between and across organisations. Externally, conservation organisations have approached proselytising and the job of persuasion in different ways.

On the other hand, many questions are of a technical order. Defining the component parts of the international conservation task is not easy. More particularly, there are overlaps with a number of other international policy areas that can loosely be grouped together as environmental. In a 1974 monograph, Lundqvist defined 'environmental problems' as referring to the results of human and societal actions perceived as undesired or as harmful to the physical or natural environment. He drew up a list of ten categories falling under this general heading:

(1) environmental education;
(2) environmental research and development;
(3) hazardous products control;
(4) land use planning;
(5) nature conservancy;
(6) pollution control;

(7) solid waste management;
(8) water resources management;
(9) weather control and modification;
(10) wildlife management.[50]

Though the list covers a lot of ground, it is considerably more compact and circumscribed than the varied definitions of the scope of the subject revealed in the national reports prepared by governments for UNCHE in 1972. These problems of definition have more than an academic significance. They have practical policy implications for international organisations, particularly the United Nations Environment Programme. In his proposed programme for 1975, for example, the Executive Director of UNEP identified 'endangered species and wildlife' as a policy area falling within a single group of closely related questions: problems of arid lands and grazing lands ecosystems; tropical woodlands and forests ecosystems; other ecosystems; ecosystems, sites and samples (or parks and reserves); soils; water; and conservation of genetic resources. This group, labelled 'terrestrial ecosystems, their management and control', he put in the context of six other sets of issues: human settlements and habitats; the health of people and the environment; environment and development; the oceans; energy; and natural disasters.[51]

Bird's-eye-view definitions, however, restrict the scope of the field of conservation of nature. As it emerged in the 1940s, for example, it was frequently defined to encompass the full range of the natural resources of the planet, and the term 'conservation' to incorporate or imply rational utilisation of them. This wider and more dynamic perspective was contrasted with what were viewed as the more narrowly circumscribed and cautious approaches of previous decades, when 'protection' of nature was the phrase in vogue, and when the focus was on national park creation and management, the protection by law of certain threatened species in various countries, revision and better enforcement of hunting laws, and education and propaganda to spread more widely appreciation of the need for such measures. Since the late 1940s, there has been a continuous process of probing, and of learning by trial and error, by international conservation bodies aimed at identifying more precisely the shifting boundary of political acceptability by states and intergovernmental actors of their work, ideas, proposals and potential. Pressures from within have also left their mark. At times, the range of tasks and aspirations of organisations like IUCN have expanded into study of those areas of human activity that have obvious implications for the wellbeing of the natural environment: pollution, energy or mineral resource development, hydroelectric schemes, or high rates of population growth. At other times, lack of resources, paucity of expertise, resistance from other actors, intellectual doubts or simply changes of personnel have compelled a retrenchment to the core areas of ecosystem conservation research and promotion activity. But the older insights of simpler ages and of non-European cultures on the value of nature have never been fully pushed aside. As one UNEP document noted in 1976: 'The least tangible, and yet important, benefit mankind derives, either consciously or unconsciously, from wilderness and wild creatures, is mental solace.... as population pressures and urbanisation increase, this aesthetic, soothing value of nature and natural beauty will increasingly be appreciated.'[52]

# Part II

# The growth of international organisation

# 3  Origins and evolution

To see the Mississippi, the Nile, or the Danube in all their quiet majesty is
an unforgettable experience; but it is still more exciting to find their
sources and watch the new-born streamlets trickle from under the rocks.
Curt Sachs, *The Wellsprings of Music*[1]

The history of international conservation has been marked by continuities.
A lurch in an apparently new direction often leaves traces of older
concerns. Some problems have been defined and tackled in broadly similar
ways for several decades. A number of organisations can locate their roots
amidst the conservationist tangle and enthusiasm of the first few years of
this century. A handful of individual scientists and naturalists, through
activities spanning long careers, have added to this sense of flow. It has been
augmented, rather than fundamentally diverted, by the growing
dependence on scientific method and attachment to the virtues of
professionalism that have characterised international conservation in more
recent years. Changes in the international system have left more indelible
imprints. Older contacts between eastern and western Europe were lost
with the onset of the cold war, though resumed in modified form later; new
international organisations have come into existence, many of them, as in
Europe and within the United Nations grouping, later incorporating
conservation into their range of tasks; decolonisation and the divide
between the industrialised and the developing countries have provided
compelling reasons for reassessing traditional approaches. Continuous
change makes it difficult to isolate a date at which the contemporary history
of international conservation can reasonably be said to have begun. The
formal establishment in 1948 of an international union designed to protect
nature on a worldwide basis, however, removes some of the arbitrariness of
such a decision. In this chapter we will search for the sources of this
development in the nineteenth century and the period between the two
world wars.

*International co-operation in the nineteenth century*

The regulated protection by governments of animal and plant species occurred long before the industrial age in Europe. There was often a sound economic impulse. The hunting of beavers was forbidden in Poland in the eleventh century to allow King Boleslas to retain a monopoly of the resource. Destruction of England's oak forests for ship-building prompted agitation for stricter controls in the sixteenth and seventeenth centuries: one Durham man in 1629 was reputed to have felled more than 30,000 oaks in his lifetime.[2] Certain species, such as the ibis or falcon in Egypt, have been protected for religious reasons; others have become cossetted symbols of state or courtly power. In imperial China's relations with lesser states, the ritualised and highly political exchange of animals (including, oddly enough, humpless camels[3]) demanded a certain amount of attention to their availability. The setting aside of protected areas, as opposed to reserves for the hunting of game, likewise has a long history in both China and Europe. A Lithuanian reserve for the protection of the European bison was set up in 1541;[4] and the history of protected areas in what is now Czechoslovakia dates back to 1721.[5] This tendency sometimes clashed with older practices. In 1569 one Swiss canton established a reserve to protect the severely depleted chamois of the Kärpfstock; a critic wrote in 1894 that although such efforts might prevent the extermination of some species, in general the democratic spirit was not one favourable to the preservation of game.[6] Birds also appeared at an early date in government regulations, decrees for their protection being issued in the German states of Lippe-Detmold in 1777 and Saxe-Coburg in 1809.[7]

It was in the nineteenth century, though, that protection of nature as an international enterprise got under way. Colonial expansion stimulated public and scientific interest in the world's wildlife. Darwin's researches on the *Beagle* in 1831–5 set a pattern of biological work in the field on a scale previously unknown. Acquisition by the new London zoo of four giraffes in 1836 was the occasion for much excitement for months.[8] Such fascination did not usually lead to concern for the survival in the wild of unusual species: the world of nature seemed too rich and diverse, and man's impact localised and, when set against the whole picture, negligible. Threats to nature from the spread of industry and human settlement inside Europe, particularly in Britain and Germany, were the decisive factor.

An interest in international regulation stemmed naturally from an interest in birds. First, growing populations were putting increased pressure on agriculture. Birds could be seen either as pests, or as aids in the control of pests. As in the inquiry of the House of Commons Select Committee on

Wild Birds Protection in 1873, much time had accordingly to be spent on the difficult question of identifying those birds which were useful to agriculture and those 'troublesome and injurious to farmers'.[9] In the Austro-Hungarian Empire five years earlier, a group of farmers and foresters had approached the Foreign Minister with the aim of initiating moves towards conclusion of an international agreement to protect birds useful to agriculture.[10] Second, the expanding trade in birds and feathers, primarily to meet the requirements of Victorian fashion, suggested to ornithologists the advisability of seeking control at the international level. In 1906–7, a total of 35,615 ospreys, birds of paradise, albatrosses, rheas, kingfishers and pheasants were offered at two London feather sales.[11] Third, bird protection organisations were beginning to be politically active in a number of countries, and to develop the argument for more universal protection of wild birds, regardless of their value in terms of food production. An Act for the protection of sea birds was passed in Britain in 1869, for example, following a campaign by the Yorkshire Association for the Protection of Sea Birds and other groups, and the British Association for the Advancement of Science.[12]

Of these issues, the first had the widest appeal. In 1872, the Swiss Federal Council proposed that an international commission be set up to work on the drafting of an international agreement on bird protection. Though not immediately acted upon, the move lent weight to the growing momentum in European ornithological circles in favour of such a treaty. (When the idea had first been put forward, at a German meeting of ornithologists in 1845, it had, in the words of one observer, been 'severely ignored'.[13]) At the International Ornithological Congress held in Vienna in 1884 a Permanent Committee was set up and given the task of clarifying those species which ought properly to be regarded as suitable for inclusion in such a convention. An international agricultural congress at the Hague in 1891 called for an agreement to protect useful birds, and the Second International Ornithological Congress, held in Budapest the same year, proposed that the Austro-Hungarian authorities prepare the way for it. The thorny issue of classification was resolved in Paris in 1895. Meeting there at the invitation of the French Government, official delegations from sixteen European countries finally reached agreement on the division of birds into three categories, described respectively as useful birds, winged game and noxious birds. Though some critics objected to this bureaucratic intrusion into the farmyard (and to a certain lack of official expertise and preparation: the head of the Sûreté was a prominent member of the French delegation, and the Russian delegate arrived only in time to sign the final document[14]) it became the foundation for the treaty 'for the protection of birds useful to agriculture' eventually signed in March 1902.

The lasting value of the agreement was limited. States were reluctant to ratify. Those that did may have been attracted less by its principles and provisions as by the latitude allowed them by Article 4, which meant, according to some ornithologists, that it could in effect be safely ignored by governments.[15] As in later nature protection treaties, there was not a high degree of correspondence between signatures and ratifications on the one hand, and pertinent domestic legislation and its enforcement on the other. It was, however, in force from December 1905, and continued to attract a measure of support at international meetings, particularly those of the Institut International d'Agriculture.[16] Its longer term importance lies more, perhaps, in the criticism which it provoked later among conservationists. Opposition to the criterion of utility embodied in the convention, and to its restriction in scope to birds, formed a rallying point for those groups seeking both a more ambitious document and also a permanent international institution to work in the area of nature protection.

An upsurge of nature protection activity in Europe, and also in North America, set the scene for this next step. Organisations in several European countries took their inspiration from the national parks movement in the United States. The Swiss League for the Protection of Nature, which had a formative influence on international developments in the late 1940s, was founded in 1909 as a fund-raising body to pay for the national park finally created in 1914.[17] The Swedish Society for the Protection of Nature was also set up in 1909,[18] and each of the Scandinavian countries passed laws protecting species and sites early in the century.[19] Scientists and amateur naturalists were similarly active in eastern Europe. As early as 1868 protection had been given in Galicia to listed species of birds and mammals for a mixture of scientific and educational, ethical, and practical agricultural reasons, and high fines and prison terms introduced as penalties for infringement of hunting and trading prohibitions in relation to these species; though the provisions of the law were never fully enforced, the scientific work and public interest which flowed from a related measure to protect the chamois and marmot of the Tatra mountains saved these from extinction in the region.[20] Russian naturalists were also influenced in the early 1900s by the expansion of the United States national parks system, which was taken as a model for the future development of their own country.[21] In Britain, a number of organisations thrived. Older bodies, such as the Plumage League, the Society for the Protection of Birds, and the British Ornithologists' Union, were joined in 1903 by the Society for the Preservation of the Fauna of the Empire (later the Fauna Preservation Society), founded by a disparate group of scientists, naturalists, hunters and game wardens who earned themselves the sobriquet of the Penitent Butchers;[22] and in 1913 by the Society for the Promotion of Nature Reserves, which later played an influential role in the evolution of official conservation activity. From 1906, Germany had its own national nature protection organisation and journal, with branches operating in Bavaria, Saxony, Baden and Württemberg.[23]

These developments — there were parallels in other countries — provided a degree of access to government, particularly where, as in London, informal associations and contacts arose between officials and the leaders of nature protection groups; and marked the beginnings of an international network maintained through attendance at international gatherings, correspondence and exchange of publications. The International Congress for the Protection of Nature held in Paris in 1909 drew together representatives of organisations across Europe. Discussion of the papers presented, which summarised progress in various countries, revealed support for the establishment of a permanent institution.[24] At the Eighth International Congress of Zoology, in Graz the following year, a committee was established with the objective of securing agreement by states, through the auspices of the Swiss Federal Council, to the formation of such a body. The great Swiss conservationist Paul Sarasin was the driving force behind these events. The sense of urgency he injected into the Graz meeting was crucial: 'toute la faune supérieure de notre planète, vivant à l'état sauvage, est vouée à une destruction complète si tous ceux qui sont capables de se rendre compte du péril, ne s'y opposent pas avec la dernière énergie'.[25] Finally, at Berne in November 1913, an Act of Foundation of a Consultative Commission for the International Protection of Nature was signed by delegates from seventeen European countries. The tasks of the Commission, on which each state was to be represented by two members, were set down in Article VI: '(1) The collecting, classifying and publishing of every item dealing with international protection of nature; (2) Propaganda for the international protection of nature'.[26]

War broke out before the Commission could begin work and the first Assembly never met. Nor did an international conference planned for August 1914 to discuss, amongst other things, whaling, international hunting regulations, prohibition of the use of poison, migratory bird protection, and international regulation of the trade in skins and feathers. By December of that year, fourteen countries had nonetheless nominated their delegates to the Commission: and it was the consensus of legal opinion later, when the foundation of a new international body was being discussed in the late 1940s, that the Commission did have a legal existence. More important, it set a precedent as being the first intergovernmental agency dealing with the protection of nature, with a structure making it broadly akin to the international technical unions of the nineteenth century. Its defined tasks prepared the ground for the activities of international non-governmental organisations in the 1920s and 1930s; and it represented a significant departure in both scope and rationale from the thinking behind the 1902 convention.

## The interwar period

War fades memories. The League of Nations envisaged no future role for itself in relation to nature protection. Tentative steps to refurbish the Consultative Commission led nowhere. In 1922, scientists from several countries, now including Canada and Japan, enquired about its status. Sarasin took his case to the Swiss Federal Council. The Minister of the Interior insisted, however, that the chances for the work of the Commission being successful were not promising in the immediate political circumstances of the day. A major International Congress for the Protection of Nature was eventually organised in Paris in 1923, and this too supported the Commission's being convened; but again this was considered not practicable.[27] Developments in the interwar years took place largely at the non-governmental level. A number of treaties emerged, notably the migratory bird agreement between Britain (for Canada) and the United States in 1916, and the London convention on African conservation of 1933, but no new initiatives were taken at the level of intergovernmental organisation.

Two major international non-governmental organisations were, however, established during this period. The founding meeting of the International Committee (later Council) for Bird Protection (later Preservation) took place in London, at the home of the then Chancellor of the Exchequer, in June 1922.[28] It was called by T. Gilbert Pearson, the American ornithologist, who had earlier been negatively impressed by the mutual ignorance that divided North American from European bird protection groups. The Committee's purpose was defined as being that of 'co-ordinating and encouraging the preservation of birds'. A statement drafted at the time noted, more particularly, the need for research, the control of shooting to prevent the depletion of certain species, the destruction of small birds of little food value, and the role played by the trade in feathers in the diminution of some species of birds. The structure of the new body was kept simple. Encouragement was given to members to form National Committees in various countries, and an Executive

Committee was later formed to link these.[29] It was also a transatlantic organisation, the leading role being taken at first by Pearson himself, as President of the National Association of Audubon Societies.[30]

The work of the ICBP in the 1920s and 1930s was an important formative influence on the later evolution of international organisation. Major gatherings of ornithologists were held in Paris in 1923 and Luxembourg in 1925. A number of specific questions came to form part of an international agenda of priorities: the small bird question, particularly where migratory species were concerned, the feather trade, and threats of severe diminution in numbers facing some species such as the egret, crowned pigeon and bird of paradise. Attention was also devoted to the question of an international regime of bird protection. Opinions were divided as to whether that loosely ushered in by the 1902 convention should be consolidated, or scrapped and replaced. The need for some kind of international regulation was emphasised at a conference attended by delegates from organisations in seventeen countries in Geneva in 1928. 'Although it is obvious that the protection of birds must largely be left to individual effort and unofficial action in the different countries, the fact that the vast majority of birds are migratory and, therefore, international in their habits, often crossing many different countries between their winter and summer homes, clearly demonstrates that international action is necessary if protection is to be really effective.'[31] Some governments were responsive. In 1927, the British Government made approaches to six other European governments with a view to securing agreement on the international protection of migrant wetland and sea birds; though officials made plain their preference for further continuation of informal moves in this direction by private organisations.[32] In 1931, Sweden and Denmark signed a protection agreement; but a 1935 draft convention between Norway, Sweden and Finland to replace that of 1902 on a regional basis was not adopted. Similarly a draft convention finalised at the ICBP meeting in Vienna in 1937 failed to get off the ground before war again intervened. Debate on this did, however, culminate in the treaty of 1950, which will be discussed in a later chapter.

The failure of the 1913 Commission left a gap that the ICBP alone could not fill. Sarasin's earlier promotion work was now taken up in the Netherlands by P. G. van Tienhoven, one of the leading figures in international conservation in the interwar period. Tienhoven had been present at the founding meeting of the ICBP in London in 1922; in 1925 he established the Netherlands Committee for International Nature Protection, which he clearly saw as the focal point of a spreading international movement that would one day produce an international institution to replace the defunct Consultative Commission.[33] He urged the setting up of national committees (parallel to the ICBP National Sections) in countries where such central networks linking existing groups were lacking. His advocacy quickly met with success. The Belgian Committee for the Protection of Nature and the French Permanent Committee for the Protection of Colonial Fauna were established in 1925–6. An attempt in 1927 to expand this small triple alliance was blocked by British conservationists, though a British Correlating Committee for the Protection of Nature had been set up in 1923 through the SPFE. At a meeting in London in April it was argued that the foundation of an 'international federation' was premature, since only a few countries at that time had some form of central co-ordinating machinery for nature protection.

Tienhoven instead pursued the idea through the General Assemblies of the International Union of Biological Sciences. A consensus was reached that an international body — preferably with some form of support from governments, but if necessary without — could usefully carry out tasks related to the gathering and dissemination of information on scientific and legal questions pertaining to the conservation of nature. Following a motion from the Dutch, Belgian and French grouping, with support from Polish delegates, the sixth IUBS Assembly in 1928 approved the setting up of an Office International de Documentation et de Corrélation pour la Protection de la Nature, with Tienhoven as its head.[34] The Office was given an annual subsidy by the Dutch government from 1929. Scientific interest in its early activity grew over the next couple of years, particularly at the 1931 meetings of the IUBS and of the Second International Congress for the Protection of Nature in Paris, and it was consolidated as the International Office for the Protection of Nature in 1934. Statutes drawn up in that year took the Office some way beyond the more circumscribed goals set by the IUBS in 1928. Its object was 'to work internationally for the progress of nature protection' (Article 2). Various means were specified: '(1) by centralizing, by classifying, by publishing and by distributing to governments, institutions and persons interested in nature protection, documents, legislative texts, scientific studies, information and data of any kind regarding nature protection and especially the conservation of fauna, flora and natural scenery in a primitive state; (2) by encouraging and facilitating international co-operation between institutions, and persons interested in [these] questions; (3) by making studies and technical investigations in the domain of nature protection; (4) by organising the propaganda for nature protection especially from an international standpoint.'[35]

In practice, information gathering and dissemination formed the core of

IOPN's work. Close links were kept up with the ICBP, in part because of Tienhoven's own earlier contacts. The ICBP was at this time pressing for a moratorium on the import, export and transit of quails as a means of securing their wider international protection, a move supported by the Seventh International Ornithological Congress of 1930; the collecting of legislative materials by the IOPN was clearly an area that lent itself to useful collaboration between the two organisations on this kind of question. An early example was a joint survey in 1930–1 of the status of various threatened species of birds.[36] A series of publications issued as an *International Review of Legislation for the Protection of Nature* concentrated on African colonial territories, with volumes appearing on the Belgian Congo, Kenya, the Cameroons, Uganda, Ruanda-Urundi and French Equatorial Africa. From 1947 a *Review of Bibliography on the International Protection of Nature* was also prepared and published by the Office for a short time.

Pearson's role in founding and leading the ICBP from 1922 was only one instance of an expanding American interest in international problems of nature protection during the interwar years. Organisations such as the Audubon Society and the Sierra Club were by then long established, and predated many of their European equivalents. These were joined in 1913 by the Permanent Wild Life Protection Fund of William Hornaday. From the early 1920s, concern for the world's fauna mounted steadily. Africa was the focal point. President Theodore Roosevelt earlier whetted the appetites of hunters for the continent: by the mid-1920s the resulting pressure on game, especially in British East Africa, was beginning to be well documented in United States journals.[37] Harold J. Coolidge, Jr., later the foremost internationalist in the conservation movement, took part in a cross-Africa expedition from Harvard University and investigated at first hand the status of gorillas and other threatened species. On his initiative, and with support from Tienhoven at the IOPN, the Boone and Crockett Club — a group formed in 1887 and having a membership keenly interested in African conservation problems — established in 1930 the American Committee for International Wild Life Protection. This Committee comprised representatives of the most important United States organisations.[38] During the 1930s and 1940s it emerged as a major actor in international conservation. Its financial support for the IOPN, combined with active representation on the Office's General Council, guaranteed that body's survival at critical junctures. It immediately set about the task of promoting wider public knowledge of nature protection problems throughout the world. Some of its publications played a crucial role in furthering American interest in the area; these assumed broader international significance during the Second World War when German occupation of Belgium halted IOPN activity. In particularly, the ACIWLP sponsored and published two volumes in the 1940s — Allen's *Extinct and Vanishing Mammals of the Western Hemisphere* and Harper's *Extinct and Vanishing Mammals of the Old World*[39] (the latter based in large part on data collected by the IOPN[40]) — which together formed a data base for international conservation in the 1950s.

Africa also occupied a central place in British concerns. The SPFE supported missions to East and West Africa with a view to establishing the facts upon which sound conservation policies could be based in British colonial territories.[41] In reports to the Royal Geographical Society, and the Second International Congress for the Protection of Nature, in 1931, R. W. G. Hingston noted particularly threats to the white rhino, gorilla, nyala and Grévy zebra, and estimated that the elephant could not survive more than fifty years at rates of destruction then current.[42] This activity in the late 1920s and early 1930s formed an essential background to the signing in London in 1933 of the Convention for the Protection of the Fauna and Flora of Africa, which was described by one government minister later as 'the Magna Charta of wildlife preservation not only in Africa ... but elsewhere also'.[43] Its general aim was to meet threats to wildlife in Africa by such measures as the creation of national parks in colonial territories, and provision for the more effective protection of those species thought to be most threatened with severe depletion in numbers in the future. The Convention replaced one signed in 1900 which had grown out of approaches from Britain to the other colonial powers in Africa; it will be assessed in the context of African conservation problems later in this book. By reaffirming that wildlife conservation was a suitable subject for agreement between the powers, the London Convention of 1933 was a significant event in the interwar period. By dealing, moreover, with that region of the world where scientists and naturalists felt the greatest threats to the world's fauna and flora existed, it also became an early vehicle for collaboration between conservation organisations and governments. The Secretary of the SPFE provided the conference with a list of mammals in danger of extinction in Africa, and this shaped in large measure the listing of threatened species contained within the Convention.[44] The network of links between international conservation bodies was also operative. Relations between the SPFE and the IOPN were good, after the earlier British doubts about the wisdom of establishing an organisation such as the Office had been overcome, and the ACIWLP took a keen interest in the work of the conference, publishing and distributing the text of the Convention in 1935.[45]

The role of international organisation was defined more explicitly in relation to a later agreement, the Pan-American Convention for the Protection of Wild Life in the Western Hemisphere signed in Washington in May 1940.[46] Its origins can be traced to the setting up in 1929 by the Fourth Pacific Science Congress of a Permanent Committee for the Protection of Nature in the Pacific, at that time one of the few international bodies in existence. Continued prodding by Coolidge, from a Pan-American Committee of the ACIWLP, was a determining factor in bringing about the Convention, which grew from a draft formulated by a committee established by the Pan-American Union following a resolution of the Eighth International Conference of American States in Lima in December 1938. Under the terms of the Convention, a section of the Pan-American Union's agriculture division was tasked specifically to help governments on matters such as surveys of wildlife populations.

*Emergence of an international union*

By the beginning of the Second World War conservation of nature had therefore become more firmly secured as an object of international attention. Two international non-governmental organisations, the ICBP and IOPN, each with extensive official contacts in various countries, had come into existence. National organisations with broader regional or world concerns were active, notably in the Netherlands, the United States and Britain. A variety of international fora provided opportunities for exchanges of ideas, and new bodies were created to link those interested in particular aspects of the field of nature protection: an international association for the protection of the European bison, for example, was set up in Berlin in 1923.[47] In some way, indeed, the international milieu was more favourable than in later decades to the promotion of conservation goals. Apart from the access afforded British, Belgian or French groups by the imperial order, conservationists were also assisted by the sympathetic atmosphere of many international scientific meetings of the period, which sometimes contrasted with the greater scientific 'respectability' of such gatherings in the 1950s and 1960s. Two major conventions dealing with conservation in different regions of the world were signed (though a conference planned by the British Government for 1934 to extend the principles of the Africa Convention into Asia and Australia was not held). These fitted into a larger international context of treaty law. The Canada–United States migratory bird agreement of 1916 came to be recognised as a pioneering example of international co-operation; though by the early 1940s criticism had mounted of some of its workings, such as the inadequacy of its system of sanctuaries to cope with threats to habitat brought about by oil exploration in the Louisiana marshes.[48] In 1936 the United States signed a similar protection agreement with Mexico. The 1911 Anglo-American Convention on sealing, the 1930 Convention for the regulation of whaling, and the succession of whaling conferences held in London in 1937–9, though falling outside the scope of this book, form a related series of developments.

Contacts patiently built up during the 1930s were severed by war. In 1940, the administrative offices of the IOPN were formally transferred from Brussels to Amsterdam. A little routine work continued during the German occupation of the Netherlands despite the death in 1943 of the Office's Manager, J. M. Derscheid, formerly General Secretary of the old Belgian Committee. Even·this ceased during most of 1946. The one significant thread of institutional continuity was provided by the threatened species research supported in the United States by the ACIWLP.

At the beginning of 1947, the Office produced a report on international wildlife protection activity during the war years with the purpose of reviving interest in the organisation and, not least, of raising funds.[49] Work had resumed in Amsterdam towards the end of 1946. A few weeks earlier, in October, the first moves towards reconstruction of the pre-war network were set in motion at the first post-war meeting of the ICBP in Brussels, attended among others by Tienhoven. Plans were made for the holding of a conference of the ICBP's European Continental Section in London the following year, and the organisation's headquarters were moved to there from Brussels.[50] Conservation activity began to revive in several European countries. In Prague the Ministry responsible for nature conservation in Czechoslovakia established contact with Tienhoven and the IOPN soon after the end of hostilities. In Britain, this recuperative process had international ramifications. Following the work of the interwar period, an influential Wildlife Conservation Committee was set up in 1947, and the official Nature Conservancy in 1949: under the leadership of E. M. Nicholson in the 1950s and 1960s, the Conservancy developed into a major force in international conservation.

But the initiative was now taken, again, by the Swiss. Early in 1946, Sir Julian Huxley, the distinguished British biologist, arranged with a colleague in Basle to bring over a group of British scientists later in the year for a visit to the Swiss national park. About the same time, Tienhoven was corresponding with Dr Charles Bernard, President of the Swiss League for the Protection of Nature, and arguing forcefully in favour of a resumption of international contacts as soon as possible. The proposed visit by Huxley and the British group provided the opportunity for Bernard and the Swiss

League to organise a conference in Basle on international nature protection problems in the post-war period.

Two central questions of substance and process arose. First, should the already existing IOPN be strengthened or replaced? The former route had the obvious advantage of building on a foundation of past achievements. A new body would have to fight for recognition in a rapidly changing world. On the other hand, there was a spirit of innovation in international organisation in the air. The United Nations had taken the place of the largely discredited League of Nations; and there was considerable support among conservationists in 1946 for a strategy of institutional change. The existence of the IOPN would have been less of a problem but for the position of Tienhoven himself, by the mid-1940s the elder statesman of international conservation in Europe. Sarasin's old 1913 Consultative Commission posed few difficulties. There were by 1946 no vested interests either for or against it. Many were ignorant of its existence — if indeed it did exist after more than three decades of life only on legal paper. Others were unclear of its nature and goals. A second issue related to the manner in which change was to be ushered in. More particularly, the fact that it was the Swiss who were taking the lead aroused latent national jealousies. There were murmurings about Swiss imperialism, allegations that the Swiss wanted to monopolise conservation and, the events of 1872 and 1913 and the work of Sarasin apparently forgotten, suggestions that the Swiss had never done anything in the past for the protection of nature to warrant their taking this kind of initiative now. As Bernard observed later, 'We found ourselves repeatedly up against obstacles ... we have been criticised and attacked from many sides, violently and, to us, incomprehensibly. We were accused of sinister projects, the worst intentions were attributed to us'.[51] Johann Büttikofer, the League's Secretary, did however identify one factor which in later years assumed much greater significance. It seemed, he wrote, 'que nous étions en quelque sort prédestinés, quoique notre pays soit éloigné des mers *et ne possède pas de colonies*, à prendre cette initiative'.[52]

The main conclusion of the Basle meeting was that: 'In order to facilitate the co-operation of national societies concerned with the protection of nature and the preservation of amenities, it is desirable that there should be an active international organisation, widely international and representative in character, adequately financed and with adequate terms of reference'.[53] This phrasing of the desideratum became the cornerstone of debate in subsequent months. It skirted over the question of whether such an organisation should be inter- or non-governmental in nature, though the reference to adequate financing suggested to some the desirability of pursuing a body comprising states as members. The complications posed by the IOPN and the 1913 Commission were left for another day. The position of the Office should be 'taken into account' in future developments, as should be the resolutions of the First International Congress for the Protection of Nature of 1923 (which, it will be recalled, had recommended amongst other things a reconvening of the Consultative Commission). Finally, the Swiss League was asked to submit to the Swiss government proposals for an initiative to promote intergovernmental collaboration in nature protection, restoration of the Commission being specifically mentioned as an appropriate first step in this direction. Bernard and his Swiss League colleagues assured a wide international distribution for the report of the Basle proceedings from November 1946, which became known as the 'red book'.

After Basle, however, the focus switched to UNESCO, under Huxley as its first Director-General. Huxley's reference in his memoirs to IUCN as 'the organisation for Nature Conservation I had founded and built up while at UNESCO'[54] contains a sufficient measure of truth for its slight exaggeration to be overlooked. At the end of 1946 he submitted to UNESCO's General Conference a programme that included conservation of areas of natural beauty as well as of sites of historical interest. Then, and over the next few months, he was engaged in a long struggle to secure wider acceptance among UNESCO's member states of the principle that nature conservation fell properly within that agency's competence. He won his point at UNESCO's General Conference in 1947. 'Delegates asked what seemed to me silly questions: Why should UNESCO try to protect rhinoceroses or rare flowers? Was not the safeguarding of grand, unspoilt scenery outside its purview? etc., etc. However, with the aid of a few nature-lovers, I persuaded the Conference that the enjoyment of nature was part of culture, and that the preservation of rare and interesting animals and plants was a scientific duty.'[55]

Huxley faced two immediate policy questions: the most appropriate way of including nature conservation, or some of its aspects, among the functions of UNESCO; and the best way to respond to developments already under way in 1946–7 for the setting up of some kind of international nature protection organisation. Convening a world conference under UNESCO's auspices on the subject appeared to be the solution to the first of these problems. The two were, however, closely intertwined.

Setting up non-governmental or semi-governmental organisations, or nurturing those established previously, in the fields of science, technology and medicine was a central preoccupation of UNESCO's scientific staff at this time. While this fell among the responsibilities of Joseph Needham, the British biologist and sinologist who largely shaped UNESCO's scientific

policy during this period, it is significant that the particular question of
bringing a nature protection organisation into existence was one handled
primarily by Huxley himself for reasons of his own personal interest in the
subject. A number of proposals emerged. Some overlapped the broader area
of conservation of the world's natural resources. Sir John Orr of FAO had
suggested the creation of an international organisation with just such a
wide definition of its goals; Professor J. D. Bernal had published a proposal
for an International Resources Office to have a similar scope.[56] More
particularly, the New York Zoological Society, later an important national
non-governmental    actor    in    the    area,    was    actively    pursuing    the
establishment of an International Conservation Foundation. The Society's
staff, under Fairfield Osborn, were corresponding with a number of British
and Belgian scientists on the idea. The aim of the new body would be 'to
promote conservation of the earth's life-supporting resources — animal life,
forests and other plant life, water sources and productive soils'. It would
'assist in the rehabilitation of the IOPN, and support especially its work on a
world survey of species of fauna and flora in danger of extinction'.[57]
Finally, there was the Basle proposal, with which Huxley had been
indirectly involved in a personal capacity, for an international nature
conservation organisation, the tasks of which were envisaged as being
much more narrowly circumscribed. On the second question of a world
conference to signify UNESCO's presence in the nature protection field,
Huxley's position was both complicated and eased by plans for a major
United Nations conference on conservation and utilisation of natural
resources to be held in 1949 in New York. This conference, known as
UNSCCUR, had originated in part in a suggestion from the late President F.
D. Roosevelt to his then Secretary of the Interior, Harold Ickes. It was
formally called by ECOSOC in a resolution of March 1947 which spoke of
'the importance of the world's natural resources ... [and] the need for continuous development and widespread application of the techniques of resource
conservation    and    utilization'.[58]    Planning    for    the    conference    already
in 1947 involved several departments of the Administration in Washington
and, more particularly, Coolidge from the Pacific Science Board.

Both Huxley and Needham held discussions with Swiss League officials
in Paris in November 1946. The outcome was a vaguely worded statement
of encouragement. UNESCO, Needham wrote, would 'follow with the
deepest interest the efforts which may be made in the immediate future to
clarify the situation in the field of international collaboration between those
interested in nature protection'. If and when a 'satisfactory International
Organisation' were set up, UNESCO's Natural Sciences Division would
'undoubtedly wish to give all possible aid, which may take a material as

well as a moral form'.[59] The question then arose of the relationship such an organisation should have with the International Council of Scientific Unions. Following correspondence between Huxley and Tienhoven, and talks in Paris between Needham and the Secretary of the IUBS (the international scientific union out of which the IOPN had sprung in the late 1920s), Needham observed in January 1947 that since the question of nature protection involved so many matters beyond the bounds of pure science, it would seem fitting that the proposed organisation should not be incorporated within the framework of the ICSU, but should be something *sui generis*: having a position 'more akin to that of such organisations as the International Meteorological Bureau, the International Hydrographic Bureau, the International Bureau of Weights and Measures, etc.'.[60] In a UNESCO explanatory note a few weeks later, however, it was given a more elevated status as one of five 'technical high order "inclusive" bodies (strictly scientific and technological)' with which UNESCO was involved, the others representing pure science (the ICSU), medical science, engineering science and agricultural science.[61]

These exchanges between senior officials of UNESCO, the Swiss League and the IUBS went a long way towards clarifying what kind of nature protection organisation should emerge. It was already accepted, for example, that a new organisation should be created, though what its relationship with the IOPN would be was not clear, and that the Basle conference represented the first step in the process towards it. (The New York Zoological Society's proposal became channelled into the establishment of the Conservation Foundation in 1948, the aims of which were geared, initially at least, much more to the requirements of conservation in the United States.[62]) The ground was thus prepared for a second international conference planned for the end of June 1947 in Brunnen. In discussions at the Swiss League's offices in Basle in March 1947, Needham identified four possible outcomes of the conference.

(1) the setting up of an international federation of nature protection bodies;

(2) the passing of a resolution calling for implementation of the 1913 Convention;

(3) approval in principle of a draft constitution for the proposed organisation (such a draft was already circulating among national groups, having been amended by the Swiss League on the basis of comments received from several departments of UNESCO[63]); or

(4) approval of, and support for, UNESCO's own plans for a world nature protection conference.

More particularly, it was UNESCO's aim to deflect the Swiss League's ambition to turn the 1947 conference into one which would actually set up the new organisation. Huxley made it clear in a letter, also in March, that the establishment of this kind of semi-governmental organisation would have to be a matter to be taken up at a separate meeting in 1948.[64] Bowing to this pressure, Bernard gave the conference a less definitive character than the Swiss League had originally anticipated.

At Brunnen, therefore, there was a certain amount of confusion about the scope and purpose of the deliberations. Some delegates saw it as a founding conference. Professor Vinding Kruse, of Denmark, took the lead among those pressing for immediate action, arguing that it would not be practical to leave to UNESCO the initiative to make decisions regarding the constitution of the proposed organisation. British delegates tended to support the more gradualist route. Still a third alternative was defended by the IUBS representative who, Needham's earlier position notwithstanding, called for the establishment of an international union which would be affiliated with the ICSU, and which would collaborate closely with the IUBS through some form of international mixed commission. Uncertainty as to UNESCO's own goals in this area prompted annoyance. It was Bernard's understanding, based on his exchanges with Huxley and Needham, that UNESCO was not planning any future direct action in relation to nature protection, apart from the projected world conference. On the other hand, Huxley's own preferences were known. And, as one delegate pointed out, one of UNESCO's offshoots, the International Council of Museums, already had under it a committee dealing with national parks, nature reserves and related matters. Partly in order to head off any future attempt by UNESCO to steal more of their thunder, the delegates to Brunnen finally arrived at the compromise of establishing there and then a *Provisional* International Union for the Protection of Nature, and appointed the Swiss League to act as its agent. In addition, UNESCO was formally requested to convene a Congress in 1948 for adoption of a Constitution, to be based on that finalised by Swiss and British delegates to Brunnen. It was recommended that this be sent to UNESCO for circulation to all governments. Finally, the Swiss Government was to be approached and asked to take the necessary steps to abrogate the 1913 Convention, on the grounds that the Consultative Commission had never functioned. In this, the Brunnen conference departed from the UNESCO view, which tended to be that revival of the Commission would be a useful step since a signed Convention did already exist in international law.[65]

On the more sensitive matter of IOPN, Bernard denied criticisms that it was the intention of the Swiss League to abolish the earlier organisation. It could, he argued, constitute one section of the new union, and as one of its members, he asked Tienhoven to convene a formal meeting of the Office's General Council on the occasion of the Brunnen meeting. Speaking for IOPN in turn, Dr Westermann confirmed that the Office would collaborate with the proposed new organisation.

Fresh difficulties arose, however, before the Paris Congress. First, UNESCO objected to the degree of governmental participation in the union suggested by the Brunnen conference. It was felt to be inappropriate to circulate the draft constitution to governments with a view to securing wider state membership for the organisation. Consultations were held with officials of several member governments. As a result, studies were initiated, as one UNESCO report put it in April 1948, on 'the possibilities of an international non-governmental organisation for the preservation of nature rather than an intergovernmental organisation as proposed by the Brunnen Conference' the year before.[66] Second, the French Government stepped in with its own plans to upstage UNESCO in the preparatory work for the conference. The resulting 'serious technical and fundamental obstacles', as Bernard called them, set back the start of the meeting from July to October 1948. An arrangement was eventually reached whereby France and UNESCO jointly invited Governments to send representatives to the conference, while the Provisional IUPN (in practice the Swiss League) issued invitations to private bodies.[67] The main work of the conference, held at Fontainebleau, centred on a Legal and Drafting Committee chaired by Dr Herbert Smith of the British delegation. The draft constitution approved at Brunnen had to be revised in the light of amendments subsequently put forward by UNESCO and also by the Foreign Office in London. Coolidge, acting for the United States delegation to the conference (and himself representing both the New York Zoological Society and its newly established Conservation Foundation) pressed successfully for major revisions in the preamble of the union's constitution to give it a more forceful, and wider, cutting edge.[68] Apart from this, the main issue to arise at Fontainebleau had to do with voting powers of members in the General Assemblies of the union. The question posed difficulties because of the mixed, semi-governmental character of the organisation. Government delegates were reluctant to commit states to an arrangement which would allow private groups in a country to outvote their own government in such meetings. It was eventually agreed that government members of the union should have two votes in General Assemblies, and private organisations combined one vote. Problems in succeeding years, however, showed that the dilemma could not be so neatly resolved.

Huxley's second longer term goal was secured more readily. At its

General Conference in 1947, UNESCO agreed to convene a technical conference on nature protection in the summer of 1949 to take place immediately after the more general one planned by the United Nations on the conservation and utilisation of resources. Some objections arose later. In September 1948, after a meeting on nature protection chaired by Coolidge had aired the issues, the Natural Sciences Panel of the United States National Commission for UNESCO argued against a separate conference on the subject. It proposed instead that UNESCO should support fully the UN resources conference and aim to ensure that the UN put special emphasis in its natural resources programme on the preservation of natural areas.[69] At UNESCO's General Conference in Beirut in November, the British, supported by New Zealand, failed in a move to decouple the two conferences. The nature protection conference, it was argued, should rather be held at some European location on the grounds that many countries lacked ample dollar resources.[70] But the original plan survived basically intact, and in the event was approved by the United States delegation at Beirut. The matter had already by then been settled. At the beginning of November, one month after Fontainebleau, UNESCO signed a contract with IUPN, based on a draft produced in earlier exchanges between Coolidge and UNESCO scientific officials, giving to the new body the financial support necessary to make the scientific and technical preparations for the proposed meeting. Known later simply as the Lake Success conference, it laid the foundation for international nature conservation work for much of the 1950s.

The Constitution of IUPN blended the aspirations of previous decades with a shrewd appreciation of the art of the possible. It was designed to have a hybrid membership. Four categories of potential members were identified: governments, agencies of governments, international inter- and non-governmental organisations, and national non-governmental organisations (Article II[1]). Under Article IV, the determination of policy was to be the responsibility of the General Assembly, with voting according to the rules noted earlier, and decisions by a simple majority of votes cast. An Executive Board, consisting of the President of the Assembly and between eight and fourteen members elected from among Assembly delegates, exercised authority at other times within limits set by the Assembly (Article V). Provision was made for Board members to be chosen from among those technically competent in the field of nature protection, and for there to be no more than two members from any country in view of the need for a balanced geographical distribution. To these component parts was added a Secretariat under a Secretary-General (Article VI). The preamble defined protection of nature in broad terms as 'the preservation of the entire world biotic community, or man's natural environment, which includes the earth's renewable natural resources of which it is composed, and on which rests the foundation of human civilisation'. (The reference to resources is important. Delegates to the 1947 and 1948 conferences were divided on the issue of whether the union should incorporate 'natural resources' somehow into its official name; this step was not taken until 1956.) IUPN's objectives were equally wide. It was, according to Article 1, to 'encourage and facilitate co-operation between governments and national and international organisations' in the area, particular reference being made to the spread of public knowledge, education, scientific research and the drawing up of 'international draft agreements' and a worldwide convention for the protection of nature.

*Growth of the network*

While IUCN, as the new body became, can realistically be treated as the central actor in the broader conservation network — its goals have been cast in global terms to encompass, where resources have allowed, threats to wild nature arising in all regions of the world — it cannot so unequivocally be viewed as the 'leader' of this network. That position has usually been left unfilled. Too many organisations of different kinds operate in the international wildlife field. Disagreements about priorities, relative abilities and the best approaches have been too numerous; the scars of past conflicts have sometimes proved difficult to heal. All organisations here have at times been subjected to criticisms of one kind or another by others: IUCN is no exception, and in addition has suffered from being the target of inflated expectations and the recipient of inadequate funds and other resources with which to carry out its work.

However, by the early 1960s a central nucleus of actors had emerged — a grouping of institutions that have been closely related, even to the point of periodically discussing formal amalgamation. The financial problems of IUPN remained a fundamental obstacle to further progress during the 1950s. In 1961 the World Wildlife Fund (WWF) was established in Britain on the initiative chiefly of several individuals who were already active in or closely in touch with IUCN affairs, and who were motivated to launch out in a new direction primarily by the wide gap that existed at the time between urgent conservation needs — threats to east African wildlife provided the immediate context — and the apparent inability of existing organisations to tackle them or to provoke others to act. The two later developed good working relations, though not without the difficulties of deciding on tunes that inevitably arise between pipers and payers. While the International Office of the 1930s became gradually incorporated within the new union, ICBP, then the senior international conservation body, retained its identity to continue as the organisation primarily responsible for bird protection questions. IUCN in practice left birds out of its range of interests. An offshoot of ICBP, the International Waterfowl Research Bureau (IWRB), has also been active in matters relating to the wider international protection of wetland habitats, notably in the preparatory moves that led to the treaty on the subject signed at Ramsar, Iran, in 1971 and in the implementation of the convention. But lack of commonly agreed ground rules, and the vulnerability of those that do exist to changes of circumstance and ambition, leaves open considerable possibilities for manoeuvre by organisations other than these four. Various national non-governmental groups have at times worked intimately with this central grouping, such as the Fauna Preservation Society (FPS) in London, whose secretary in the early 1960s headed IUCN's key scientific advisory body on endangered species. So have intergovernmental organisations. In the 1950s UNESCO provided the new union with much needed contract funding on conservation education questions; FAO collaborated with it on African conservation problems in the 1960s until a dispute later in the decade brought about a temporary break in relations. Other groups have gone their own way, with occasional contacts. The New York Zoological Society's proposals in the late 1940s for a new international conservation body were noted earlier in this chapter; this and the Frankfurt Zoological Society have since been among the leading national actors. Several private organisations, among them the Jersey Wildlife Preservation Trust, have concentrated on the captive breeding of endangered species and have played their own international roles. The Council of Europe was the first intergovernmental institution outside the UN system to undertake conservation of nature responsibilities (though the Nordic Council had earlier held discussions on migratory bird protection questions). The European Community later expanded its environmental interests to examine migratory bird problems in its member states.

It is not possible, though, to do justice in a brief sketch to the variety and extent of the conservation network. Organisations will be brought into the discussion at appropriate points in the chapters following. While there is some virtue in proliferation — small, independent, specialised bodies can often tackle problems with greater vigour and freedom than the subunits of bigger institutions — the problems of co-ordination have also at times seemed insuperable. In some cases co-ordination, even in the tacit sense of *de facto* recognition of niches, is just not feasible. The large fund-raising bodies, for example, have not usually found it to be in their interests to be associated in the public mind with smaller radical groups; though even here, the passage of time and the appreciation of some commonality of ultimate aims have produced a variety of relationships from grudging toleration to active partnership on particular problems. The creation of UNEP in 1973 raised some expectations of a more concerted attack on this question. In connection with wildlife conservation and threatened species and ecosystems, some tentative steps towards a greater degree of co-ordination were made through the Ecosystem Conservation Group (ECG), comprising IUCN, FAO, UNESCO and UNEP. IUCN's design of a World Conservation Strategy in the late 1970s served a similar purpose by aiming to express a consensus on conservation priorities and needs. These larger kinds of questions will be raised in greater depth in a later chapter. The two immediately following look for the most part at IUCN and WWF in their scientific and political roles.

# 4 Scientific development: knowledge and its uses

'What do Jagulars do?' asked Piglet, hoping that they wouldn't.
'They hide in the branches of trees, and drop on you as you go
underneath,' said Pooh.
A. A. Milne, *The House at Pooh Corner*[1]

From the outset the IUPN was faced with a data gap of awesome proportions. Despite the backlog of work from the 1930s in Europe and the 1940s in the United States, simply not enough was known about the status of various species of wild fauna and flora thought to be threatened with severe depletion of numbers or outright extinction. Further, research in ecology and in cognate disciplines of the biological sciences had not advanced sufficiently for there to be on hand a useful corpus of knowledge applicable to the task of conservation. Specialists with reliable information on threatened species either did not exist, or else were scattered in institutes in several countries without working networks of communication to link them. From this period the conviction grew that the international conservation of nature was inherently a science-based enterprise. At least a modicum of scientific expertise in the gathering and handling of data, and in the relating of findings to gaps and concerns in the pertinent literature, increasingly came to be perceived as an index of legitimacy, or political acceptability, in a competitive world. Some of the implications — greater caution in the making of public statements, greater professionalism in the internal workings of organisations, greater interest in habitats and ecosystems than in particular species — produced at times a certain tension between the scientific and the public faces of the conservation movement. These problems are taken up in later chapters. By the 1960s, this process was overtaken, though not replaced, by the growing emphasis on development issues that followed the influx of new states into the United Nations and its related agencies. The changing atmosphere affected conservation as it did other functional areas. The evolution of the intellectual basis of international conservation is the theme of the present chapter; special emphasis is placed on the formative years of IUCN in this regard.

## Science and conservation

We have already seen that UNESCO considered it inappropriate, in 1947, that the projected international nature protection organisation should be affiliated with the ICSU and structured like one of its member scientific unions. As Needham foresaw, the new organisation was interested in a broader range of questions than those of scientific research. But science was the cornerstone. Tienhoven in 1947 described the International Office as 'a scientific centre of the international movement'.[2] This kind of self-image translated easily into the early work of the IUPN. It was given an occasional bolstering by individual scientists such as Frank Fraser Darling, connected in a variety of capacities both with the new union and with the Conservation Foundation in the United States, and by the union's at first informal associations with bodies like the IUBS. Jean-Paul Harroy, the distinguished Belgian conservationist and colonial administrator who became the IUPN's first Secretary-General, wrote in 1952 of the requirement that the union 'should systematically accentuate its activities in scientific matters in such a manner as to merit being ranked among international scientific organisations'.[3] Lack of adequate resources during the 1950s, however, prevented it from acting as a sponsor of research, and constrained its ability to play a role either as a    clearing-house of information on conservation or as a forum of scientific deliberation. The goal was restated, and pursued more vigorously, in the early and middle 1960s under Sir Hugh Elliott as Secretary-General; while the potential for secure and long-term funding contained in the establishment of the World Wildlife Fund at the beginning of the decade underscored fresh optimism on the point. The objective, IUCN's Executive Board stated, should be 'to fill the need for an international technical advisory body or scientific "brains-trust", specialising in applying the ecological approach to conservation problems'.[4]

Two interrelated factors influenced the course of this scientific development. First, the new organisation had to devise appropriate, and feasible, decision-making structures within which scientific policy could be shaped. Its constitution made specific provision for technical competence, as well as geographical spread, as a criterion for elections to its chief executive body. In practice too, many members, governmental or non-governmental, were represented at General Assemblies by individuals who brought different kinds of scientific and technical expertise to bear on policy problems; though because of the mixed character of the membership of the union, such fora were also marked by a diversity of interests and approaches to conservation. More centrally, there gradually emerged during the 1950s and 1960s the basic structure of a scientific advisory network linking individual specialists in different countries. Voluntarism was a key organising principle, partly because of recurrent financial difficulties, but in part also because it was felt that this approach better reflected the underlying conception of international conservation as a 'movement'. Two such networks are central to the topics dealt with in this chapter: the Survival Service Commission, established on Coolidge's initiative as a natural consequence of his promotion activity in the United States in the 1940s on behalf of the world's threatened species, and further developed in the 1960s and 1970s by Sir Peter Scott; and the Commission on Ecology, intended to draw in and make available to the union's constituent organs findings and insights on a broader front of scientific research. Though the latter was designed as the union's chief scientific advisory body, over the longer term it was in practice rather the SSC that became a focal point of advice and recommendations on scientific policy. One reason was the greater immediacy and excitement of its work in terms of the outside world of conservation. These and other IUCN Commissions have faced many problems. In organisational terms, a particular constraint was the slow pace of development of parallel support facilities within the Secretariat: itself, when resources eventually allowed, an important source of scientific policy in the organisation.

A second factor was change and development in the science of ecology. This meant, among other things, that whereas threatened species of fauna and flora remained a paramount concern of the union, attention had increasingly to be given to wider contexts. In a paper reviewing the work of the SSC presented to the International Zoological Congress in London in 1958, Coolidge noted in particular the 'greater realisation of the importance of preserving habitats instead of individual species on a living specimen basis'. There had also been, he said, a change in the significance attached to preserving endangered species by the general public 'from treating them as local curiosities to the development of a climate increasingly favourable for making them a focus of world attention'.[5] Ecology as a science, though, proceeded with a certain degree of caution which did not always endear its practitioners to active conservationists. Landmark publications, such as Elton's *The Ecology of Invasions by Animals and Plants*,[6] appeared at intervals during the 1950s and 1960s. The intellectual basis of conservation, that is, was being slowly put together piecemeal at a time when the urgency of the threat facing the world's wildlife seemed to many to be approaching crisis proportions. Periodic attempts were made by individuals active both in the conservation and academic scientific worlds to accelerate this process. But the formal discipline of ecology embraced concerns wider than the application of knowledge to conservation. As one speaker observed at the 1961 General Assembly of the IUBS, IUCN's Commission on Ecology could not be considered as representing all ecologists.[7] Further, and particularly after the environmentalist atmosphere of the early 1970s had put unprecedented pressures on it, the field was being criticised from the inside as being already too diffuse and overextended.[8] Where both the pure and applied threads have been woven together well, as in the early volumes of the journal *Biological Conservation*, the combination was a strong and effective one; but the higher syntheses, that also incorporate knowledge from the social sciences, have been notoriously difficult to achieve.

*Conservation of species*

Many organisations at the national and international levels have supported or made use of scientific research relevant to conservation problems. In relation to both species and ecosystems, a considerable degree of disagreement on issues between specialists has shown itself to be possible, indeed normal. In this section we will look at the development of knowledge concerning threatened species of plants and animals, and concentrate more particularly on the work of IUCN in this area.

In 1948, a few scattered scientists and amateur conservationists had some familiarity with the plight of a handful of the species of mammals thought possibly or probably to be threatened with extinction or decline. Evidence came from hearsay, personal reporting, anecdotes, observations by colonial administrators interested in wildlife or by scientists in the course of other work, and occasional research reports. Use could also be made of the IOPN card index on threatened species drawn up under Tienhoven's guidance by Colonel Rasmus Hoier, formerly of the Parc National Albert. Information on the status of some species existed in some journals, for example the *Zoological Record* of the London Zoological Society. The volumes on threatened species in the old and new worlds by, respectively, Harper and Allen, published by the ACIWLP in the 1940s were in addition a basic data source;[9] and in its 1947 report, IOPN continued this kind of work by publishing notes on the gorilla, European and American bisons, and mammal species in the Malaysian archipelago, New Guinea and Australia.[10] Some data had been generated by the various international conventions then in existence, for example in relation to whales. The 1900 London Convention on African conservation included Schedules which listed species needing some form of protection; a similar device was adopted in the 1933 Convention. Here, though, the problem was that the data on which the lists were drawn up were not adequate, particularly by the late 1940s, and there had been varying motives for including particular mammal species in Schedules, including that of trying to impress on local and colonial authorities the need for stricter enforcement of conservation legislation. More solid steps towards the identification of regional problems had, however, been taken in the context of the provisions of the 1940 Washington Convention on wildlife preservation in the Americas.

Even so, this constituted a flimsy basis on which the IUPN could begin work on threatened species of mammals. Hence the importance of the conference on international nature protection problems scheduled by UNESCO, and prepared by IUPN, for the end of August 1949, immediately after the more general United Nations conference on the conservation and utilisation of the world's natural resources (UNSCCUR). From the start this was planned by Harroy and Coolidge as a trailblazing endeavour. The union's Executive Board 'took the risk of deliberately breaking away from the tradi- tional practice of devoting most of the discussion at such gatherings to questions of perfecting conservation legislation and of managing reserve areas'.[11]

One of the four sections of the programme of the Lake Success conference was devoted instead to the subject of international co-operation in the stimulation of ecological research. It treated, amongst other topics, emergency action for preserving vanishing species of fauna and flora. Coolidge himself was the prime mover on this particular question, but the meeting generally ·served to bring together leading scientists interested in problems of conservation, including Fraser Darling and Theodore Monod. Discussion ranged broadly over a wide range of causal factors: the introduction of exotic species, modification of agricultural practices, hunting, intensive harvesting of wild species, collecting, trophy collection, the introduction and spread of disease, pollution and, in related sessions on birds, the impact of lighthouses, high-tension cables and other technological developments. The longer term significance of the Lake Success conference, however, lay in its production of lists of threatened species. That for mammals was based in part on status reports on ten vanishing species drawn up by Antoon de Vos, then of the Department of Lands and Forests in Canada, and on threatened species of European fauna and flora prepared by Helmut Gams.[12] After further deliberation, those considered to be most in danger of extinction were listed as the Javan and Indian rhinoceroses, Asiatic lion, Burmese brow-antlered deer, giant sable antelope, North African bubal, Tasmanian wolf, marsupial banded anteater, wisent (the European bison) and the various species of chinchilla; together with the mountain zebra, Caribbean monk seal, Mediterranean seal and Addo bush elephant. The list, it was emphasised, was provisional and further additions were intended. The aim was to cite prominent examples of threatened mammals in order to draw wider public and scientific attention to the precarious state of the world's fauna. Resolutions of the conference as a whole drew particular attention to the need for additional information on orang-utans, both the Javan and Sumatran rhinoceros and other Indonesian species, and the status of the great Indian one-horned rhinoceros in Assam. The world, it was concluded, faced 'an increasing list of threatened and vanishing species of fauna and flora'.[13]

The meeting also formally proposed that the IUPN maintain an 'open list' of rare and threatened animal species. This was in effect already under way, since the working arrangement agreed to by IUPN and the International Office included provision for future use and development of the various lists of threatened species on which work had begun in the 1930s. The task was pursued by the union's Survival Service network under Coolidge, which was formally designated as a Commission in 1956. However, after the excitement and sense of anticipation generated by the conferences of the late 1940s, including that at Lake Success, the pace was now necessarily slower. The gap between needed information and the resources available to get it was a daunting one. It was accordingly decided to restrict attention initially to those species on the Lake Success list of mammals. (According to the listing in Resolution 16 of the conference, this included the Cuban solenodon, which had taken the place of the Mediterranean seal.) Countries that had representation in the union, whether officially or at the non-governmental level, were encouraged to draw up their own lists — a suggestion that was not to take root for more than two decades. Individuals with information on any of the Lake Success mammals were encouraged to bring it forward. Publication of a *Bulletin* by the IUPN from 1952 onwards was for this reason an important step. Information sent in from the Netherlands in 1953, for example, led to the inclusion of the oryx in a revised list of threatened mammals issued in July of that year.[14] Ten additions had already been made to the Lake Success list by the time of the union's Third General Assembly in September 1952, and with the growth of knowledge and a steady expansion of the web of contacts, it had been proposed that a provisional list also be set up to cover species on which sufficient information was still not available.

This pattern of the first half of the 1950s fell short of the expectations of the pioneering decade before it. And, as action in the field to halt destruction of habitats had been still less forthcoming, murmurings of discontent on the part of some members grew louder, especially in the United States. Lack of the adequate financial base set as a criterion by the Brunnen conference in 1947 constrained the new organisation's activities in every direction except those, most notably conservation education, where specific external funding was more readily available. Scientific work, Harroy lamented in 1954, was non-existent.[15]

From 1955 the search for data shifted to the offensive. Appreciation of the union's difficulties, combined with a sharpening of American conservationists' anxieties about the African environment — particularly the Serengeti in Tanganyika — and some discreet pushing by internationalists like Coolidge, opened up new channels of support. In particular, funding from Russell M. Arundel allowed IUPN for the first time to engage in research on the spot on questions of threatened species. Lee M. Talbot, a young ecologist from Berkeley whose father and grandfather had both been active in conservation in the United States, was tasked to survey the status of a number of threatened species of large mammals, notably those on the augmented Lake Success list, on which data were lacking because of their inaccessibility. Talbot travelled extensively in the Near and Middle East, southern Asia and Africa in 1956–7, after reviewing the Survival Service data collection work of Jean-Jacques Petter, of the Musée National d'Histoire Naturel in Paris. His report, *A Look at Threatened Species*, he described as 'of necessity a compromise between a scientific paper and a popular work'. Apart from surveys of problems and developments in the countries visited, it gave particular attention to six mammal species: the Sumatran, great Indian and Javan rhinos, Indian lion, Arabian oryx, and Syrian wild ass.[16] The project did more, however, than merely add to the stock of information available to conservation organisations, important though that outcome was. Its results were put to immediate educational and propaganda use by IUCN (the change of official title of the organisation was approved by its 1956 General Assembly), for example in its publication *Fossils of Tomorrow*. Talbot himself gave publicity to the project and to the activities of the union in a series of articles written for *The Times*, *National Geographic* and other journals; the collaboration it entailed between IUCN and the Fauna Preservation Society in London, which published the report, helped to consolidate a significant link between IUCN and conservation groups in the United Kingdom; and over the long term, a new pattern of initiative, and a regained sense of urgency, had emerged.

Other projects in the late 1950s were of a similar mould. Extensive research on threatened Indonesian species was carried out by Pierre Pfeffer in 1958; E. P. Gee investigated the status of the great Indian rhinoceros and brow-antlered deer, two of the species on the original Lake Success list of a decade earlier, in Nepal and Manipur in 1959–60; a survey of the status of the black rhinoceros was undertaken in the same period using data from correspondents in several African countries, following a proposal by Mervin Cowie, then Director of the Royal National Parks of Kenya; and, more dramatically, 'Operation Oryx' was launched in 1962 by Major I. R. Grimwood, Chief Game Warden of Kenya, and the FPS and resulted in the successful translocation of a breeding herd of the threatened Arabian species to the United States.[17]

But as IUCN's Secretary-General, M. C. Bloemers, commented in 1960 on the work of the organisation: the 'foremost item is collecting and classifying information'.[18] Co-operation with the FPS in London formed a key component of the strategy. Its Secretary, Colonel C. L. Boyle, took over responsibility for managing and developing the SSC's data collection on rare and endangered species, which still in practice usually meant mammals. There arose, however, the policy question of what to do with the collection. During the 1950s, it had generally been assumed that such information needed to be gathered and organised by IUCN for its own purposes, in order that it could better promote the interests of wildlife conservation on a worldwide basis. In the early 1960s, by contrast, the question began to be raised from various directions of the data being published essentially in a raw form to allow interested national conservation organisations to shape more rationalised research and educational programmes, and also policy recommendations to their governments that might be that much more effective. The union was experiencing significant changes in this period. The establishment, in London in September 1961, of the World Wildlife Fund, and the publicity the event attracted, gave new impetus to the drive for adequate and accurate data on threatened species, as, in a slightly different fashion, did the beginnings in 1961–2 of a major concentration by IUCN on problems of African conservation and on wetlands.

A list of thirty-four endangered species had already been put together in 1958 as a means of stimulating further information for the General Assembly of IUCN held in Warsaw in 1960. After this Assembly, a list of 135 species of mammals was duplicated in loose-leaf form as a 'Red Data Book', and a small number — forty-four — circulated to scientists and specialist institutions. The issue of distribution was still unresolved after the subsequent Assembly in Nairobi in 1963, though the consensus there was that circulation should be as wide as was financially feasible. By 1964, the SSC was in process of being reorganised by Scott and looked into the possibility of producing a revisable printed volume that would 'become a "Who's Who" dealing with rare creatures'.[19] A 'preliminary list' of 204 rare mammals was published that year in the *Bulletin*, and a more finalised list of 210 appeared in 1966 as the first of a projected series of *Red Data Books*.[20]

These volumes, in various forms and editions, became a central vehicle, if at times a controversial one, of IUCN operations. The format was designed to facilitate periodic updating. Sheets described species individually under such headings as distinguishing characteristics, distribution, estimates of numbers, status, breeding rate in the wild, reasons for decline, protective measures already undertaken or proposed, number held and breeding potential in captivity, and other relevant remarks and references. The greatest value of the *Red Data Books* lay in their constituting a basic, reliable and objective source of information which could readily be cited by other bodies, particularly by WWF.[21] The information was exploited more generally as a base for educational and promotion work. One of the issues that had arisen in the debate on publication of the series centred on the unsuitability of this kind of technical data as an instrument of conservation education directed towards a wider public audience. After further deliberation a popular, and successful, version of the *Red Data Book* series then available or in preparation was published in 1969 as *Wildlife in Danger*, edited by James Fisher, Noel Simon and Jack Vincent.[22] The more technical sheets, however, continued to serve as reference points for research, including that being undertaken by scientists and researchers in the SSC network of specialist groups. Preparation of the threatened species data for wider circulation also compelled further refinement of the various categories of endangeredness that had been traditionally employed as aids to data collation. In the early 1950s, for example, IUPN had devised a simple threefold scheme: (1) vanishing species, (2) threatened species, and (3) species which needed local protection to preserve representatives in certain areas.[23] This eventually evolved, after revision had been made to a classification worked out by the SSC in 1963, into a standard set of four categories: extinct, endangered, vulnerable and rare. More careful definitions and criteria were set for each.

This clarification of the language with which threats to the world's wildlife could be discussed both in scientific and non-scientific settings can itself be regarded as one of the key contributions made by the SSC under Scott's leadership in the 1960s. It also reflected his instinct for the effective communication of facts and ideas. It was the SSC's thesis, Scott said in

1966, 'that the present rate of extinction — not less that one higher vertebrate animal from each year — could be substantially reduced without delaying the progress of mankind, simply by making more people aware of what is happening, by the exercise of ingenuity, by the application of scientific knowledge, and by the promotion of a little foresight'.[24] In the longer term, reverberations inside countries were significant, as different kinds of national *Red Data Books* began to appear to give form to Harroy's forgotten proposal of 1952.[25]

The *Red Data Books* did, however, encounter difficulties and criticisms. One was practical. The format was not one popular with libraries because of the extra work entailed in replacing the colour-coded sheets at intervals (though the ease with which they could be removed attracted those students working to deadlines who were less troubled than others by their consciences). More substantially, the political implications of the inclusion, exclusion or recategorising of a species made for problems on the part of compilers. Writing in 1971 of the hazards involved in preparing the volume on threatened birds, Colonel Jack Vincent noted that of 'resisting pressures to have species included ... by those whose motives are somewhat ulterior' who were advocating the inclusion of a species 'in order to "twist the arm" of some local authorities towards generally better conservation procedures'.[26] Dropping a species could be an equally sensitive matter. Soviet scientists protested against, as being premature, the removal of the polar bear from the endangered mammal list at a critical phase of the developments that eventually culminated in the signing in 1973 of an international convention for protection of the species. There were periodic complaints from specialists of factual errors, perhaps only to be expected in an enterprise of such an ambitious scope; of the initial emphasis, corrected later, being simply on mammals and birds; or of the lack of attention given to regional or local problems (as opposed to the world population of a species), to species in the wild that had not yet shown signs of becoming rare (the compilers of the volume on amphibia and reptiles used the innovation of a list of taxa thought likely to move into the endangered category in the near future if causal factors then at work continued), or to wider arguments and debates on conservation problems and approaches. The format also proved to be one unsuited to the special needs of threatened plants — we will come back to this question shortly. Finally, it could also by the 1970s be argued that the vocabulary of crisis bred indifference. Commenting in 1978 on the status of the Mediterranean monk seal, Keith Ronald, head of the SSC's seal group of specialists, said that 'It would be tempting to ascribe the terms "endangered" or "threatened" ' to the species, 'but these are terms of overuse and hence liable to be read and passed by'.[27]

The idea of a regularly appearing journal as an alternative to the volumes was first raised in 1964 and explored again in 1976–7, but met with apparently insuperable publishing obstacles.

Particular species of mammals have at times been singled out for attention, in parallel with the development by the SSC of a network of specialist working groups of scientists and conservationists. The reasons for such focusing of effort have varied. Information could reveal a new level of threat to a species. While Indonesian species had long (at least since the 1930s) been a matter of concern, a report on the international trade in orang-utans and on their severely depleted status presented to IUCN's General Assembly in 1963 gave the animal fresh prominence.[28] In other cases, the organisation was called upon to develop greater interest in certain species. A symposium held in Prague in 1959, for example, recommended greater involvement of the union with Soviet and Mongolian scientists working on the Przewalski horse.[29] From the middle 1960s the number of scientific and technical meetings held to deal with this kind of question grew steadily. Several such gatherings emphasised lack of knowledge as a major factor hindering conservation. In these cases — as in conferences on ungulates held in Alberta in 1971, or on wolves in Stockholm in 1973[30] — the conference came to be recognised as a forum that itself generated new information as well as insights into the problems of better management and conservation of species. The pattern set at the Lake Success meetings in 1949 of using conference resolutions as an instrument for highlighting threats to the status of particular species also persisted in later decades. While sceptics cast doubt on the efficacy of this device in terms of changes brought about in government policies, it is likely that the sustained momentum developed by some issues in this way, through repetition at successive fora and echoes in a variety of different organisations, has had a discernible impact. Apart from the orang and the polar bear, cases in point are whales and the tiger. The receptivity of states and intergovernmental organisations to such prodding is a topic taken up in the next two chapters.

Increasingly by the middle and late 1970s, though, species were securing a position at the centre of the stage more by virtue of their significance in terms of broader programmes of ecosystem conservation. Marine mammals are a good example. Before turning to these broader perspectives, and to the continuing debate on conservation strategies and methods in relation to particular species, it will be useful to look briefly at the development of knowledge of the circumstances of rarer species of birds, other animals and plants.

The Lake Success conference of 1949 must again be taken as the post-war starting-point for international policy on threatened birds. The ICBP, however, was by 1949 a long-established body. It had had an active interest in this question at least as far back as its collaboration with the International Office in the early 1930s. Before the foundation of IUPN it had already begun to pick up the threads of pre-war activity in Europe. Therefore, for ornithologists the 1949 conference more clearly represented one step in a longer historical evolution than it did for mammal specialists. The approach was also different. In drawing up a list of those of the rarest species of birds which seemed to be threatened with extinction, the participants decided to exclude a number of species: some that were extremely rare were in fact omitted, either because their situation seemed to be hopeless, or else because it was considered that everything possible was already being done. As with mammals, the list of birds was aimed primarily at arousing wider interest: comprehensiveness and exactitude could come later. Twelve were identified: the Arabian ostrich, Hawaiian goose, New Caledonian kagon, Indian pink-headed duck, Australian ground parakeet, Laysan duck, Marianas mallard, Cuban ivory-billed woodpecker, Bermuda petrel of Cahow, Marianas megapode, California condor and Eskimo curlew. The North American whooping crane was added after discussion and examination of available data on its status.[31]

The ICBP was the natural institution to pursue further investigations, though the early relationship with IUPN was not without its frictions. The limitations of the Lake Success list were readily acknowledged. In the future many birds would be threatened, ICBP's President stated in 1950: it would be easier to add a hundred more species to the list than two or three.[32] At IUPN's 1952 General Assembly in Caracas, twenty-five species were placed on a provisional list for possible inclusion, and ICBP was formally invited to gather information and make recommendations with regard to species on the original Lake Success list.[33] One complicating factor was work already under way in the United States by James Greenway, who was preparing a companion volume on birds to those published in the 1940s by Harper and Allen on mammals. His survey, *Extinct and Vanishing Birds of the World*, appeared in 1958 as a special publication of the ACIWLP.[34] This became a standard source, and augmented more conventional ornithological materials such as regional or species monographs, or Peters' *Check List of Birds of the World*, then still incomplete.[35] But there was no real equivalent here of the impact on mammal data collection of Talbot's project. Collection of data at Dillon Ripley's offices in Washington, and at the ICBP Secretariat in London, moved ahead gradually; updated reports on the world's threatened bird species were prepared for IUCN and ICBP Assemblies and Conferences from 1954.[36]

During the following decade, the core list of those felt to be threatened with extinction was consolidated and a lengthier list of rarer birds prepared for publication in the *Red Data Book* series. Steller's albatross, for example, had been added to the Lake Success list at IUCN's 1958 Assembly in Athens. Others were deleted in 1960 on the basis of a report to ICBP's Congress in Tokyo by George Merck: the Arabian ostrich was already extinct, and the population of the Laysan duck was held to be as large as the habitat would hold. Two were added: the kakapo and Japanese crested ibis. The Philippine golden-backed hanging parakeet, another candidate, was turned down on the grounds that it was a subspecies probably extinct with other forms still abundant.[37] But, in line with the changing thinking behind the work of the SSC from 1963–4, it seemed increasingly evident that exclusive emphasis on the direst cases was too narrow, and also that greater publicity to threatened species was needed outside the still rather circumscribed world of international conservation. Data collection on a wider front was already being undertaken by Vincent in London, following work there by H. G. Alexander in the late 1950s. Under Vincent's tutelage it grew into a major enterprise. Early in 1965 ICBP issued a revised list of 'rare' birds, comprising 335 species and subspecies. This enlargement of scope allowed greater flexibility, and more room for reasonable doubt, than the more restricted list of species thought to be on the verge of extinction. Vincent also drew up a list of 162 species and subspecies extinct since 1600 in parallel with a similar IUCN list on mammals.[38] In 1966 *Aves* finally appeared as the second volume of the *Red Data Book*.

The emergence of specialist working groups of ICBP, particularly from 1969–70, then assisted the process of filling out the known facts about the rarer species and families of birds. As Vincent admitted in 1966, the task was far from easy: it was difficult to be precise about which rare birds should be included in collections such as the *Red Data Book*. Many species were known only from a few specimens, with recorded knowledge so scanty that it was impossible to guess at the status of a population.[39] During the 1970s groups were established to investigate further, amongst others, bustards, pheasants, flamingoes, birds of paradise, cranes and parrots. The development and organisation of this network is explored further in a later chapter.

Other parts of the animal kingdom got off to a late start in international conservation. Mammals and birds have always managed to hold on to the lead because of the powerful combination that each could exploit of active and extensive scientific interest and public fascination. The tortoise may have won his race against the hare, but in the real world defined by human priorities reptiles for a long time barely reached the starting line. Early in the 1950s, the Survival Service of IUPN defined its scope as being threatened mammals, plants and 'other animals'. Nor was there much pressure from member organisations or from outside to develop expertise within the last category. A change of emphasis, or at least a growing appreciation that a certain imbalance had entered into international conservation research, began to appear later in the 1950s. In 1957 a group of more than 120 scientists from various countries sent a petition to IUCN stressing, with some urgency, the dangers of extinction facing crocodiles.[40] But progress in the more obscure areas was slow in the 1960s. Lack of conservationist interest in species of fish threatened with extinction (other than those of economic value) was noted in the 1969 *Red Book*.[41] *Red Data Book* volumes on amphibia and reptilia were, however, published in 1970; and by this time the SSC had specialist groups dealing with crocodiles, freshwater fish and marine turtles. In the years following, a number of species attracted wider scientific and public interest because of their importance in relation to more broadly defined problems: crocodiles in the context of issues arising in the international trade in endangered species, for example, or marine turtles in those pertaining to ocean research and conservation. Despite this, sustained and determined pushing on their behalf by a few key individuals seemed to remain a condition for further concentration of effort.

Plants were likewise for long a neglected subject. Lack of much conservation interest in them (apart, again, from those of economic importance) until the late 1960s and early 1970s did not, however, reflect a lack of appreciation of their ecological significance by international organisations. Indeed, there was considerable discussion of threatened plant species at Lake Success in 1949. Botanists at the conference gave it as their opinion that most of the thousands of species of insular plants were endangered, and that the situation of others was serious. It was practical difficulties, rather, that stood in the way of the kind of data-gathering work that followed the conference on birds and mammals. Vast numbers of species were involved. These could not be listed in the same manner as were threatened mammals and birds, each of which began at around a dozen and grew to no more than a few hundred. There were, further, problems of a theoretical or conceptual kind. It was more useful, and realistic, to talk in terms of communities of plants: preserving threatened plants was essentially a matter of preserving environments, which, as Roger Heim, Vice-President of IUPN, pointed out, made it difficult to start the business of compiling lists of particular species. Even protection of areas was problematic, others added, since many plants belonged to subclimax stages and would tend to disappear in time. The botanists nonetheless followed the lead of the mammalogists and ornithologists and noted what appeared to be the most urgent threats, in particular those facing certain Alpine plants and the rubber liana of tropical regions. A resolution of the conference as a whole called on IUPN to recommend to governments that they take action to protect areas supporting plant communities which contained rare or vanishing plant species, and proposed that the union should maintain an open list of such species.[42]

Some moves were made in the early 1950s to implement this strategy, but it was a full two decades before threatened plants emerged as a priority concern of IUCN. At IUPN's Assemblies in 1950 and 1952, the view continued to be that little could in practice be done on the question of lists. Procedures for collecting data on threatened mammals were felt not to be applicable; work should rather be done, it was argued, on the ecological processes involved in declines of species, on descriptions of plant communities, or on related questions to do with habitats. The fact that FAO was already engaged in extensive research on problems of plants of economic interest, including threatened species, created some difficulties of defining an appropriate niche for the union. Threats to certain plants in Madagascar and South Africa in particular were, however, identified.[43] The Survival Service of IUPN took the general question sufficiently seriously to urge the convening of a symposium on vanishing and rare plant species and habitats; this eventually took shape in modified form as part of the meetings in Paris in July 1954 of the Eighth International Botanical Congress, one of the most important post-war botanical fora.

Work on plants then fell into abeyance, although the neglect was periodically noticed by conservationists. In 1962, a small botanical subcommittee of the SSC was set up under Sir George Taylor, who organised the carrying out of a survey of botanists with a view to discovering the scale of the problem of threatened plant species. Over the next three or four years, appreciation mounted of the ecological significance and the importance of the conservation of plants and their habitats, and the issue was again raised at the Assembly of IUCN in Lucerne in 1966. Discussions between staff of IUCN and of the Royal Botanic Gardens, Kew, and support from the Royal Society in London, led finally to the commencement of research in 1968 aimed at the compilation of lists of threatened plants. This work, carried out by Ronald Melville, culminated two years later in the production of a *Red Data Book* volume on angiosperms.[44] Out of it also came the statistic than an estimated 20,000 species of plants were threatened in one way or another in the world, a large proportion of them being on the edge of extinction. The sheer immensity of the problem, combined with a growing realisation of the practical value to man of many hitherto unutilised — even undiscovered —

species, served to make threatened plants a high priority of IUCN in the middle and later 1970s. The SSC established a Threatened Plants Committee (TPC) in 1974 under Professor J. Heslop-Harrison, Director of the Royal Botanic Gardens, Kew, and a small secretariat headed by Grenville Lucas and Hugh Synge collected data eventually used as the base for a new *Red Data Book* published in 1978, consisting of 250 sheets, each a case history of a particular threatened species.[45] By then, the TPC estimated, a minimum of 25,000 species of plants were either dangerously rare or under serious threat.[46]

*Conservation of ecosystems*

We have so far been looking at approaches to the conservation of species of mammals, birds, other animals and plants that have rested first and foremost on the construction of an adequate foundation of facts on which actions, and recommendations for action, could be built. A similar route can be traced out for habitats. It was not only in relation to the special problems of plants that conservationists repeatedly underscored the requirement of habitat protection. Deterioration of habitat was a central factor consistently and increasingly referred to in studies of threats to mammal and other animal species. Further, though this concern was slower to get off the ground, the goal of conserving distinctive and representative samples of different ecosystems in themselves drew greater recognition. Its origins can be discerned in the broader ecological interests of IUPN, and also to some extent of UNESCO, in the early 1950s, and more particularly in the activities of both organisations connected with conservation and development issues in arid regions. The IUPN Commission on Ecology, founded in 1954, became under the American ecologist Edward Graham an important forum in which these questions were tackled. At meetings of the Commission in London in 1955 and at the IUCN General Assembly held in Edinburgh in 1956, for example, ideas were mooted — including the needs for an inventory of islands, and for a uniform system of habitat descriptions — that acquired momentum only in the 1960s and 1970s.[47]

Wetlands were for the 1960s what arid regions had been for the early 1950s: a cohering and aggregating focus around which a variety of sometimes divergent concerns could gather. By the end of the 1950s, several organisations were moving separately towards making different aspects of wetlands conservation central to their plans for the following decade. In 1960–1, IWRB's Executive Board was increasingly seized with the issue of threats to birds posed by the draining of marshland in Europe, especially ⸱ in France and Spain. The vulnerability of the marismas of Guadelquivir provided the Bureau with an immediate and urgent question that sharpened its attention to this problem. In this as in other similar cases, however, the constraint of lack of data soon became frustratingly evident.[48] Graham's Ecology Commission was also discussing wetlands at this time. On its initiative, IUCN decided early in 1961 to embark on a major programme dealing with their conservation and management. The aims of Project MAR, as it was labelled, were to publicise threats to these habitats, assemble data on the means of conserving wetlands, make an inventory and classification of all European and north-west African wetlands of international importance, and ultimately to offer technical assistance for the establishment by governments of reserves in such areas.[49]

A conference held in the Camargue (to where IWRB had moved its headquarters under Luc Hoffman[50]) in November 1962 established the underlying philosophy of the project and initiated the international scientific research programme connected with it. Development of an appropriate classification scheme was a central problem. Without this a useful list of wetlands of international importance in Europe and north Africa clearly could not be compiled. It was agreed that every kind of shallow marine, coastal or inland wetland was encompassed within the project's objectives; deeper waters were less in danger of being drained. The scheme thus comprised (1) coastal waters, (2) shallow coastal lagoons, (3) coastal marshes, (4) shallow inland salt, brackish or alkaline water, (5) shallow static inland fresh water, (6) shallow flowing inland fresh water, (7) inland freshwater mineral marshes, and (8) peatland. A list of European and north African wetlands classified according to this scheme was drawn up and published by IUCN in 1965.[51] By the mid-1960s participating scientists were drawing attention to the requirement that coverage be extended to include wetlands in the Near and Middle East. Both IWRB and IUCN's Ecology Commission were making plans for such an expansion of their range of research and conservation interests, and after a division of labour had been worked out, a conference held in Turkey in 1967 took the MAR project in this direction.[52] Two related projects followed close on the heels of MAR concerns: TELMA on threatened peatlands; and AQUA, aimed at production of an inventory leading to the conservation of aquatic habitats of international importance to science.[53]

By the late 1960s, however, data collection on international wetlands was being harnessed more to the preparation of an international convention on the subject. This possibility had been foreseen, and advocated, by the MAR conference of 1962. It took shape as a treaty on wetlands of international importance (the phraseology itself reflecting its antecedents in that conference) signed at Ramsar, in Iran, in 1971. The sequence of events involved in this process of convention-making will be studied more closely later.

The International Biological Programme (IBP) was more ambitious. Proposals for an international research programme on 'the biological basis of productivity and human welfare' were hammered out within IUBS in 1959, and, when finalised, endorsed by ICSU. The way in which the programme was structured was also in part an outcome of discussions held with IUCN officials and Commission specialists. The programme as a whole can be summarised briefly. It was eventually divided into seven sections: three on primary and secondary production in, respectively, terrestrial, freshwater and marine environments; one on fundamental aspects of primary production; two on human adaptability, including problems of the use and management of biological resources; finally, a section on the conservation of terrestrial biological communities (IBP/CT).

In scope, the IBP thus stretched considerably wider than a concern with ecosystem conservation. It did, however, have more than a tangential connection with the objectives of IUCN. Particularly in light of the union's wetlands work in the 1960s, great effort was made to try to ensure that IUBS and IUCN would not overlap unnecessarily in the conservation areas of the programme. The relatively small number of scientists and conservationists involved at the outset in defining the aims of the IBP/CT section, and the informal meshing of the IUCN and IUBS networks at the level of contacts maintained between individuals, facilitated this task. And, largely through Graham's own initiative after exchanges with key groups such as the British Ecological Society and the Ecological Society of America, the ecology component of IUBS was formally strengthened at its 1961 General Assembly in Amsterdam.[54] The move both brought more into the open, and mellowed somewhat, earlier IUBS reservations about IUCN's representativeness of the field of ecology and, perhaps, on the part of some members, its scientific standing. The goal of IBP/CT was accordingly an amalgam of the distinctive approaches of the two organisations: 'The establishment of the necessary scientific basis for a comprehensive programme of preservation and safeguarding of areas of biological or physiographical importance for future scientists.'[55] Its work centred on use of a check list as a basis for collecting information for a world survey and classification of 'ecological types of environment and their variants'. This survey was to record both habitats and their representation, or lack of representation, in the protected natural areas of the world. Research for this section fitted in well, therefore, with IUCN's own preparation, after the Seattle national parks conference of 1962, of a standard list for the United Nations of the world's national parks and equivalent areas. Following the conclusion of the five-year programme in 1970, IUCN took over responsibility for the IBP/CT Check Sheet Survey. Its duration also saw a number of collaborative efforts, for example the joint IUCN–IBP sponsorship of an important conference on tundra productivity and conservation held in Edmonton in 1969,[56] and the AQUA project on aquatic habitats.

This kind of pattern, of IUCN participation in and pressure for greater emphasis to be given to the conservation aspects of international scientific endeavours, was repeated for UNESCO's Man and the Biosphere (MAB) programme of the 1970s. Because of the scale of the programme, however, and the intergovernmental character of that organisation, the union's role tended to be more limited. The programme was launched in 1970. Its origins lay in the 'biosphere conference' organised by UNESCO in 1968, a seminal forum anticipation of which coloured much international conservation activity in the 1960s, and to which, in turn, can be traced one source of the Stockholm environment conference of 1972. The aim of MAB was described as being 'to develop within the natural and social sciences a basis for the rational use and conservation of the resources of the biosphere and for the improvement of the relationship between man and the environment'. Fourteen central themes were tackled. Of these, one on 'conservation of natural areas and of the genetic material they contain' (Project 8) was most germane to IUCN's interests. In exchanges between IUCN and UNESCO officials, particularly at a meeting in Morges in September 1973, this project was accorded a certain prominence within the programme as a whole because of its logistic and conceptual relevance to other projects, such as those promoting research on undisturbed ecosystems, genetic and demographic change, perception of environmental quality, and environmental education.[57] Like the IBP, though, to which it can in some ways be regarded as a successor, the MAB programme encompassed a broad-ranging gamut of tasks that went far beyond those related to the conservation of nature.

One of its ultimate aims, on the other hand, echoed around international conservation bodies during the 1970s. This was the creation of an international network of biosphere reserves, or protected and representative ecosystems. Especially in the first half of the decade, ground-clearing classificatory work tied to this kind of goal was given high priority by IUCN. Schemes such as that by Wallace on the world's faunal regions were a traditional part of biology, but were generally considered inadequate as a basis for conservation in the 1970s. Fundamental taxonomic questions thus constrained the pursuit of ecosystem conservation goals; in relation to species, these problems had either already been resolved or else were amenable to easy handling through established international procedures. Ray Dasmann, then senior ecologist with IUCN, set out a biome classification scheme, with further subdivision into biotic provinces distinguished by vegetation, fauna or flora, in an article published in 1972; he then related it more specifically to IUCN's continuing activity of listing on behalf of the UN the world's national parks and protected areas.[58] Given not only the preoccupations of the MAB secretariat at UNESCO, but also the growing environmental conservation interests of other organisations such as the Council of Europe, attempts by IUCN staff to develop and refine such frameworks grew under the Director-Generalship of Gerardo Budowski. In 1975, for example, the union published a monograph by Miklos Udvardy which aimed to number consecutively each of the world's biogeographic provinces according to realm (Nearctic, Indomalayan, Australian, and so on) and biome type (kinds of forests or woodlands, deserts, tundra, grasslands, islands or lakes); and the American biologist G. Carleton Ray produced a scheme for the classification of the world's coastal and marine environments that was used in conjunction with international meetings held in 1975 in Tokyo and Tehran on marine park management.[59]

The gaps in the conservationist's arsenal of conceptual tools that these were designed to fill were hardly insignificant ones. Their genesis often highlighted the interconnectedness between different organisations and programmes. A habitat classification used at a (pre-MAR) symposium of 1958 on brackish waters was later modified and extended by the United States part of the IBP, and became incorporated in revised form as a source of Ray's IUCN coastal and marine classification; similarly, IBP work on vegetation was taken up later in world mapping efforts by both IUCN and the MAB programme.[60] The necessarily provisional character of the scheme made them vulnerable to criticisms of their alleged shortcomings. Professional conservationists dealing with specific areas of the world, for example in Europe, saw a need for greater subtlety and discriminations. UNESCO made use of IUCN classifications, particularly that by Udvardy, but, as MAB's International Co-ordination Council observed at the end of 1977, the value of this lay at a very general level: countries were therefore encouraged to develop compatible regional classifications as bases for their research and conservation activities.[62] Further, agreement was often difficult to reach on the criteria to be used for differentiating habitats. Interest in vegetation in the 1970s was in part a response to criticisms of the inadequacies of earlier zoogeographic schemes that were felt to have been weighted too heavily towards certain taxa. This definitional question had policy significance. In preparations for and implementation of the 1971 wetlands treaty, for example, some critics argued that too much reliance was being placed on migratory waterfowl and other bird populations as indicator species. Birds, that is, had a political clout that others lacked: and at the back of such debates in the technical arena frequently lay the inescapable fact that habitats fared poorly as vehicles for mobilising the kind of public interest and support that conservation groups sought.

*Conservation policy and ecodevelopment*

This brief survey has been able to do no more than skim the surface of the ecosystem conservation interests even of one organisation — albeit the major one in the area. Particular concerns have risen, got shuffled, and, though usually only temporarily, sunk. Some have managed the difficult feat of taking off and enjoying a political life of their own. The question of wetlands conservation did this for a time in the early 1970s, particularly, in Europe, in the context of an educational campaign mounted by the Council of Europe in Strasbourg. Similarly, IUCN and WWF stress on tropical rain forests in the mid-1970s touched a responsive chord among western publics becoming gradually more attuned to the character of ecological argument applied to questions of planetary survival. Where conservation requirements have overlapped with development needs — as in the case of marine issues or, though apparently with less staying power, desertification — the mixture could be a heady one.

The construction of new and the refurbishing of old rationales for conservation of nature has been an unavoidable accompaniment of research and data collection. Facts need the nourishment of argument if they are to live in a political milieu. Not even in the nineteenth and early twentieth-century heyday of the traditional nature-protection ethic could a basic set of assumptions and values, in the light of which facts about threatened species of flora and fauna could make sense, be taken for granted by the international organisations that gave high priority to education and propaganda in the pursuit of the goals of conservation. This has been still less true of the post-1945 period. In a world of expanding population and finite resources, the wellbeing of animals and plants — unless obviously useful to man — seemed a topic best relegated to a low position on the agenda of international issues. From the late 1950s and early 1960s began a process of adaptation by conservation organisations to the imperatives of economic development.

Two threads of a later synthesis came early. First, as we saw in the last chapter, debate in the immediate post-war period, particularly in the United States and Britain, often tied questions of nature protection to far broader issues of the management and utilisation of the earth's natural resources. A number of conservationists, among them Westermann of the International Office, advocated inclusion of some reference to this wider scope in the official title of the international body projected in the gatherings of 1946–8;[62] and other proposals of that time took this line of reasoning still further in their organisational designs. Harroy, Fraser Darling and others used IUCN fora and publications during the 1950s to press the view that economic and social objectives could be fully attained only if due recognition were given to ecological realities. Second, modestly couched suggestions were made about ways in which technological development could accommodate, at little cost, provisions for wildlife conservation. Lighthouses, to use a favourite ICBP example of the 1950s, could be constructed so as to avoid or minimise injury to seabirds; in Britain, various organisations put forward schemes for the linking by underpasses of habitats disrupted by new roads, or for greater exploitation of the potential for protecting waterfowl populations of reservoirs.[63] This kind of thinking had a longer term significance over and above the specific issues dealt with. It did, however, cause problems. No one organisation could nurture recognised expertise in all areas of human activity that had significant repercussions on the natural environment. The resources were simply not available. IUCN's Ecology Commission developed a sustained interest from the mid-1950s in pesticides and their effects on wildlife; ICBP became an effective voice on matters of oil pollution at sea, particularly as regards the consequences for seabirds. But many questions in practice lay tantalisingly out of reach.

The spread of development issues through UN organs and agencies in the 1960s, a product of the influx of new member states from the developing world, added a further twist to the dilemma. Former colonial territories contained a large proportion of the world's rare, beautiful and scientifically interesting creatures: but political élites in the newly independent countries showed few signs of sharing the preoccupations of western environmentalists. As early as 1956, IUCN was looking for ways in which conservation and development concerns could be reconciled. The basic principle was expounded that 'within the framework of financial and technical assistance to underdeveloped countries, landscape-planning based on ecological research should be the starting-point of the development programmes to be prepared'.[64] A further shift was effected at the union's 1960 Assembly in Poland. It was decided that the Executive Board should 'give more specific attention to the economic aspects of conservation, insofar as they relate to the responsibilities and functions of the Union'. Mention was made more particularly of the desirability of 'relating affairs of the Union to the work of international agencies and organisations concerned with the more practical aspects of resources management'.[65]

This momentum was reinforced in later years by several factors. IUCN meetings and conferences elaborated on the basic theme. At the world conference on national parks held in Seattle in 1962, two resolutions drew attention, respectively, to the importance of conservation in development programmes and to the need for international agencies to incorporate ecological studies into their planning.[66] Attempts by UN institutions to come to terms with these kinds of arguments were likewise a source of change. In 1962, UNESCO's General Conference and the UN General Assembly both passed key resolutions on the relationship between conservation and development that noted especially the need for aid to be given to developing countries for the conservation of their flora and fauna.[67] Contacts between IUCN and development agencies grew in this period; in 1961-2, for example, its Secretary-General, Gerald Watterson, was provided by FAO. Its increasing emphasis on African problems in the early 1960s provided much grist for the mill of conservationist self-questioning. Further, the membership of the union was altering. Greater representation from Third World countries assured the debate a regular airing. Zafar Futehally, then a Vice-President of IUCN, told its 1972 Assembly in Banff: 'To ask a starving man to conserve rather than exploit is, of course, pointless.' But this moved the focus from education and persuasion to economics: 'in most places trees will cease to be cut down only when kerosene or something similar is supplied free to the people'.[68] More attention to development needs was also urged by some members from the socialist states. The prestige of the union, argued B. N. Bogdanov, a Soviet member of IUCN's Executive Board, would be 'much enhanced by further strengthening of its attention to the social and economic aspects of nature conservation'.[69]

Yet the process of change has been gradual. More traditional concerns still tend to have the most vitality. Talk of wildlife as a 'resource', or of species in terms of 'harvesting' — on no matter what sound management principles — can raise hackles and open up concealed fissures in the conservation network. One catalyst has been expediency. Scott in 1962 summed up the consensus of one meeting as being that 'ethical and aesthetic considerations were probably more important than economic considerations but that in the present stage of civilisation the economic arguments would still be needed for some time, and it was therefore important to arm ourselves with these economic facts'.[70] Another has been the aggregating of typically conservationist and developmental issues in broader syntheses. This process was, in more general terms, an important feature of the preparations for the UN Conference on the Human Environment of 1972. Maurice Strong, Secretary-General of the Conference and later Chairman of the Bureau in IUCN's revised post-1977 constitution, used the term 'ecodevelopment' as a shorthand label for this kind of tack. According to Dasmann in 1977, this meant that development should be ecologically sustainable; appropriate in terms of both the ecological relationships and constraints of a bioregion, and its local cultures and energy resources; and should take account of and provide for nature conservation (a point, he added, often in danger of being overlooked by more technologically or urban oriented environmentalists).[71]

The upshot of this internal debate was increasing attention to specific development issues: something of a contrast to the macrolevel arguments of the early 1950s about the global balance of population, resource and environmental factors. A Virginia conference of 1968 on the ecological implications of technological development led eventually, after talks with members of the World Bank and UN Development Programme staffs, to the publication in 1973 by IUCN and the Conservation Foundation of a volume coauthored by Dasmann on *Ecological Principles for Economic Development*.[72] This was not intended to break new ground, but rather to meet the requirement for a compact textbook of ecological guidelines for development planners. It set out in very general terms ecological and development needs in humid tropical lands and pastoral lands in semi-arid and semi-humid regions, and discussed problems connected with agricultural development projects and river basin projects. It was followed up in subsequent years by preparation by IUCN of a series of guidelines for development planning, each dealing with a particular topic. The organisation's technical meetings in the 1970s continued to explore these themes, particularly at the Banff General Assembly of 1972, which reiterated that 'comprehensive and competent scientific and technical evaluation of relevant ecological factors normally be made publicly available as a prior condition before any such project be accepted or acted upon'.[73] But history, as well as the character of the subject of nature conservation, checked a full-fledged transition to its becoming a development-oriented body. Its role in 1977–9 was rather that of prodding such agencies where possible, particularly in the UN system, into greater awareness of the ecological dimension of their activities. As such, it occasionally in return met criticism of its own relative weaknesses in the development area. The relationship between conserving and developing, in other words, was still being worked out.

Conservation of nature, to be effective, must rest on scientific research of formidable scope and diversity. Given the fact of meagre resources for carrying out even such preliminary functions as data collection and the locating and co-opting of independently existing expertise, IUCN, like other conservation bodies with broadly similar aspirations, was faced in its early years with difficult choices. Its scientific policy dilemmas were rendered still more acute by the stress on holistic thinking inherent in the discipline of ecology. Yet specialisation was necessary: not only because a free rein was not financially viable, but also because the process of legitimisation tended to put a premium on distinctiveness and the exclusive possession of special skills. The core areas, then, are the threatened species and ecosystems of the world, but no watertight definitions of scope are possible. On occasions, through its technical meetings and publications series, IUCN has been a significant forum of debate on a variety of matters: the management and administration of protected areas, for example, including national parks; problems of pollution and the effects on wildlife populations of pesticides, areas investigated by the union's ecology commission from the late 1950s; the introduction of species, on a planned or accidental basis; game ranching, tsetse fly control, and threats to crops from birds, elephants and other animals in Africa; the captive breeding of endangered species. On topics such as the last, links have been forged with other more specialised institutes. On others, such as criticism of the Maximum Sustainable Yield (MSY) concept as a foundation for the managing of stocks of exploited wild species, notably whales, IUCN debates and positions have both drawn from and had an impact on the wider policy arena.

To the extent, however, that scientific expertise in key areas was not available to it — either through the advisory commission structure or in the secretariat itself — the making of the union's scientific policy has been seriously constrained. This has been a periodic complaint of biologists working in specific fields: specialist advice on a particular threatened species was being ignored; the union lacked the capacity to make sound judgments on many questions ostensibly within its competence. Such nagging, it should be added, has been less prominent in the 1970s than it was earlier. A similar difficulty arose with the growing shift towards a development focus. The questions here called for different batteries of expertise drawing on economics and the social sciences. Some critics pointed to a failure to cultivate even minimal skills in such fields, and related this to the problems the union was encountering in dealings with intergovernmental bodies, particularly in the UN network. UNEP, for example, was more development-oriented than IUCN, and the gap between the two on this criterion occasionally made for friction, for example over the union's approach to the design of the World Conservation Strategy in 1978–9. And no significant contribution was made to the debates on the New International Economic Order (NIEO), the notion around which, for good or ill, world development questions tended to congregate in the middle and late 1970s. It is rather in the continuation and augmenting of the research by international organisations of the 1930s on the world's threatened species of wild fauna and flora that the union has made most impact. How this accumulating body of knowledge could best be applied in practice is the theme of the next chapter.

# 5  Political development: constraints and influence

Oh Monsieur si j'avois jamais pû écrire le quart de ce que j'ai vû et senti
sous cet arbre ... avec quelle simplicité j'aurois demontré que l'homme
est bon naturellement et que c'est par ces institutions seules que les
hommes deviennent méchans.
J.-J. Rousseau, 'Lettre à M. de
Malesherbes' (21 January 1762)[1]

Tienhoven's International Office defined its tasks in the 1930s largely in
terms of the gathering of information. So, in varying degrees, have
conservation organisations since then. For none, though, has the amassing
of facts been an end in itself. Still less have debates on the rationales for
conserving nature, or on guides for action by governments and other
bodies, been intended to take place in a vacuum. Knowledge has been
directed towards change: ultimately towards political and legal change. The
goal has been approached directly, through attempts to discover and plug
gaps in the domestic and international laws and practices of states, and
indirectly, by way of education and the seepage of ideas. The capacity of
these organisations to bring about change in the real world is the subject of
the present chapter.

*Conservation and states*

Any international organisation has essentially one aim only, IUCN's
Secretary-General, M. C. Bloemers, remarked in 1960: to provoke action
by authorities.[2] In the less forceful language of the 1970s, the appropriate
metaphor was seen to be the catalyst. But either way, the primary focus
was on states. These were the targets of persuasion. Given the facts of
sovereignty in the international system, however, it was readily apparent to
conservation organisations of an international character that the potential
for influence was limited, and that the constraints defining the art of the

possible were more intractable than they sometimes appeared to local and national groups. Overt attempts at influence were likely to fail, argued the voice of caution, and in the process to bring discredit, and a lessened capacity for future influence, on those concerned. For IUCN, ironically, state membership and the cultivation of scientific prestige provided additional constraints. A purely non-governmental organisation could expose the sins of wrongdoers with zeal: one whose membership comprised a hybrid mixture of states, government agencies and private bodies was denied much taste of this luxury. Some conservationists came to argue, therefore, that pursuit by IUCN of an expanded state membership as a means of furthering its goals was self-contradictory. Prestige defined in terms of scientific competence and impartiality was similarly perceived as an attribute desirable because it would nurture the power to persuade. But it was one that restricted the number of instruments available. A declaration that more research is needed to determine the status of a threatened species of flora or fauna might be good science, but is hardly the stuff of rhetoric.

Therefore, while the work of IUCN forms the point of departure for this chapter, it should be remembered that this is only one of many conservation organisations active at the international level, though one with just claim to be regarded as the linchpin of the system. Others have been less inhibited. The World Wildlife Fund, for example, though in a symbiotic relationship with IUCN, has been, or felt itself to be, considerably freer to publicise and criticise: some of its constituent National Appeals still more so. A more radical pitch was cornered for a time by Friends of the Earth International; while national components of the international Greenpeace movement have combined argument with physical efforts to intervene to disrupt seal culls, hunting and whaling. And IUCN itself, viewed from some angles, is less an organisation than an umbrella arrangement. A variety of member organisations, both state and non-state actors, bring a diversity of viewpoints to bear on conservation questions. Because of this some issues have proved impossible to resolve satisfactorily or for long. Should hunters' organisations committed to conservation be treated as like-minded bodies, to be admitted to the same clubs because of the opportunities for moulding and quiet diplomacy that these provide? Or do their ulterior motives put them beyond the pale?

If some conservation organisations are openly, even joyously, political in their orientations — in the sense of seeing themselves as being actively engaged in the political process — others are as consciously non-political. The terms 'political' and 'non-political' have meaning in this context not so much as ways of describing the policies and goals of different actors, as of understanding their perceptions of their place in the world. Thus IUCN was firmly identified by its President in 1963 as an organisation that enjoyed 'complete independence of all forms of political influence' and whose activities were 'directed by men chosen for their scientific standing, outstanding contributions to conservation and a willingness to co-operate regardless of other considerations'.[3] Stress on the non-political character both of IUCN and of the subject matter of nature conservation has been a recurrent theme. In the sense in which such statements are intended to be understood, they are essentially true. As was noted in an earlier chapter, IUCN has not been shaken by the conflicts that have intruded into UNESCO and other technical agencies of the United Nations system; nor, despite its western image, has conservation of nature been a question irrevocably or inevitably fastened to the interests of any one group of states or actors in the international system, or to any one ideology. Falls from grace have been few and minor. South African delegates were excluded from one General Assembly (the immediate context of Bourlière's remarks in 1963); membership of a small Taiwan non-governmental body was discontinued at one point in order to pave the way, it was hoped, for participation by representatives of the People's Republic of China; Soviet and West German delegates were embroiled in a protracted dispute in the early 1970s over membership of an organisation from the German Democratic Republic, an issue which, though multifaceted, could not be fully divorced from the currents of world politics.

On the other hand, too earnest a clinging to a belief in the separability of science and politics can betray misunderstandings of the nature of the latter. No organisations that can call for such fundamental changes in the ways people think, and in the manner in which governments make decisions, as have conservation bodies, can reasonably be regarded as apolitical. 'Thus conservation,' argued David Munro, IUCN Director General, in 1979, '— action aimed at the sustainable use of resources — is no fringe movement. The issues are inextricably bound up with human welfare and even survival. And inevitably they are political.'[4] The implications of this kind of characterisation, however, have been a nettle not so easy to grasp. IUCN's political roles, moreover, have changed as the organisation itself has changed. Its General Assemblies have been likened to the successive metamorphoses of an insect. From being a small grouping dedicated chiefly to opening up and maintaining channels of communication between conservationists in different countries, it had become by the late 1970s a central actor among intergovernmental agencies working in environmental policy areas. Players and bystanders see things differently.

In the next chapter, we will explore the relations and patterns of influence between the various intergovernmental and non-governmental organisations in the conservation network. Here, attention is directed towards states: first, attempts by IUCN and other bodies to bring about changes in national policy and legislation; second, approaches to conservation by way of developments in international law; and third, the more indirect routes of education and the patient fostering of more enlightened public attitudes.

*States and national policy-making*

The condition of some threatened species of wildlife seemed sufficiently urgent in the late 1940s to warrant the taking of immediate steps. In the two years between the founding of IUPN in 1948 and the convening of its second General Assembly in 1950, a total of twelve approaches were made to governments. Many were in connection with specific resolutions of the Lake Success conference. The governments of Indonesia, India and Belgium were approached by Harroy on questions pertaining, respectively, to orang-utans and rhinos, the Indian rhinoceros, and the Sart-Tilman forest. Other governments in western Europe were contacted and informed of the threats to nature posed by military manoeuvres. The experience was a sobering one. Over the next two-year period, only seven such direct approaches were made, for example over elephants in Indonesia threatened by a local extermination campaign and the condition of the rhinoceros in Nepal. Between 1952–4, the number was reduced to six, on national parks, dams, and certain species under investigation by the union's Survival Service. Polite rebuffs, disguised either as bland encouragement or the forwarding of notes to other government departments, made for greater reluctance on the part of Harroy to involve the prestige of the union in any and every situation. Extreme urgency, the chance of a successful outcome, or the absence of sensitive local toes, remained circumstances in which this strategy might be considered. In 1950, it was decided that IUPN should intervene in principle 'only in cases where local protection committees, incapable of effective action themselves, appeal to the Union for help'. Harroy reiterated the need for restraint two years later. Intervention in the affairs of states needed serious thought: the union was at risk of displeasing its friends by such activities. Approaches to governments were thus to be made only after careful study, he added in 1954, 'in order to avoid possible *faux pas*'.[5]

But therein lay a dilemma. Caution made good strategic sense. It did, however, risk arousing the indignation of a still largely unofficial membership. Lack of visible results in the early 1950s, and of an apparent willingness on the part of the union to embark on courses that might secure them, led to the resignation of the American Society of Mammalogists. The event was a serious one for the new organisation, in view of the past tradition of United States support for international conservation, IUPN's desire to gain wider recognition from scientific bodies, and its own preoccupations with the problems of threatened mammals. Combined with what looked in 1954–5 like an irreversible descent into financial insolvency, this sense of thwarted expectations produced what Roger Heim, then the union's President, described as 'une dure crise de croissance'.[6] The issue remained after recovery of the union's fortunes. Local organisations fighting local battles could see IUCN as a valuable ally, on the theory that governments would have rather more qualms about offending an organisation that could be introduced as a semi-official embodiment of world opinion. The government concerned, though, might also be an IUCN member, or one that the union wished to entice into membership. In 1966 a committee chaired by Scott produced a series of guidelines on Assembly resolutions. It was best 'not to become involved in local or highly detailed and specialised questions unless there are exceptional arguments for expecting that such interventions will achieve results not otherwise obtainable'. It was also best to avoid reiteration of previous resolutions. Some situations could better be handled not by a resolution and publicity but by a letter from the President or some other direct contact.[7]

Various forms of direct contact had already appeared. Following approaches from and discussions with ICBP in 1954, new arrangements were made by the British Government for RAF bombers in West Germany with a view to reducing threats to birds; an IUCN telegram to the Ministry of Foreign Affairs in Paris was instrumental in persuading the French authorities to postpone the opening of the wildfowl shooting season after the harsh European winter of 1962–3.[8] Individuals at Presidential or Secretary-General level have frequently been well placed by virtue of their other activities to initiate informal approaches to governments. Harroy, for example, came to IUPN in 1948 from a career of research in central Africa, and left in 1956 to become Governor of Ruanda-Urundi and Vice Governor-General of the Belgian Congo, returning in the 1960s while still a university professor in Brussels to work on national parks questions for the union. Apart from his abilities and unequalled past experience, one argument for recruiting Maurice Strong to fill a newly created senior position in IUCN's revised 1977 structure was precisely that his range of international contacts among governments afforded him an invaluable degree of ready access for promotion of world conservation goals. The effectiveness of Assembly resolutions was thus often a function of the extent to which road work had been done in advance, and of the availability of support and repair vehicles to follow behind. A 1960 resolution in general terms on international trade in rare species lent weight to earlier IUCN overtures to Nepali officials, particularly in the context of Gee's 1959 mission; as a result, game department inspectors were appointed in the larger towns to assist customs and local authorities in the control of the export trade in rare Nepali species.

This kind of strategy was from the start much more a part of WWF's armoury. A central objective was to 'use its influence to draw the attention of governments and local authorities concerned to the issues involved and to persuade them to take the necessary steps'.[9] The Boards of Trustees of WWF National Appeals in various countries have tended to have an active membership drawn from individuals prepared and able to undertake this task of persuasion. A number of successful personal interventions have been made by Prince Bernhard of the Netherlands as the Fund's President. From 1971 he also set about gathering together an international group of 1000 'influential men and women from 48 countries into what amounts to a working club for conservation'. Members of 'the 1001' were chosen on the basis of their capacity to carry influence in business or government; while at the same time, with a figure of $10,000 being set for membership, a capital fund of $10 million was being created.[10] A variety of other methods have been used by both IUCN and WWF to publicise questions. Meetings of WWF's Board of Trustees have used the formal passage and promotion of resolutions as a means of highlighting particular issues; like those of IUCN Assemblies, these have where possible incorporated complimentary pats on the back for governments or organisations thought to be moving in the right direction. (For both bodies, though, the constraints noted earlier have served to overrule suggestions for a more full-fledged moral equivalent of stick-and-carrot behaviourism.) Scott's advocacy of ingenuity as a tool of international conservation has also made its mark. By 1969, eleven governments had been approached by IUCN and asked to accept 'ultimate responsibility' for a particular species for which there was widespread international concern, and five of these had accepted.[11]

But neither IUCN nor WWF can be viewed simply as groups endeavouring to bring pressure to bear on wayward or forgetful governments. Like the technical agencies of the United Nations system, they have also acted increasingly as participants in the framing or implementation of national conservation and development policies. Three aspects of this relationship are useful to examine more closely: the provision of aid and technical assistance to countries or organisations;

development of a series of policy aids, particularly in relation to the creation and management of national parks and other protected areas, the framing of legislative instruments and the making of development policy; finally, the preparation on request from governments of specific policy recommendations pertaining to conservation and development plans. Though this work was more characteristic of the later 1960s and the 1970s, a couple of earlier departures from an exclusively research and education orientation deserve mention. In 1955 deposits of high-grade iron ore were discovered in the Mount Nimba region straddling the Liberia and Guinea borders. IUCN approached the authorities in Guinea in 1958 in connection with prospecting threats to the nature reserve established there by the French in 1944, and more particularly the disbandment of a research station constructed under the auspices of IFAN. The greater threat, however, appeared likely to arise on the Liberian side. A Swedish-American consortium, LAMCO, began mining operations there in 1963. The problem was raised more urgently by IUCN conservationists familiar with the uniqueness and scientific importance of the area, notably Monod and Kai Curry-Lindahl. The Swedish and Liberian Governments were contacted, and discussions held with LAMCO representatives. These resulted in a grant of $50,000 from the consortium for support of a two-year programme of ecological research. Details of this were worked out in talks between Curry-Lindahl and Liberian officials in 1963, and centred on suggestions for the establishment of a forest reserve similar to that which IUCN had been encouraging Conakry to maintain on its side of the border. Research directed towards advising the government on a long-term mining programme that would take account of conservation requirements began in 1964, and Mount Nimba remained an important IUCN priority during the rest of the decade.[12] The Fauna Preservation Society's 'Operation Oryx' of 1961–2 was a second, and rather different, instance. As we saw in the last chapter, the oryx had been added to IUPN's Lake Success list of threatened mammals on the basis of local information secured after 1949. Its decline was also noted in Talbot's research in the late 1950s; and subsequent reports confirmed its acutely threatened status. In August 1961, FPS, whose Secretary was also at that time Chairman of IUCN's Survival Service Commission, decided to launch an operation in what was then the British Eastern Aden Protectorate to capture a sufficient number of the animals to form a breeding herd. An impressive measure of collaboration between local Arab and British officials, rulers and armed forces units, and interested conservation groups such as the East African Wild Life Society, concerted by Major I. R. Grimwood, led to the successful establishment of a breeding group in Arizona.[13]

The Nimba and oryx ventures had as much psychological as practical significance. Morale was boosted by this evidence that international conservation bodies could successfully seize the initiative in relation to potentially delicate local situations and, through consultations with governments, push through plans for the protection of vulnerable species or habitats.

Provision of aid and technical assistance was clearly one way in which such programmes and operations could be mounted on a more secure, sustained and longer term basis. This was not an option that had been open to IUPN. Its own survival was sometimes a more pressing problem than that of wild animals. One central objective of WWF from its foundation in 1961 was to raise funds that would permit existing conservation organisations, particularly IUCN and ICBP, to avoid spending too much time immersed in depressing bank statements and to pursue their conservation goals more effectively. The Fund's success in raising money came quickly. By 1967 it had supported a total of 183 conservation projects in various countries totalling $2.2 million. This included funds for scientific research on a number of threatened mammals and birds in which IUCN and ICBP had long had an interest, such as the lynx, aye-aye, Javan rhino and crested ibis. Financial support was also given during WWF's first few years towards the establishment or better maintenance of national parks and protected areas, including the Coto Donana reserve in Spain (a focal point of concern for several years), Momela National Park in Tanzania, and the Kalabagh Wildlife Reserve in Pakistan. In line with the African preoccupations of the 1960s — IUCN in the early years of the decade was engaged in its African Special Project, and WWF itself was conceived in an atmosphere of widespread western fears for the future of east African wildlife — most attention was given to that continent (65 of the 183 projects), and relatively less (in terms of the numbers of projects funded) to, respectively, Asia, Europe, North and Central America (which region absorbed, however, the largest proportion of funds — 29.9 per cent) and South America.[14]

It is not possible both to summarise adequately and to do justice to the variety and extent of WWF-supported projects. The total amount of funds allocated increased steadily, with occasional step-level jumps. In 1968, the value of projects grant-aided by WWF more than doubled that of the previous year to reach nearly $1.4 million; in 1974 the figure exceeded $2 million for the first time.[15] Many scientific projects were supported over periods of several years, as in the yearly census of rhinos carried out in the Udjong Kulon reserve in Java from 1967, the results of which indicated a fairly steady increase of numbers of the creature. Funding for educational purposes has been a regular item, for example in aid (together with other conservation bodies) for the Wildlife Clubs of Kenya, a secondary school movement begun in 1968 with the aim of instilling in that country's future citizens a greater appreciation of the needs for conservation in the context of land-use policy. Assistance towards the purchase of land for use as protected habitat has continued, as has the provision of vehicles, fencing, binoculars, other equipment, or wardens' salaries in connection with existing national parks or protected areas. In this kind of work WWF has been able to blend to an unusual degree action at the international level with grassroots voluntarism: a campaign launched in 1968–9 by the Birmingham and Eastbourne groups of the WWF British National Appeal, for example, led to purchase of Cousin Island in the Seychelles as a reserve by ICBP.[16] The organisations in the central conservation network linked to WWF — IUCN itself, ICBP and IWRB — have also continued to benefit from the Fund's campaigning vigour.

There is a two-way link between WWF's capability to raise and dispense funds on the one hand, and to exercise influence on the policies of governments on the other. While in its first years WWF was necessarily restricted to allocating scarce funds to individual conservation projects, one review of its work observed, 'it has since built up such achievements and reputation that it can use its weight in the balance of decisions by governments and conservation authorities'. A total of thirty-one instances of interventions by the Fund's President, individual Trustees, or senior WWF staff were cited which during the course of one year had produced concrete results in the form of greater protective measures by governments. 'Whereas these "high level" approaches often take some time to bring results, and whereas such results are always difficult to evaluate, many led to actual achievements which may well reach — if not surpass — in importance the impact of the WWF's hard core activity, the allocation of grants to conservation projects.'[17] In some cases, policy recommendations have been made by IUCN and WWF on a sustained and regular basis over the course of several years. We will return to this facet of the relationship shortly.

Development of a series of policy aids, the second of the ways in which IUCN has attempted, rather more indirectly, to influence the course of government policy, has proceeded in several directions. One characteristic and long-established method has been the monitoring of the world's protected areas. This was already a well-worn topic by the time of the Lake Success conference in 1949. One section of this conference dealt with the specific problems of national parks bordering on frontiers between states or territories. Shortly afterwards plans took shape for publication of an *Atlas* of the nature reserves of the world, which eventually appeared in 1957.[18] Coolidge in particular was now actively pressing for a greater commitment by the union to this type of work. In 1958 it formally established an International Commission on National Parks to be headed by him. He was then the key figure in securing UN recognition of a more general international need for the kind of inventory which IUCN had compiled. The idea was aired at the union's 1958 Assembly. In October, its President, Jean Baer, wrote to UN Secretary-General Hammarskjoeld and offered the services of the union in the preparation and maintenance of a world list of national parks. Coolidge obtained wider official United States support for the proposal from his national parks commission offices in Washington. On a request from the United States, the subject was raised at ECOSOC's session in Mexico City in 1959, with Coolidge himself taking part in the discussion. A resolution was passed which requested the UN Secretary-General to establish in co-operation with UNESCO, FAO and other interested specialised agencies 'a list of national parks and equivalent reserves' for consideration by the Council at a later meeting, and to bring forward recommendations for maintaining and developing the list. IUCN and other organisations were invited to assist in the preparation of the proposed list.[19]

Work on the list was described by Bloemers, IUCN Secretary-General, in 1960 as 'the most important task the Union has ever undertaken'.[20] An initial list, based on replies to a questionnaire circulated to governments by the UN Secretariat on advice from IUCN, was adopted by ECOSOC in February 1961; a fuller one, based also in part on comments by UNESCO and FAO, became the principal reference document for the world conference on national parks held in Seattle, the site of the world exposition, in 1962. The Seattle conference, of which Coolidge was the prime mover, was something of a landmark in the post-1945 history of international conservation. Over the longer term, it stimulated the idea for a parallel world conference on threatened species; this surfaced eventually, in a considerably altered form, as UNESCO's biosphere conference of 1968, the immediate forerunner of the Stockholm environment conference of 1972. Seattle affirmed the principle that for every threatened animal or plant, an appropriate area of natural habitat should be provided in a national park or other protected area as an official sanctuary; it also resolved that IUCN should further develop a technical assistance role to advise countries on national parks programmes, and that the union should draw up for each main region of the world a preliminary list of the most representative habitats, which should be included in an official world list.[21]

The Seattle conference was intended, however, to be a forum that would focus wider attention on the question of national parks and their relation to world conservation requirements. The list prepared for it in two parts by the UN Secretariat and Coolidge's ICNP in 1961–2 was done quickly; given that it covered eighty countries, it is not surprising that on reflection afterwards it was thought to be insufficiently critical and found to contain some inaccuracies. The job of developing it into a more reliable and usable tool was taken on by Harroy. Two further points needed to be tackled. First, data on world habitats generated by the International Biological Programme's conservation section (IBP/CT) in the 1960s had to be incorporated if judgments about the representativeness of existing or planned protected areas were to be made. Second, definitions had to be sharpened. The 1961–2 list included a wide variety of different kinds of areas which enjoyed some measure of official protection, but which differed considerably in use and function. Not until 1969 was IUCN's Assembly, meeting in New Delhi, able to approve finally a scheme which distinguished carefully between national parks, scientific reserves, nature reserves, 'special reserves' (a term used in the 1968 convention on conservation in Africa) and recreation areas. Criteria for each were noted. The term 'national park', for example, was to refer to 'a relatively large area (1) where one or several ecosystems are not materially altered by human exploitation and occupation, where plant and animal species, geomorphological sites and habitats are of special scientific, educative and recreative interest or which contains a natural landscape of great beauty and (2) where the highest component authority of the country has taken steps to prevent or to eliminate as soon as possible exploitation or occupation in the whole area and to enforce effectively the respect of ecological, geomorphological or aesthetic features ... and (3) where visitors are allowed to enter, under special conditions, for inspirational, educative, cultural or recreative purposes.'[22] Such an extended definition was as much normative as it was a guide for the collection of data. Many areas officially labelled as national parks could fall short of the standards. Compilers of such lists could in principle, therefore, find themselves in the embarrassing and politically delicate situation of demoting a national park to another category or of excluding it altogether.

These problems notwithstanding, a second edition was published as a *UN List of National Parks and Equivalent Reserves* in 1971. This appeared in time for distribution before the Second World Conference on National Parks held in Yellowstone National Park, on the occasion of the centennial of its establishment, in September 1972. The event prompted assessments and stocktaking of national parks developments in the decade since Seattle. Most of the major problems were by then well known: increasing numbers of visitors, and the dwindling world resources of park-quality areas because of exploitation or casual destruction. As many as forty-three countries had no national parks at all, and some thirty others had only primitive parks systems.[23] From 1973, the *UN List* was published on a yearly basis — though in a considerably simplified format which excluded much of the detailed information of earlier editions. The provision of such detail was the function of a *World Directory of National Parks and Other Protected Areas*, the first issue of which appeared in 1975, and which adopted the loose-leaf format of IUCN's *Red Data Books*. A second instalment published in 1978 brought the *World Directory*'s coverage of countries to sixty. By the late 1970s, then, IUCN had available for circulation to governments, planning authorities and organisations two continuing series of publications on protected areas of the world that constituted potentially invaluable aids in the formulation of national park policies.

A second, and related, kind of aid for policy-making has been in relation to the domestic and international legislation of states. The IOPN had begun the systematic collection of legal instruments relating to wildlife conservation in the 1930s. Lack of resources prevented IUPN from devoting much energy to this kind of task. It was one early aim of the new organisation, however, to draft a standard national law that could be used as a model for the official conservation of threatened species. For the most part, though, legal data collection was a function carried out elsewhere, notably by FAO in the context of its wider interests — it too having inherited the work from its predecessor of the interwar years. A general review, *The Position of Nature Protection throughout the World in 1950*, was published by IUPN in 1951, with an Addendum in 1954. This summarised, on the unavoidably sketchy information then available, both the conservation problems and the legislative measures and policies of sixty-nine countries and territories.[24]

Lack of a follow-up to this book did not cause IUCN much anguish during the 1950s. In terms of data gathering, by far the more compelling need lay with threatened species. Increasingly, though, IUCN was becoming more involved in questions of law and policy as the conservation problems of countries were probed more deeply. Advice on how best to conserve wildlife could not be given, even if sought by governments, unless the union had at its disposal a firm base of comparative legal data on which to draw. The case for a fuller commitment on the part of IUCN to this kind of activity was pressed as a matter of some urgency by Wolfgang Burhenne. A Committee on Legislation and Administration was created in 1960. Its terms of reference were defined as being the collecting of information on laws and administrative ordnances in the field of conservation of nature and natural resources.[25] Burhenne immediately set about approaching governments for complete information on their conservation legislation; replies and documentation had been received from sixty-five by September 1963. From the spring of that year, data gathering was begun on matters related to the import, export and transit of endangered species of wildlife. This was then a developing area of IUCN's interests that culminated in the following decade in the Convention on International Trade in Endangered Species (CITES). Work at first seemed directed towards production of a loose-leaf compilation akin to the *Red Data Books* on threatened species. By 1966, however, with some 15,000 documents collected, the virtues of computer storage appeared unassailable. A pilot project initiated in 1968 led to development of a system by 1972 for the storage of information on the legal status of certain species of wild fauna and flora, again in part with a view to the endangered species trade convention.[26] The system was demonstrated at the Stockholm conference on the environment in 1972; and plans were made for the data collection, still housed in Bonn but designated the Environmental Law Information System (ELIS), to become an integral part of UNEP's own global environmental data-gathering work in the new organisation's Information Referral Service (IRS). Publication during the 1970s of a series of monographs on international environmental law was an important offshoot of this activity.[27]

Thirdly, the production of guidelines for the making of development policy has been a feature of the more development-oriented conservation approaches of the 1970s. The joint IUCN–Conservation Foundation volume co-authored by Dasmann on ecological principles and development planning was touched on in the last chapter. It led on directly to meetings and publications dealing with specific ecodevelopment policy issues, the former involving representatives of governments of developing countries as well as IUCN and other specialists, beginning with Latin America and South East Asia in 1974.[28]

We have so far looked briefly at some of the work of IUCN and WWF in relation to the provision of aid and assistance on matters of threatened species and protected areas, and the development of a series of instruments of various kinds having potential value for governments. A final aspect of the relationship has been the preparation of specific policy recommendations. This has been a natural spin-off of some of these other activities, and indeed a clear dividing line between these is not always possible. By the middle 1970s, for example, the Environmental Law Centre in Bonn was increasingly being drawn on by governments both as a data resource on legal questions and as a source of advice on the framing of domestic conservation legislation.[29] The union's commissions, notably that on legislation and the SSC, were instrumental in the late 1960s and early 1970s in securing the introduction of legislation or additional regulations governing the protection — particularly in connection with the export trade — of marine turtles and crocodiles from Ceylon, Surinam and Sabah, and of crocodiles in several Latin American countries. A still earlier example followed a 1963 Assembly resolution which foresaw the extinction of orangs 'within a few years': an Orang-utan Recovery Service (OURS) was set up in Malaysia with the aim initially of taking young orangs into care and forwarding them to zoos in the hope of improving the prospects of their being bred in captivity. Later the union acted as an advisory body to the Indonesian government in connection with the export trade in orangs.[30]

The creation and maintenance of protected areas is a question that has lent itself more readily to performance of this kind of function. The determination of Coolidge in the early 1960s to secure for IUCN an authoritative position in relation to the world's national parks, particularly in their role as habitats for threatened species of wildlife, produced several instances of the union acting in an advisory capacity. A detailed management plan was devised, for example, for the Uladag National Park in Turkey in 1965–6.[31] Research and conservation policy in the Galapagos Islands has been a long-standing interest in collaboration with officials of the government of Ecuador. Advice on management and policy questions has also been an inextricable component of the WWF-funded Operation Tiger from the early 1970s. This was aimed essentially at ensuring 'the maintenance of a viable population of the tiger in India' and the preservation of the areas concerned as part of that country's national heritage. Specific projects supported by WWF have included ones focusing primarily on education, the provision of equipment for national park maintenance, training and research. The last two in particular have spilled over, whether directly or through relations established with funded intermediaries, into management and policy areas, for example in the support provided for ecological and behavioural research to obtain basic data and to assist in the formation of a management structure to deal with tiger populations in the Royal Chitawan National Park in 1973–5.[32]

*States and international law*

We have looked to this point at the role IUCN and WWF have attempted to play in relation to the making of policies by governments. States, though, can be stubborn. Interference by well-meaning outsiders may be at best grudgingly welcomed. Advice accepted one week may be quietly forgotten the next. Or attempts to persuade, as IUPN discovered in the early 1950s, may be viewed simply as gratuitous meddling. Thus while an impressive number of local successes has been notched up in this way, other methods, that confront the reality of sovereignty by more roundabout routes, have proved useful to exploit or at least explore. One such means is the securing of friends and allies among the other intergovernmental and non-governmental actors of the conservation network. This is the theme of the next chapter. Another is the pursuit of change in the legal framework governing the relations of states in the international system. This is the question to which we now turn. Some international agreements are discussed in later chapters: in particular, those on conservation of the polar bear (Chapter 7), on conservation of African fauna and flora (Chapter 8) and on wetlands of international importance (Chapter 9). The examples with which we shall be most concerned here are CITES, and the 1979 Bonn convention on migratory species.

Several international agreements preceded IUPN's establishment in 1948. The African convention of 1933 and the 1940 Pan-American convention were still much discussed in the late 1940s as models or precedents. For ICBP, the defects of the 1902 convention on the protection of birds useful to agriculture had in the 1930s provoked the beginnings of a process that ended with its replacement by a new treaty in 1950. Given this backlog, the progressive accumulation of effective international conservation agreements seemed a worthwhile goal to pursue. At Lake Success in 1949, the British Government and the OAS were asked to convene meetings of the signatories of, respectively, the 1933 and 1940 agreements.[33] One section of the conference was also devoted to preliminary study of the idea of drafting a world convention on nature protection. This was specifically listed under Article I(2) of IUPN's 1948 Constitution as one of the objectives of the new union. On balance, however, it was decided that the time was not yet ripe for such a move. World conventions, it was argued, needed solid foundations. Further, experience had shown that it was difficult to reach agreement on the many technical questions that such a convention would entail. Regional arrangements comprising specific and manageable commitments, such as those of 1933 and 1940, were to be preferred. A 'World Manifesto on the Protection of Nature' was nevertheless drawn up shortly afterwards by IUPN. This was more, however, a document of aspiration and exhortation. Seven articles noted in general terms problems of the protection of nature, industrialisation, the survival of the world's species of wild flora and fauna, the wise use of natural resources, and related matters. However, UNESCO, to which the manifesto was sent as the basis for one that governments could sign, declined to circulate it or suggest revisions on the grounds that it contained no practical measures and was of a purely idealistic character.[34] Some steps were taken towards the preparation of a more concrete text, but the world convention idea soon fizzled out.

The manifesto concept, though, came to light again, in the cyclical manner of developments in world conservation, in 1975. In his opening remarks to the IUCN General Assembly then being held in Kinshasa, the President of Zaire called for a 'Charter of Nature'. While a resolution supporting the proposal was passed by the Assembly, the prospect of the union preparing such a charter was not one universally welcomed by member organisations or officials of the IUCN Secretariat. A draft was finally put together and discussed at a technical session at its Assembly in Ashkhabad in October 1978. The generality of the language that had to be employed for such a truncated statement of faith caused insuperable difficulties, and the document was returned to the Secretariat for redrafting.[35]

It was during the 1950s, however, that the groundwork was laid for the convention on endangered species (CITES) signed in 1973. This agreement ranks among the major achievements of IUCN. Focusing on the deleterious consequences for threatened species of international trade was, of course, not new. British conservation groups in the late nineteenth century seized on the problem of the trade in birds and feathers in their campaigns against the millinery trade; and ICBP had urged tighter trade controls in the 1930s with respect to species known to be threatened or vulnerable in the wild. Trade issues slowly gathered momentum in the 1950s. IUPN's 1952 General Assembly passed a resolution advocating the prohibition of the importation by states of animals of protected species.[36] International commerce in wild animals was increasingly identified by the SSC as an important factor causing declines in the populations of some species, for example the orang-utan. At its 1960 Assembly IUCN concluded on the basis of this research that 'a major threat to the existence of some rare animals is their illegal exportation from the country of origin, followed by their legal importation into other countries'. Restriction of the importation of such species by governments in the countries concerned, by implication the leading European and North American importing nations, was proposed as the best method to deal with the problem.[37]

The starting-point of the road to an international convention was the Arusha conference of 1961. This was the main event of IUCN's African Special Project of the early 1960s. It was designed to bring together conservation experts and officials from newly independent African nations and to assess future conservation requirements on the continent. One session, chaired by Talbot, tackled the trade question. Investigations carried out by Grimwood for the SSC already seemed to indicate expansion of the trade in skins and trophies, for example in leopard skins and birds of paradise feathers. Talbot's group, following the lead taken by other members of the United States delegation to Arusha, proposed an international convention to control the trade in endangered species. The idea was taken up by IUCN at its 1963 Assembly in Nairobi. Further study of the illegal export of species was recommended, and a resolution called on IUCN to draft an international convention on the trade in such species, and their trophies and skins.[38] The projected world conference on threatened species, the counterpart to the Seattle meeting on national parks, was suggested as a possible occasion at which the convention could be presented to governments. Other developments of the early 1960s fitted into this broader pattern. Attempts to persuade exporting nations to impose stricter controls were meeting with some success, for example in Nepal; the SSC was operating the Orang-utan Recovery Service (OURS) in Malaysia, acting as a screening agency for requests for the export of Indonesian species, and collecting data which continued to point to increased traffic in curios, particularly of turtles, alligators and spotted skins; IUCN's Legislation Commission under Burhenne was from 1963 engaged in gathering customs and trade law data; and the British Government, acting on advice from, among others, Boyle of the SSC and FPS, was preparing to tighten its own import controls. The upshot, the Animals (Restriction of Importation) Act, 1964, was widely regarded at the time as a model for the conservation of threatened species by way of restrictions on their importation.

A first draft of the proposed convention was produced quickly, during 1964. A long process of revision and change followed. After internal examination by the SSC, the Commission on Legislation, and IUCN's Executive Board — in the light of new information that was by then steadily increasing in volume — and extensive discussion at the union's 1966 Assembly in Lucerne, a third version of the draft was circulated to governments in September 1967. A total of thirty-nine governments and eighteen international organisations sent back comments. Further examination within IUCN resulted in a second draft, sent to governments by Secretary-General E. J. H. Berwick in August 1969. Two main kinds of problems were arising at this time. First, some difficult questions of the domestic legislation of states were involved. Countries differed considerably in their approaches to the regulation of their foreign trade. The legal protection status of different wild species also varied from government to government. And, while the projected treaty did not run counter to the General Agreement on Tariffs and Trade (GATT) — because of the exemptions allowed under Article 20 — a convention on international trade did raise questions that went beyond the competence of nature conservation agencies of government to involve trade officials as well as foreign ministries. Second, it was evident that the success of the convention would rest not only on its subsequent ratification and implementation by states, but also on the adequacy of its own definitions of what constituted an endangered species. On this point experts could reasonably disagree. In 1967–9, for example, SSC specialists had not a little difficulty in listing species that should appropriately fall under one or other of the Annexes to the convention. For some, admittedly, categorisation was relatively straightforward. In 1969, IUCN's New Delhi Assembly called on countries that had not already done so to prohibit the importation, retention and exportation of the species concerned without official documentation from Indonesia or the Malaysian states of Sarawak and Sabah.[39] The SSC's files on the legal commerce in and smuggling of Indonesian and eastern Malaysian species in particular were becoming bulky.

During the course of consultations on a third draft circulated to governments in the spring of 1971, the United States let it be known that it was willing to convene an intergovernmental conference at which the endangered species convention could formally be presented for signature and remaining differences of opinion ironed out. The background to this offer lay in the changes that had occurred during the 1960s in the official United States approach to endangered species policy. Congress passed the Endangered Species Preservation Act in 1966, following an initiative taken by Secretary of the Interior Udall which was itself a direct response to the Seattle principle of 1962 that each threatened animal or plant should have a protected habitat. The measure was strengthened by the Endangered Species Conservation Act of 1969. This had a more international orientation, a reflection, perhaps, of Udall's own brand of internationalism earlier in the decade: he had been an active participant, for example, at the Nairobi Assembly of IUCN in 1963 which had called for an international convention to outlaw trade in endangered species. The 1969 Act provided, amongst other things, for the establishment of a list of animals and animal products the import of which would be prohibited in order to lessen the possibility of the wildlife of other nations being eliminated.[40] Trying to identify which of the world's wild species were threatened with extinction thus became one of the functions of the Department of the Interior. The development was a significant one in the history of conservation politics in the United States: for many species in which conservation groups were interested, such as elephants or the larger cats, international trade was the critical factor. In addition, the newly created Council on Environmental

Quality was to become increasingly involved in world environmental conservation issues as these impinged on United States policies. More particularly, Talbot was able to press effectively for Washington to take a lead in bringing the endangered species convention to a successful conclusion. He had moved from the Smithsonian Institution in 1970 to become the Council's senior scientist, and, as a member also (from 1969) of IUCN's Executive Board, was well placed to keep contact with and affect the convention-making process he had played a large part in initiating in 1961. The vitality of the United States connection was itself a factor in developments at this time: Russell Train, Chairman of the CEQ, was another IUCN Executive Board member who had been present at the creation at Arusha and Nairobi in 1961 and 1963; and Coolidge was the union's President.

Soundings taken by IUCN in connection with the third draft in 1971 indicated a willingness on the part of a sufficient number of countries to sign the convention as it then stood.[41] Several problems still needed ironing out, though; and sustained United States criticism of the IUCN approach clearly had to be accommodated, in view of the importance of the testing ground of Washington's domestic endangered species trade legislation. Various conservation groups had taken part in steps to implement the provisions of the 1969 Act. Staff of the New York Zoological Society, for example, took part as expert witnesses in court cases in 1971; the Society, with other environmental groups, successfully secured the addition of many animals, including most big cats, to the protected list; and it published an aid for federal agents dealing with identification of commercial crocodilian hides.[42] Wayne King, the Society's Curator, was in 1972–4 chairman of a committee advising the US Office of Endangered Species and International Activities on applications for import permits (as well as, from 1973, chairman of the SSC's crocodile group). American criticisms, expressed during Senate Committee hearings in 1971–2, centred on weaknesses of the IUCN draft treaty as far as enforcement details were concerned. United States proposals accordingly called for a tightening to bring the provisions of the treaty more in line with those of existing United States importation laws. Similar points were made in Kenyan official comments.[43] Because of the character of the projected treaty, suggestions were also incorporated into the final United States working document from the GATT and the Customs Co-operation Council, as well as from FAO and international conservation bodies. Trade and customs officials in some countries, including Britain, had earlier raised objections concerning the relation of the convention to existing international trade regulations, the practicability of its enforcement as regards identification by customs officials of parts and derivatives of the animals and plants to be listed in appendices, and the conditions and provisions for re-export and other aspects of customs control procedures. Agreement was reached on some of these technical points only at the conference itself.

This was held in Washington in February–March 1973. In the immediate post-Stockholm period, it was a meeting which attracted considerable public attention in the United States. Some of the key issues that arose both reflected and sustained this, and the large United States delegation, headed by Train, included officials of a number of conservation groups that had been active in the pre-conference phase. Marine species, for example, proved difficult to handle; eventually only the five species of whales already given complete protection by the IWC were listed under Appendix I of the convention. There was disagreement between delegates on the extent to which animal or plant parts and derivates should, or could realistically, be incorporated within its scope. Disputes arose between representatives of wildlife producer and consumer nations, and between those of countries in both groupings either willing or reluctant to be bound by the treaty's provisions.

The document that finally emerged was lengthy and complex. The preamble stated that 'peoples and States are and should be the best protectors of their own wild fauna and flora' but that 'international co-operation is essential for the protection of certain species of wild fauna and flora against over-exploitation through international trade'. Article II provided for the 'particularly strict regulation' of trade in species threatened with extinction; these were listed in Appendix I. A second Appendix included species that might become threatened with extinction unless trade in them was strictly regulated (and others that had to be subject to regulation in order that this provision could be made effective). Appendix III allowed parties to list species regulated within their own jurisdiction which required the co-operation of other parties to secure trade control. Under Article II(4) the parties undertook not to allow trade in specimens of species listed in these Appendices except in accordance with the provisions of the convention. The provisions were set out in subsequent articles, which outlined procedures for the regulation of trade in specimens of species falling under each appendix (Articles III–V). These centred on the issuing of permits and certificates (described in Article VI) by appropriate bodies, that is, the Management Authorities competent to grant permits or certificates and advisory Scientific Authorities which were to be set up by each party under Article IX. A major feature of the convention lay in its provision for continuing machinery. Under Article VIII(6 and 7) each party was required to maintain trade records and prepare reports summarising both these data, and any legislative or other measures taken to enforce the provisions of the convention. UNEP's Executive Director was to provide a Secretariat, the functions of which included arranging for the periodic conferences of the parties provided for by Article XI, undertaking technical studies, informing the parties of the current listings of species in the appendices, preparing annual reports on its work and on the implementation of the convention, and inviting 'the attention of the Parties to any matter pertaining to the aims' of the convention (Article XII).[44]

The landmark importance of CITES in the history of international wildlife conservation rests primarily on three factors. First, it was a well-constructed and carefully prepared instrument that drew not only on the pre-conference drafting work initiated by IUCN, but also on the long history of data gathering by the union which had firmly established the point that international trade was a factor in the continued decline in numbers of at least some threatened species. It entered into force in July 1975 after ten states had ratified it. The United States was among this first batch, and the convention had by that date been signed by fifty-eight countries. Article VII provided for certain exemptions, for example for travelling zoos and exhibitions if a Managing Authority allowed, or for exchanges between scientific institutions, but for the most part these were not such as to undermine the effectiveness of the convention.

Second, provision for continuing machinery to oversee its operations ensured that CITES did not merely gather dust in government archives. UNEP contracted IUCN to carry out the secretariat duties, and a small unit was set up in Morges to perform this function. It quickly became tied in to those parts of the IUCN network that had been among the original movers of the convention. The SSC's trade monitoring activity, for example, had earlier been formalised with the establishment of the TRAFFIC group. Operating from headquarters in the FPS offices in London, this now acted chiefly as a data bank on trade in wildlife and wildlife products through a consultancy agreement concluded with it in 1978 by the CITES secretariat; but in addition TRAFFIC had a life of its own, publishing a monthly bulletin from 1979, and expressing the hope that conservation groups as well as government departments would make use of its information to carry out more detailed investigations and, where necessary, take legal proceedings.[45] The meetings of the parties provided for under Article XI have been vital to the continued success of the treaty: the first was held in Berne in 1976 and the second at San José, Costa Rica, in March 1979, with in the interim a special working session on technical problems in Geneva late in 1977. Some of the difficulties encountered had been anticipated during the drafting phase, such as the need for identification aids to facilitate enforcement by customs officials and the special problems raised in control of the 'readily recognizable parts and derivatives' of species. Further clarification of the basis for determining the appropriate appendix for particular species was also needed; the Berne meeting agreed on more carefully defined criteria for the addition of species and other taxa to Appendices I and II, for their deletion, and for their transfer from the second to the first.[46] The machinery, further, did not only have an existence during such meetings. The obligation on parties to keep records and submit reports went a long way towards ensuring effective monitoring of trade; in addition discrepancies between official statistics and evidence of trade flows arrived at independently from other sources provided opportunities for probing by alert conservationists. Further, a communications network was created which linked state authorities and the secretariat directly without diversions through foreign ministries; this greatly facilitated the secretariat's information-gathering and dispersal role, and its capacity to secure speedy answers to questions related to the provisions of the treaty.

Thirdly, CITES became a central focus of world conservation politics. The agreement and its workings proved to be a useful way of attracting media attention to wildlife issues. Smugglers make good copy. While some interest in trade regulation had arisen earlier — the Canadian Broadcasting Corporation made a film on the question in 1971 for example — this expanded considerably later in the decade. Stories highlighting threats to endangered species associated with the pet or exotic plant trade, the cruelty frequently inseparable from the commerce in specimens, and the evasive movements of dealers as fewer centres remained free from interference by the governments of states which had ratified the convention, were all valuable implements in the conservationist's tool kit. The specificity of the convention also sharpened the demands of environmental groups. From seeking necessarily diffuse goals such as the more effective protection of a species, they could pursue new sets of more explicit objectives: transfer of a species from the second to the first appendix, for instance.

The impetus towards its more rapid conclusion in something like its final form by the United States notwithstanding, the endangered species convention thus stands out as a substantial achievement of IUCN. The union was engaged in preparatory work in the early and middle 1970s on several other conventions. A Convention on Conservation of World Heritage was signed in 1972 and entered into force in December 1975. Based originally on a draft produced by IUCN in 1971, and on a later version drawn up the following year in exchanges with UNESCO, this provided for protection of both natural and cultural sites. IUCN acted as advisor with respect to the former, with UNESCO carrying out the overall secretariat duties. Regionally based and other more specific conventions were also either initiated or developed by the union. It prepared a draft agreement on conservation in the South Pacific designed to promote the creation of reserves and the protection of indigenous fauna and flora; this was adopted at an intergovernmental meeting in Samoa in 1976, and provided for the South Pacific Commission to act as secretariat. Preparatory work on conventions governing islands of value to science, and the Wadden Sea — an area the further protection of which required the collaboration of Denmark, West Germany and the Netherlands — was also a prominent feature of IUCN's work during this period.[47] But the other treaty which came near to rivalling the endangered species convention in scope and potential significance was that on migratory species signed in Bonn in June 1979.

From the start the Convention on the Conservation of Migratory Species of Wild Animals was a more controversial enterprise than CITES. The fundamental concept was both simple and ecologically sound. Some species migrate across national frontiers: their conservation required co-operation between the states concerned. That there should be an international convention to handle such matters was proposed by UNCHE in 1972 in Recommendation 32 of the Action Plan adopted at Stockholm. Following an initiative taken by delegates of the Federal Republic of Germany at the second session of UNEP's Governing Council in 1974, IUCN prepared a draft of such a convention which was circulated to governments the following September. A preliminary intergovernmental conference to evaluate the draft and the legal and political issues involved in drawing up a migratory species treaty was then held in Bonn in July 1976.[48] The difficulties that arose, however, delayed the convening of the plenipotentiary conference for three years. There were major problems of definition. Some species crossed international boundaries at different stages of their life cycles. The existing legal environment was complex. A number of treaties governed certain aspects of the problem, for example bilateral agreements on the protection of birds. Others were planned, including a regional migratory species convention by the Council of Europe. Special obstacles surrounded marine species, many states being reluctant to countenance restriction of potential harvests.

The convention, conceived as a broad framework document, was adopted at the 1979 Bonn conference. Disputes between contending states at the meeting seemed to indicate that the process of ratification, however, would be far from easy. The term 'migratory species' was defined to encompass 'the entire population or any geographically separate part of the population of any species or lower taxon of wild animals, a significant proportion of whose members cyclically and predictably cross one or more national jurisdictional boundaries' (Article I[1]). The parties acknowledged the need 'to take action to avoid any migratory species becoming endangered' (Article II[2]). As for CITES two appendices were attached. The first dealt with endangered migratory species, and included various provisions for Range States (defined in Article I[1] as 'any State ... that exercises jurisdiction over any part of the range of [a] migratory species') to endeavour to conserve the habitats of such species and to prohibit their taking (Article III). For species not in this category, however, the convention was more permissive. Under the terms of Article IV, Appendix II listed migratory species 'which have an unfavourable conservation status and which require international agreements for their conservation and management, as well as those which have a conservation status which would significantly benefit from the international co-operation that could be achieved by an international agreement'. Parties that were Range States of Appendix II species would endeavour to conclude such agreements, guidelines for the design of which were set down in Article V. Continuing machinery was provided for: a conference of the parties (described as the decision-making organ of the convention); a Scientific Council, to provide advice on scientific matters for the conference; and a secretariat, to be provided by the Executive Director of UNEP (Articles VII–IX).[49] The Bonn convention thus drew in a number of respects on the CITES experience, and indeed there was a consensus at the conference that implementation and the carrying out of secretariat functions for the two should rest on an appreciation of their close relationship. The disagreements over the place of marine species in particular at the conference — the United States, the USSR and a handful of other states wanted them excluded — meant, however, that the treaty did not start life on a happy note: the United States finally registered a vote of abstention, though conservationist pressure aimed at signature resumed immediately.

### States, élites and publics

Promotion of a wider public, and scientific, interest in conservation of nature can in some ways be regarded as the most significant aspect of the work of bodies like IUCN and WWF. It has at least been an enduring motif. 'Even if the process is slower,' Harroy argued in 1956, 'it is much more effective to get people ... to set their minds in motion to observe for themselves the truths of their natural surroundings, to observe how things are generated and to perceive their own real relations to them'.[50] Treatment of wild animals could arguably be held to be a symptom of deeply rooted cultural fears, beliefs and habits. Change, in this analysis, could best — perhaps only — be secured by education. The difficulties of enforcement of even the most carefully designed laws were well appreciated by the conservationists of the 1930s and 1940s. Not new laws, but rather new ways of thinking seemed to many to be the goal to work towards. The work of Enrique Beltran in Mexico on conservation education was a seminal influence on United States thinking on international nature protection in the late 1940s.[51] It seemed increasingly evident that one function of international conservation organisations was to teach people that there were alternatives to traditional practices; that it was not necessary, to use one of Beltran's Mexican examples, to manage the resources of rivers by dynamiting lizards.

For IUPN, this rationale had also a more expedient base. Huxley's UNESCO, while it had not exactly created the new body single-handedly, was at least a godparent; in the 1950s, its perceptions of IUPN's proper role tended to be rather more restricted. The union accordingly placed emphasis on education 'inasmuch as UNESCO had indicated that it was particularly disposed to underwrite such enterprises'.[52] Harroy and his colleagues were obliged to defer or discard projects closer to the hearts of IUPN's founders: the ecological problems of bushfires, for example, or the implications of the failed West African groundnut scheme. Reviewing the achievements of the decade in 1960, Bloemers observed that the most important work had been done under contract and that this had 'tended to push the Union's other activities into the background'.[53]

The first, and most prominent, section of the 1949 Lake Success conference dealt with conservation education. A wide variety of problems was raised. Educational films produced for western audiences, for example, could, it was argued, have little relevance in the colonial territories of the world, where the more fascinating yet also the most threatened forms of wildlife existed. The meeting reaffirmed the commitment of IUPN to an educational role, in relation both to formal systems and mass publics. Needs were identified for an international youth organisation; for the sponsoring of international fellowships by organisations like UNESCO and FAO; for the progress of nature protection education in the curricula of schools, universities and technical colleges; and, touching on a wider issue of particular concern at that time to UNESCO, for the duty-free exchange of films, books and other materials.[54] Much of the educational activity of the 1950s, and indeed of later years, flowed from this pioneering foray into a complex and hazardous area. It is convenient to view the evolution of this educational role at three levels: formal educational institutions, broader publics and scientific communities.

An Education Commission was in fact established, somewhat hurriedly, at Fontainebleau in 1948. But it failed to function.[55] A similar body emerged early in the 1950s. It undertook various projects, chiefly, at least at first, with financial assistance from UNESCO. These included production of a booklet for use by teachers in Italian schools, distribution of a standard lesson on conservation and of a document on problems of adult education, and research on a survey of the status of conservation education throughout the world. By 1958, some key problem areas had been mapped out at the primary and lower secondary school levels, in teacher training, and in terms of postgraduate research. Developing countries were more of a priority from the early 1960s. This was in line with the changing interests of IUCN more generally during that period, and also with those of UNESCO educationalists. It also reflected a change of leadership. The Soviet conservationist L. K. Shaposhnikov took over the Education Commission from Ira Gabrielson of the United States and encouraged the trend towards a more developmental focus. The work of the commission, as he noted in 1966, was 'based on the idea that nature conservation is a vital economic and social problem of all nations'.[56] Pathbreaking conferences on conservation education in Africa and tropical south-east Asia were held in conjunction with IUCN's 1963 Assembly in Nairobi and in Bangkok at the end of 1965. Technical education and training needs in Africa were a special concern. In general, then, the role of IUCN here was twofold. First, aids for education were produced: a general programme for a course of studies on conservation of nature was developed in 1961–2, for example; a review of educational aids in the conservation area was published later by UNESCO on the basis of research by the commission; and an international methods handbook for the primary and secondary school level was written by Robert Saveland for the union following a joint IUCN–UNESCO meeting on environmental education in the school curriculum held in Nevada in mid-1970. Second, IUCN's commitment to this kind of work stimulated the planning and convening of some important international conferences of the period; apart from Nevada in 1970, for example, key meetings were held on environmental education at Rüschlikon in 1971 and Tbilisi in 1976.

One longer term means towards this dual function has been the creation of regional networks of teachers and educational researchers. Regionalisation was a solution turned to in the late 1950s when low levels of funding in practice tended to rule out regular meetings of the full Education Commission. A north-west European group met for the first time in Copenhagen in 1960. An active east European equivalent was established in Prague in 1967; a *Bulletin* was issued in Poland from 1969, and frequent meetings held during the 1970s. From his office in the Conservation Foundation in Washington, Fraser Darling inaugurated a North American committee in 1968.

This approach inevitably spilled over into a broader one. Implanting a delight in nature by way of the curriculum suffered from the limitations encountered by all other attempts to reform man by reaching him first in the classroom. Outside influences were often more potent. There was the Dickens effect: forced feeding could dull palates. Nature conservation could be equated with the other childish things put aside by good citizens. These were not, of course, necessary or unavoidable consequences. But however the tasks of educational reform were evaluated, their incompleteness without complementing measures aimed at public opinion was clear. If certain assumptions were made about the character of the political process, indeed, this second level could be portrayed as the crucial strategic arena within which the educational battle should be fought. In a paper to the International Zoological Congress held in London in 1958, Coolidge argued that there was convincing evidence that focusing the spotlight of public opinion on threatened species could stimulate government action; he cited in particular the introduction of protective measures for the Javan rhino by the Dutch colonial authorities.[57]

Two audiences were possible targets: member organisations of IUCN and individuals who were actively or passively interested in conservation of nature, and others who were not. The first response of IUPN to the evident need for some publication to carry out at least the first, and preferably both, of these functions was to attempt to resuscitate the magazine *Pro Natura*. The Swiss League, then agents of the so-called Provisional IUPN, had published two issues in 1948. Approaches both to publishers and to UNESCO, however, suggested that this was not a viable enterprise.[58] The title was retained for occasional publications on particular topics in the early 1950s. IUPN members continued, however, to call for a liaising and propaganda organ. In September 1951, Richard Westwood, President of the American Nature Association, agreed to launch a propaganda campaign. A short-lived Public Information Commission was created, and for a few years this played a role in publicising the aims of IUPN in the United States. Appearance of the union's *Bulletin* early in 1952 was a direct result of this concern. It has since been a central instrument of the organisation. Information from members was sought through it by Harroy in 1952 'in order to allow the IUPN to play its natural role as an information centre', and by Munro in 1978 in order both to inform public opinion and to facilitate IUCN interventions with governments 'before mistaken policy is acted on'.[59] A series of articles by Harroy from May 1952 dealt with various categories of threats to the world's wildlife. Later, with wider news coverage, book reviews and articles by specialists, the *Bulletin* increasingly became an agent for the dissemination of evolving IUCN views on conservation issues. A resolution of the 1954 Assembly, though, called on the union to play a greater role in giving publicity to nature protection, for example through films and other media. But such a general publication directed towards non-members never appeared. Several other journals — such as *Oryx, Terre et Vie* and *Zooléo* — carried items on a regular basis from the *Bulletin* to a wider, though also converted and still relatively small, audience. Occasional pieces surfaced in the press and news magazines. Some of the union's own publications of the 1950s, notably *Fossiles de Demain*,[60] achieved a certain prominence. Limited resources, however, combined perhaps with a measure of reticence on the part of practising scientists to engage in the simplification, distortion and compromise inseparable in some degree from the business of propaganda, constrained the pursuit of visibility.

The founding of WWF in 1961 broke this pattern. Indeed one factor leading to the Fund's creation was precisely the low level of public attention to urgent conservation questions, particularly in east Africa, that existing conservation organisations were managing to generate. Their respective approaches to the question of emblems typified the different styles. IUPN at the outset did not have one. The question was explored desultorily until 1954, when a contest of *Bulletin* readers produced a design. However, intended to represent blossoming and growth, in practice in the 1960s it became more of a source of puzzlement, or of embarrassment at its phallic overtones, and was gradually replaced on publications in the 1970s by a three-dimensional row of block capitals of the union's acronym, readable in either its English or its French forms. By contrast, WWF moved speedily towards its effective and highly successful giant panda symbol, drawn by Scott — himself a distinguished wildlife artist with no mean flair for publicity — from a design by Watterson. While the result irked some conservationists (it was not a threatened species, it was a mammal, and as sketched was unashamedly cuddly) the panda's recognisability, ease of monotone reproducibility, and sheer attractiveness, were undoubtedly major contributing factors in the campaigning accomplishments of WWF in the 1960s and 1970s.

While a sensible division of the educational labour thus suggested itself in the 1960s, IUCN did not entirely relinquish a more public role. It was sensitive to the need, for example, to balance the more technical sheets of the *Red Data Book* with the more approachable *Wildlife in Danger* of 1969.[61] But gradually its information role came to concentrate on the world conservation network and on scientists working in related areas of ecology. In 1978, at $85, the two-part *World Directory* was obviously not aimed at the interested layman. Heim observed in 1956 that 'les nécessités scientifiques de la protection de la faune ou de la flore n'apparaissent qu'aux yeux d'une élite éduquée et malheureusement limitée'.[62] This was a group small not only in relation to wider publics, but also in relation to the international scientific community itself, and the union's standing was not always as secure as it would have liked within the world conservation network. Rather than take up a propaganda role outside this network — this hat fitted WWF more snugly — it made greater sense for IUCN to devote its more limited resources to the mobilisation of the converted and, where possible, to expand their ranks, especially with practising scientists. It is in this context that the goal of securing wider recognition as a scientific institution has assumed a more practical significance. The union's publications have accordingly been primarily of a specialised and technical character, though the *Bulletin* has, particularly in the late 1970s, tended to adopt a more activist stance. Missing, however, has been a regularly appearing journal. This was one option discussed as a possible alternative format for the *Red Data Book* sheets in the mid-1960s and again just over a decade later. The task of providing such a forum for exchange of scientific findings and conservation views has tended to be taken up outside, for example by *Environmental Conservation*, a journal to which IUCN and WWF have lent support. A *Multilingual Dictionary of Environmental Conservation Terms*, produced in 1976 by Shapashnikov's educational commission after exchanges between IUCN and the Central Laboratory for Nature Conservation of the USSR Ministry of Agriculture in Moscow, represents another way in which the objective of promoting co-operation and communication between specialists in different countries has been pursued.[63]

Sovereignty represents a major constraint on the working of any international organisation. Those dealing with wildlife conservation — the generally low priority of the subject and its allegedly non-political character notwithstanding — are not immune to this condition. Some matters have therefore to be approached with a degree of caution. The MAB Council has argued 'that a country's sovereignty is in no way affected by creation of a biosphere reserve within its territory'.[64] A dispute over the concept of 'shared resources' arose in relation to the Bonn convention on migratory species: acceptance of this kind of phraseology was held to imply some right on the part of other states to interfere in a country's domestic affairs. CITES, similarly, laid emphasis on states themselves being the best protectors of their own wild fauna and flora. The Bonn convention's use of the term Range State went beyond this, but the framework character of that treaty restrained a more rigorous interpretation of its meaning. Attempts on the part of international conservation organisations directly to influence the behaviour of states have had mixed results. Still more difficult to assess are the consequences of attempts to galvanise public opinion. Nature conservation groups operate in a favourable milieu of diffuse public interest, if the post-1950s explosion of nature book publishing and news media attention is any indication. But even in a country where this situation is combined with a proliferation of active amateur bodies, the task of mobilising opinion in specific directions — towards a government's signature of a particular treaty for instance — has never been easy. On the other hand, the ledger has its positive entries. IUCN has been a significant initiator of conventions. It provides the secretariat for CITES. WWF's informal contacts with governments have strengthened national parks threatened with deterioration into a paper status. Ideas such as the *Red Data Book* have been adopted by national organisations. IUCN/WWF projects, particularly in developing countries, constitute a significant international presence. This activity has not, however, been carried out in a vacuum. Other bodies than IUCN and WWF operate internationally. Some are competitors. This brings us to the subject of the next chapter.

# 6 Network development: policy-making in a complex milieu

> Remedying the disturbances of government is like unravelling a knotted rope. Don't hurry, but first examine the knot carefully and then undo it.
>
> Dōgen, *Shōbōgenzō Zuimonki*

The milieu in which international conservation organisations operate is one of considerable complexity. It is unrealistic to focus exclusively on any one organisation as a means of obtaining an adequate picture of the whole. The policies and thinking of any given organisation can usually be found to have drawn at least some of their inspiration from the web of its relations with other actors — even if the relationship concerned is one of mutual distancing and rivalry. The number of actors is large. 'To each species its pressure group' has seemed at times to be a main operating slogan in the process of network formation. Diverse organisations co-exist. The present chapter keeps a guiderope firmly attached to IUCN in order to make a necessarily brief excursion into this wider arena.

## *States and other actors*

During the 1930s an extensive network linking North American with European conservation bodies came into existence. The pioneering work of the early ICBP and of IOPN was examined in an earlier chapter. The Second World War revealed the fragility of relationships patiently forged in the interwar years. Institutions persisted into the post-1945 period. But conditions were such that older patterns had lost much of their appropriateness. The founding of IUPN in 1948 was one response. Many of the far-reaching changes in world politics that have since influenced the course of international conservation activity were already beginning to be evident: the emergence of new intergovernmental organisations, consolidation of cold war divisions and decolonisation. The primary task in the late 1940s, however, was the creation of links. Writing in 1973 of the period of IUPN's establishment, Harroy commented: 'one must consider the conditions prevailing at that time. There were still very few countries where organisations devoted all their time to the conservation of nature. A few isolated individuals working in universities and museums were launching lonely battles, with little contact among them. There was no international centralised mechanism on which these individuals could rely to overcome their isolation.'[1] The union thus had a twin function: to establish contacts among such institutes and individuals, primarily by acting as a device for the exchange of information; and to set up some kind of procedure whereby common platforms and goals could be articulated, and, ultimately, a measure of influence exerted on the policies of states.

Connections were a prerequisite. Even in these early years of the union's life, other bodies with overlapping objectives existed. Most were non- or semi-governmental. Two major intergovernmental agencies, UNESCO and FAO, were lodestones that affected the movements of IUPN. A more broadly based membership comprising both unofficial and state agencies at the national level had to be sought if expertise were to be pooled, information obtained and dispersed, and funding put on a more secure footing. Three closely related topics will be pursued here: the structuring of IUCN's relations with the three other international bodies identified at the end of Chapter 3 as forming with it a central nucleus within the world conservation network; the web of non-governmental actors; and the involvement of both global and regional intergovernmental organisations in conservation of nature questions, and the manner in which the problem of more effective co-ordination has been approached.

*Actors and institutionalisation*

There was a widespread appreciation after the end of the Second World War of the need to set up a new international conservation body, though no clear consensus existed on the precise form that this should take. The need for change was spelled out in the NYZS proposals and in the discussions at the Brunnen and Basle meetings in 1946–7. It could not so readily be agreed that Tienhoven's IOPN should be disbanded. But the role taken by Tienhoven himself and by other individuals active in the affairs of the Office in the moves that led to the establishment of IUPN in 1948 guaranteed that no obstructions from the past would stand in the way of the new union. However, while emphasising that IOPN would collaborate fully with IUPN, Westermann and others insisted that the senior partner in this enterprise be granted due recognition. 'Broadly speaking,' an IOPN report stated later, 'the Union chose the role of an organ of action, leaving the task of assembling documentation to the Office.'[2] At Lake Success in 1949, Westermann argued that the earlier work of IOPN should be continued and that, given its data collection and library holdings, the Office should be accepted and supported as an integral part of IUPN: the efficient interchange of facts, that is, should be one of the outstanding features of the international movement for the protection of nature.[3] The union's Survival Service under Coolidge, for example, began its work with old IOPN records on the world's threatened species, and formal links were devised, such as Harroy's appointment in 1949 as a member of the IOPN's General Council. But the dwindling autonomous role of the Office was clear. The two organisations were formally merged in 1957, four years after Tienhoven's death.

Relations between the four main international conservation organisations of the 1960s and 1970s — IUCN, WWF, ICBP and IWRB — have been rather more complex, and troublesome at times. Indeed, such have been the close links between them that they can from some angles be viewed as a single institution. Formally they are not, and the term institution has a ring of rigidity and bureaucracy about it that would not sit well on most of the shoulders involved. However, it is useful to see their relations with each other in terms of a slow process of institutionalisation, in the sociological sense: the links, that is, have become steadily closer and more regularised. Amalgamation has been periodically discussed, especially in the 1970s, and in 1979–80 a move was begun to a common administrative headquarters near Geneva.

In view of the seniority of ICBP, the traditional vigour of bird protection groups, the speed with which its network had been resuscitated after the ending of hostilities in 1945, and the determination of its leading officials that its identity and freedom of manoeuvre should be protected, the option of a merger with the fledgling IUPN was just not feasible in 1948. ICBP's Conference approved in 1950 the draft of an agreement between the two organisations drawn up by its executive body. This was couched in terms that would in practice have reserved for ICBP an exclusive conservation role in relation to birds. The text met with resistance, accordingly, from IUPN's Executive Board. The union wanted a more explicit recognition of its right to operate on a broader front, or, as Tienhoven put it, of its freedom to act in circumstances affecting nature generally, even though birds might be involved. A phrasing was eventually hit upon under which the union would 'co-operate with the ICBP in matters concerning bird preservation' and would 'as far as possible call upon it for assistance in dealing with all matters in the field of international bird preservation in which it is widely recognised as the principal international agency'.[4] A division of labour was in fact already one outcome of the 1949 Lake Success conference, the threatened birds list agreed on there forming one focus of ICBP's work. When IUPN's Executive Board tried in 1950 to institutionalise the tackling of threatened species data collection, it set up three committees on, respectively, mammals, other animals and plants; birds were tacitly acknowledged to be an ICBP responsibility. At its 1952 General Assembly, IUPN formally invited ICBP to gather information and to make recommendations with respect to the Lake Success birds, and to forward the results to the union's Survival Service.[5]

Thus ICBP retained its distinctive character. Some of its work of this and later periods will be discussed in a subsequent chapter: its ambition of the 1930s to reshape the 1902 convention for the protection of birds useful to agriculture led directly to the 1950 Paris treaty; it was one of several European organisations in the middle and later 1970s to lobby for EEC regulation of the destruction of migratory birds; and it was an active pressure group and source of expertise in relation to oil damage to seabirds, particularly for the North Sea countries.[6] For much of the post-war period too, its identity in the world of international conservation was in part a function of the personal stature of the leading individuals associated with it, including Phyllis Barclay-Smith in ICBP's secretariat in the British Museum (Natural History) in London, and S. Dillon Ripley as President in the Smithsonian in Washington. But equally there was considerable scope for collaborative work between ICBP and IUCN, for example on the ecology of the Camargue in 1955 or on the trade in endangered bird species in connection with CITES in the 1970s. And while recognising the primary role of ICBP, the union has also intervened on some controversial issues, for example in the wider debate in 1954–5 on the grain-eating weaver bird in Africa. IUCN similarly assumed overall responsibility for the *Red Data Book* series; the first part of a revised version of the 1960s *Aves* volume appeared in 1978. Some of the convention preparation work likewise rested on a co-operative sharing of tasks, notably in relation to the Ramsar convention of 1971 on wetlands.

The simplicity of ICBP's structure was emphasised by Pearson early in its history.[7] The National Section, comprising members in a given country, was defined as the basic unit: there were twenty-six of these by 1935, forty-five by 1958, and sixty by 1971. From 1936, Continental Sections were added, at first for Europe and for the Americas and later for Asia. Periodic Conferences have constituted the main policy-making arena, and provision has also been made for continuing executive and secretariat machinery. But it is through its specialist working groups that ICBP has erected some of the more durable connections with the IUCN network. The formation of these paralleled, somewhat more slowly, those of the SSC. At its 1974 Conference in Canberra, for example, reports were presented by groups on, respectively, birds of paradise, birds of prey, bustards, cranes, flamingoes and pheasants; in 1977 a parrot group met for the first time.[8] This kind of work can be seen as an extension of IUCN's data-gathering tasks in relation to threatened species, and it constituted the basis for listings in the *Red Data Book* and the Appendices of the Bonn and endangered species conventions. One such area of specialisation in the 1930s and 1940s was in relation to migratory wildfowl. Research carried out through the British Section of ICBP led to the establishment in 1947 of the International Wildfowl Research Institute to act, especially after 1954, primarily as an information centre; its headquarters were in the Camargue from 1962, and since 1969 have been in Slimbridge, Gloucestershire, alongside Scott's Wildfowl Trust. IWRB — the change of title to 'Bureau' was made in 1954 when it was realised that lack of funds would inhibit the pursuit of earlier research goals — developed in turn its own specialist group structure, for example on geese, ducks and waders.[9] The patterns of Palaearctic (old world) waterfowl migration compelled IWRB to turn its attention increasingly to western Asia and north Africa from the mid-1960s; indeed the choice of Tunis in 1978 as the site of the IWRB Board's first non-European annual meeting was made very much with the need for expanded co-operation with African and Arab countries in mind.

Thus the links between ICBP and IUCN have traditionally been close, with only occasional irritants. Apart from the interrelated threatened species group structure, the relationship has been periodically strengthened by such means as mutual reporting of activities in the publications of each organisation, membership of ICBP personnel on IUCN's Executive Board, or Vincent's formally being designated a liaison officer between the two during his work from 1963 on threatened bird species for the *Aves* volume. In the mid-1970s, however, a need for greater co-ordination was identified. At its 1978 meeting in Ohrid, Yugoslavia, ICBP approved the outlines of a longer term conservation programme to mesh with IUCN's continuing preparation of its World Conservation Strategy document.[10] Agreement was also reached on the sharing of the new Geneva headquarters by the secretariats of the two bodies.

The World Wildlife Fund was not set up in 1961 as a rival to IUCN. One of its central goals, indeed, was to secure more adequate financial support for existing organisations such as IUCN and ICBP. But some of the criticism of IUCN's passivity implicit in its foundation played a part in shaping the relationship between the two. Money, though, was the central question. One IUCN Executive Board member of the late 1950s has commented that discussion of endangered species could revolve around the issue of whether or not the budget could stand the cost of contacting experts by mail. The cycle was difficult to break out of: sparse funds affected performance; lack of effectiveness deterred potential funders. Meetings of executive and scientific bodies were irregular, and often poorly attended; the secretariat was unable to develop as a base of scientific competence and for the administrative servicing of the commissions; the union seemed headed in the direction of being a loose association of members exchanging hopes, fears and postage stamps. As he had been for IUPN in 1948, Huxley was, through a series of articles written for *The Observer* on threats to east African wildlife, a prime mover of events in 1960–1. Others, including Scott, Nicholson and a businessman, Guy Mountfort, took up the call, and in April 1961 IUCN's Executive Board formally acknowledged the need for a new fund-raising body. The objectives of WWF, established later that year, were, amongst other things, '(a) to collect, manage and disburse funds through suitable international or national bodies or individuals for the conservation of world fauna, flora, forests, landscape, water, soils, and other natural resources' and '(b) to review the long term financial requirements of world conservation and to study and develop adequate means of meeting these requirements insofar as they are not currently met by existing efforts'.[11]

At that stage, it was obviously uncertain whether this strategy would succeed. WWF could thus be viewed essentially as a body that might allow IUCN at last to fulfil its proper role. Existing organisations, said Watterson, then IUCN Secretary-General, in 1961, were 'rather like a car with a tiny fuel tank, replenished only by an occasional half-cupful'. What was needed was 'not a new organisation to duplicate and compete with the work of existing bodies, but a new co-operative international project to make their efforts effective by providing them with adequate resources'.[12] During the next two decades, a rather more complex process of mutual accommodation took place.

While IUCN retained earlier sources of financing and later added others – UNEP from 1974 — help from WWF effected a dramatic change in its potential to act that contrasted markedly with the situation of the 1950s. In the first and second three-year periods (1962–4 and 1965–7), WWF support for IUCN totalled, respectively, SF429,560 and SF592,519. In 1968–72, the yearly average virtually tripled to SF526,894; it almost doubled again, to SF973,301, in 1973–5.[13] In addition, WWF became a major conservation actor in its own right. Not only was it an international organisation dispensing funds for conservation projects, it also had a quasi-federal structure that allowed considerable freedom of movement for National Appeals, the basic constituent units of the global WWF network. The rule of thumb devised at the outset was that one-third of funds raised would be retained by the National Appeal concerned, and one-third forwarded to WWF International, leaving one-third to be negotiated.[14] Further, the triennial International Congresses of WWF, such as the Second in London in 1970 and the Fourth in San Francisco in 1976, developed into important world forums of debate on environmental conservation issues, more heavily publicised than the Assemblies of IUCN, and more accessible to the spirit of activism that stood some risk of being quenched by sobriety in such gatherings.

But the relationship was one of interdependence rather than competitiveness. For its part, WWF needed the information and expertise that IUCN had long been developing, sought a more positive role in the formulation of a common conservation policy, and required, ultimately, its own source of conservation advice both to deal with IUCN on more equal terms and also to fulfil obligations to those individuals and organisations supplying it with funds. From 1962, when the WWF Secretariat also moved to Morges, informal co-ordination was formalised in various ways, such as the practice of holding meetings of the WWF International Trustees immediately after those of the IUCN Executive Board. A refurbishing of the union's capacity to collect, organise and have readily available information on conservation issues was also a feature of the 1960s. Difficulties arose later in the decade, however, particularly over the conservation projects funded by WWF. Agreement was reached towards the end of 1972 on measures to promote the more effective planning of joint projects, and the ordering of priorities to fit longer term conservation requirements.[15] The general pattern that emerged in the late 1960s and early 1970s was of IUCN giving advice to WWF on programmes and undertaking the screening of projects for funding decisions. In 1978, a further step was taken with WWF's relinquishing to IUCN of its management responsibilities in relation to continuing projects. But at the same time moves were made to strengthen in other ways WWF's own capability to evaluate conservation issues. These included creation of a senior conservationist slot in its Morges secretariat, to which Talbot, then still with the CEQ in Washington, was appointed.[16]

By the late 1970s, then, IUCN and WWF had in effect been fused, if not into a unified spearhead then at least into the twin prongs of a fondue fork. Proposals for formal union of the two, together with ICBP and IWRB, were mooted at various times. A single body would arguably wield more political clout. But such ideas usually floundered, probably rightly so. Each of the four major groupings has carried out a distinct set of roles. And their interconnectedness — not the least aspect of which has been multiple hat-wearing by a few leading individuals — has become an effective guard against conflict.

*Actors, competition and co-operation*

The number and diversity of groups active at any given time in the environmental field defy simple summary. A total of 3200 were listed in a 1976 publication.[17] Many have some form of international interest. Environmentalism breeds globalism. Many, too, include threats to wildlife within their range of concerns, even if their main focus lies elsewhere. In the United States — which may, admittedly, by atypical — several of the larger environmental organisations have increasingly engaged indirectly in international activity by virtue of lobbying the Administration or Congress with a view to securing changes of official external policy, for instance on certain conventions or in relation to the United States' part in the international trade in endangered species. Even the more restricted field of nature conservation, as traditionally or widely defined, is an extensive one. Since disputes about approaches and means can erupt easily, the job of co-ordination, liaison even, is a formidable one. These are not tasks, furthermore, that have fallen unequivocally to any particular organisation. The conservation network has no central government. A condition of anarchy is qualified, however, by the ways in which the organisations have themselves structured their relations with each other. As we saw in the last section, constellations of actors can emerge from these processes and have an impressive durability. Links, though, can also snap. This potential for conflict has always put a strain on organisations like IUCN. The union's objectives from the start hinged on action and the precipitating of change. It thus evolved into an arena in which contending opinions could clash and, perhaps, be resolved. Non-governmental diversity has sometimes been viewed, of necessity, as a virtue. On the other hand, Harroy tended to regard 'the mixed framework of Nature defenders' as 'rather more a weakness than strength' because of the difficulties he encountered in trying to reconcile differences.[18] And the framework has become still more mixed since 1953.

Before looking further into these relationships, some impression is needed of the kinds of non-governmental organisations which are engaged in the international conservation of nature. First, a number of nationally based conservation groups have traditionally taken an active interest in international issues. For some, the spread of membership and affiliations across national boundaries makes a dividing line between 'national' and 'international' bodies difficult to draw. The Fauna Preservation Society is a good example; it has long-standing Commonwealth connections stemming from its origins as a group intent on preserving the fauna of a worldwide empire. In the United States, groups like the Sierra Club, founded in 1892, also encompass some foreign membership; this in addition has a network of volunteer observers based in several major world centres, including Geneva, who pass back information to its New York headquarters on matters related to the international programme formalised in 1972. A scientific advisory structure brings in expertise on a variety of world conservation topics such as tropical forest development, the marine environment, tourism, international environmental law and Antarctica.[19] Publications such as its *World Directory of Environmental Organisations* have further enhanced its pursuit of a more pivotal information role in international conservation. A second category of actors similarly began to be significant in the 1920s. These are the various international scientific associations that either directly or tangentially have dealt with certain aspects of nature conservation. The interwar International Office was in large measure a product of such debates in IUBS meetings; the International Biological Programme, touched on in an earlier chapter, was in turn a forerunner of the environmental projects of ICSU in the 1970s. Zoological, botanical and ecological congresses have throughout this period also acted as forums at which those scientists interested in conservation issues could meet; though the resistance of IUBS, for example, to the brand of applied ecology endorsed by bodies like IUCN restricted their impact at times.

Zoos and the societies linked to them form a third grouping. The former maintain their own transnational networks, through the International Union of Directors of Zoological Gardens for example. But conservationists have traditionally been ambivalent towards zoos.[20] Some have been criticised for using conservation rationales as façades behind which to make profits in this potentially lucrative branch of the mass entertainment industry. Charges of cruelty or of inadequate appreciation of the needs of wild animals have been made periodically. On the other hand, some zoos clearly perform valuable scientific and educational roles. Several have been pioneers in the captive breeding of endangered species. Some institutions have indeed been designed with this goal in view.  In Britain, the Jersey Wildlife Preservation Trust has been a leader in this area, and one that has attracted a wider public interest through the writings of its founder, the author Gerald Durrell. Specific breeding programmes have been designed in conjunction with governments, for example those of Mauritius, Assam and St Lucia, with regard to particular threatened species.[21] Of zoological societies, that of New York has a lengthy history of involvement in international conservation. From its establishment in 1895 the NYZS directed its attention chiefly at conservation issues in the United States. In the 1940s, though, its President, Fairfield Osborn, gave it an increasingly international outlook: its proposals at this time for a new world body to bolster IOPN were mentioned earlier. The Conservation Foundation was set up by the Society in 1948, and this in turn embarked on an autonomous career in international conservation; it was a body with which Fraser Darling was associated for several years. The Society itself proceeded to develop an active funding role, in relation to conservation projects in Africa for example, from 1956.[22] Africa was also a central target of the Frankfurt Zoological Society, largely because of the work in Tanzania and Kenya of Bernhard Grzimek.[23]

These few instances are by no means representative of the whole field of international conservation, but they indicate the kind of problems that IUCN, designed as a focal point of the network, has faced. Two in particular need further examination: the union's role as an arena in which different NGOs can resolve conflicts and be mobilised into a more coherent force, and its position as one actor among many at the non- or semi-governmental level with which its relations have to be worked out.

These raise separate questions, in part because IUCN's own membership is not universal. In 1950, its Secretary-General reported that its membership was 'too small to permit the Union fully to achieve its aims'.[24] It followed not only that more members were needed, but also that a broader geographical spread of members would better serve its interests. This meant, more particularly, departing from the traditional bases in North America and western Europe. In 1955 the union's President, Roger Heim, approached Soviet scientists and encouraged their participation as a natural follow-up to the Academy of Sciences' establishment of a nature conservation commission. A major east European symposium held in Berlin in 1957 recommended that all countries join IUCN.[25] Several Soviet scientists became active in the union's affairs, both in executive capacities and in relation to particular topics like conservation education or polar bear protection. IUCN's 1978 General Assembly was held in Ashkhabad. Tentative overtures to China, though, met with little success until the general improvement of Sino-Western relations in the late 1970s. In 1979 Scott and a small WWF delegation held talks in Peking with environmental officials and scientists that led to agreement on Chinese membership in IUCN, signature of CITES, and the setting up of a joint committee of WWF and scientists of the Chinese Association for Environmental Sciences.[26] Extension into the developing countries of Africa, Asia and Latin America has been a persistent problem. As Budowski noted in 1975, 'We must ... get away from the impression of IUCN as a European-centred organisation'.[27] By that time, membership had spread considerably. Twenty African countries were represented in IUCN in 1976 either as state members, or through government agencies or NGOs. A large proportion of members from North America and western Europe, however, still reflected the bigger environmental NGO presence in these regions. Of a total of 244 national NGO members, fifty-seven came from the United States, fifteen from Britain, and fourteen from Canada.[28]

An expanding membership brought with it fresh problems: a larger pool of support certainly, but also more demands for a say in IUCN policy-making and higher expectations with regard to the organisation's effectiveness. Not all NGOs, for example, could afford to send delegates regularly to the union's General Assembly, its central policy-making institution; some could find themselves in sharp disagreement with their own government, which might also be represented in their country's delegation. The sheer size of the United States contingent caused problems at some Assemblies. Disgruntlement with IUCN has expressed itself in various ways: some more radically minded groups have simply not joined; memberships lapse; there have been pointed resignations, and that of the American Society of Mammalogists in 1954 Harroy counted as the union's first failure.[29] Lack of consultation was a stock complaint in the early 1970s, a spin-off from Stockholm that caught the union's leadership off its guard. In these circumstances it is not surprising that the issue that proved among the most difficult to resolve at Fontainebleau in 1948 — that of the voting powers of members in General Assemblies — was one around which much heat was still being generated three decades later. Revisions of the voting arrangements or decision rules were made in 1963, at Banff in 1972, Geneva in 1977 and Ashkhabad in 1978.[30] Assertiveness on the part of members also produced some checks for union policy, as in the Assembly's refusal at Banff in 1972 to go along with the more conservative line on whaling evolved by the secretariat and executive. Two possible costs of democracy were revealed. Efforts from 1972 to secure more adequate channels of communication between members and officials placed some strain on an already overtaxed secretariat; and the blocking power of the

Assembly put the continuity of union policy in some jeopardy.

Debate on the union's executive body has revolved around both its representativeness and its effectiveness. The Fontainebleau statutes provided for 'balanced geographical distribution' as a criterion for Executive Board membership (Article V[A]). In practice this was difficult to achieve. Western Europe and North America were the habitat of the conservationist. In the period 1948–72, these regions together accounted for between six and ten Board members. Apart from a gap in the 1950s, one member typically came from the Soviet Union or eastern Europe during this time, with a peak of three in the late 1960s. Other regions were represented by one, and occasionally two, members. Criticism of the geographical distribution of Board members was voiced by the Kenyan delegation to the union's 1969 Assembly in New Delhi; the Soviet Union later unsuccessfully proposed a formal listing of the world's regions along lines common in United Nations bodies. Changes were already evident, however, by the time of IUCN's constitutional review conference in Geneva in 1977. The trend was confirmed in the new statutes that emerged from its deliberations. The Executive Board was redesignated the Council under Article VI. Its membership was expanded, provision being made in particular for three Councillors to be elected from each of eight regions (Africa, Central and South America, North America and the Caribbean, east Asia, west Asia, Australia and Oceania, east Europe and west Europe).[31] The question of geographical distribution was closely related to those of effectiveness and efficiency of decision-making, qualities for which large committees are not usually noted. Some weaknesses were characteristic of the 1950s and 1960s. A desire for geographical spread could produce inactive Board members; lack of resources led to irregular attendance at meetings; there was at times a tendency to interpret membership as an honour, a reward for services rendered rather than an invitation to take up arms. A small Executive Committee drawn from its ranks was formally set up in 1972. The creation in 1977 of a large and geographically representative Council was then combined with that of a more compact and high-level Bureau, Strong being brought in as its first Chairman.

The largely anglophone character of the secretariat, once the shift from Brussels had been made in 1961, has occasionally ruffled some feathers; but other organisational questions have been more pressing. IUPN at first operated with what Harroy himself termed 'a necessarily very part-time Secretary-General'[32] — before taking up his colonial posting in Africa he was, from 1953, Professor of Colonial Economy at Brussels and held various other scientific and administrative positions — and a secretariat consisting essentially of its head, Marguerite Caram. The transition to a staff of thirty-eight by 1977, almost all full-time in Morges and with a closely interwoven relationship with the nearby WWF secretariat, was not accomplished without difficulty. A spirit of voluntarism seemed to many to be the key to organisations like IUCN: the timbre of the new professionalism rankled. Addressing these concerns in 1972, President-elect D. J. Kuenen commented on the past role of part-time amateurs but argued that in the interests of efficiency and continuity change was necessary. 'Expertise in matters of nature conservation is no longer a thing we pick up as we go along. We are moving into a period in which conservation is a professional job.[33] Secondment of staff from government agencies, for example from Britain and Canada, has been one feature of this process which has itself been an indication of the growing recognition of the organisation by states.

One crucial role of the secretariat has been that of servicing the union's advisory Commissions. When working well, these have been its main forward engines. In the spring of 1948, Coolidge proposed the establishment of an 'International Survival Office' as a central co-ordinator of information that the future IUPN should maintain.[34] The Survival Service was formally designated a permanent Commission in 1956, and under Scott's leadership from 1964 developed into a world network of experts on endangered species. By 1975 there were a total of twenty-six specialist groups dealing with different species or groups of animals, plants (in the form of the newly established Threatened Plants Committee) and other topics such as trade records and zoo liaison. On occasion, though, groups have had merely a paper existence and have required resuscitation to come to life. Indeed, the record of the Commissions as a whole has been varied. In 1952 it was reported that of the three then existing, only that on Education had a real existence; in 1969 the SSC was identified, with the Commission on Legislation, as the most successful in having real effects on wildlife conservation; in 1978, when the Commission structure was being investigated, these two (the latter having evolved into the Commission on Environmental Policy, Law and Administration) together with the Commission on National Parks and Protected Areas (originally established in 1958 as Coolidge's national parks commission) seemed clearly to be those which had had greatest impact in IUCN's history.[35] Of the others, the ecology commission, founded in 1954, had not become the union's principal scientific advisory body, as it was once described;[36] and that on education had appeared to some to be too firmly rooted in certain technical areas at times to play a bigger role in the affairs of the union.

Of all the reasons for this variation — the subject matter being handled, the quality of leadership, the capacity to attract independent sources of funding, the readiness of IUCN to underwrite specialist meetings of experts — one has been a constant preoccupation: the availability of a co-ordinating support facility within the secretariat. Whether its presence or absence correlated well with the performance of any particular Commission remained, however, a moot point. Still less satisfactorily resolved has been the question of co-ordination between the various Commissions, a problem raised at the 1969 Assembly.[37] There have, though, been a number of instances of productive co-operation, for example between the SSC and the legislation commission on the preparation of international conventions.

The potential for leadership in the world conservation network is thus restricted. Certainly IUCN is in no position to impose policy stands on even its own diverse, and sometimes turbulent, membership. Member organisations have their own fields to plough. They can sometimes be coaxed, persuaded or mobilised. But equally, some have developed the skill of edging the union in preferred directions that better fit their own sense of conservation priorities. Indifference or resistance on the part of others can cut the fuel supply for either process. IUCN can be viewed secondly, then, as one actor among many — a *primus inter pares*, perhaps, but without Prime Ministerial power. Relationships in the network have evolved at three levels.

First, various kinds of co-operative links have emerged.

(1) While most actors retain independent sources of financial support, primarily from members, funding relations between some — from WWF for example — can be important factors in the structuring of the network.

(2) So can patterns of membership, as in NGO participation in IUCN deliberations. In the 1970s, the union moved a step in the direction of the ICBP National Section structure by encouraging the formation of national groupings of members — a Canadian Committee for IUCN was established in 1976. Interestingly, devices such as this had been frowned upon as divisive in the early days of IUPN.

(3) Multiple role-taking by leading individuals — Scott's acting concurrently in the 1970s as Chairman of WWF, FPS and the SSC, for example — has been an especially useful method of establishing links and of attempting to ensure a measure of tacit co-ordination. The personal and informal network comprising the relatively few such individuals who have played the major part in the shaping of the post-1945 history of international conservation can, indeed, be

regarded as a central component of the movement's infrastructure.
(4) Groups may also habitually report the work of others in their
publications; or take an organisation like IUCN as a fundamental
reference point in the determination of their own policies; or, more
particularly, phrase the resolutions passed by their policy-making
bodies in such a way as to highlight their lineage in the concerns of
other actors. This last method has in some cases, such as wetlands
conservation, constituted a significant part of the dynamic of change,
even though apparent lack of response to a particular resolution can
hide the momentum.
(5) Some collaborative projects, such as IBP and MAB, or co-operation
on threatened species data between FPS and the SSC in the early
1960s, have already been mentioned.
(6) A few relationships — notably those between IUCN, WWF, ICBP
and IWRB — have taken on a longer term institutional significance.
(7) Other kinds of organisations provide exploitable overlaps with the
concerns of conservationists. Seal culls, for example, are approached
by IUCN in the light of the general problem of the conservation and
management of species, particularly of those threatened with
extinction; and by bodies like the International Society for the
Protection of Animals as cases involving questions of cruelty and the
just treatment by man of members of other species. Clearly, however,
the issues are related, not least in the minds of those urging wider
protection of seals.
(8) Finally, organisations may adhere to broadly similar viewpoints. In a
variety of ways from the early 1970s in particular, IUCN has
attempted to cultivate such agreement: on the kinds of priorities set
down in its own larger or longer term programmes, for example, or
in its World Conservation Strategy document from 1980.

Second, there is also an inevitable element of competition in the network.
Funds are not limitless; the attention spans of publics or governments are
not infinitely elastic; and not all bodies can bask in the triumph of a
particular achievement. Actors occupy niches defined as much by imagery
and stereotyping as by their actual work. Some have been fragmented by
internal pressures for change. Some have inadvertently spawned rivals:
Friends of the Earth emerged in part out of internal debate on activist
options within the Sierra Club; in Britain, the World Pheasant Association
was founded as an ostensibly more dynamic body than the Pheasant Trust;
the large San Francisco branch of the Greenpeace Foundation took its
Vancouver parent body to court in 1979 in a struggle to gain greater

autonomy.[38] A certain mutual accommodation has been possible between moderates and radicals. A shared commitment to the grounding of policy in the findings of scientific research blurs this distinction. The personnel of older, more firmly established bodies may at times value the outspokenness, freedom to simplify and exaggerate, and ability to attract public attention of younger organisations — while at the same time maintaining some official distance from them. On the other hand, they have to manoeuvre carefully. Getting tarred with the same brush as groups that have risked public disfavour, or boredom, by overstating their case can tarnish the scientific legitimacy of a body like IUCN or, though less unequivocally, the fund-raising capability of one like WWF.

Third, conservation organisations may include among their aims the influencing of other kinds of NGOs. Some are potential allies, as in the case of WWF agreements with the world scouting movement. Others raise more controversial issues. IUCN's Tenth and Eleventh General Assemblies in 1969 and 1972 were forums for a protracted dispute over the application for membership of the United States National Rifle Association. Many hunters' organisations do indeed have wide-ranging conservation programmes, albeit for motives other than a desire simply to contemplate the beauties of wild fauna. The argument has been put successfully in British nature conservation politics that association is a more productive and responsible relationship than mutual shunning, but the proposition has not translated well to the international level. Difficulties have likewise arisen in attempts by WWF and IUCN to reach understandings with fur traders' associations on the endangered species most threatened by the industry.

*Actors and interagency co-ordination*

IUCN has always been what one former President has called a 'unique hybrid'.[39] Officially a non-governmental body, it has also a growing state membership. Its fiftieth member state joined in 1978. Other countries are represented by government wildlife protection or forestry agencies that have taken out their own memberships in the union. Its status in relation to some intergovernmental organisations — or, perhaps more accurately, with those departments in them that have undertaken nature conservation tasks — has on occasion, therefore, been more that of an equal. This increasingly dual character has not been easy to handle. Some NGO members have looked on governmentalism, whether in the form of an expanding state membership or of the deepening of ties with intergovernmental organisations, as an unwelcome constraint. From its inception the union was regarded by some conservationists as a mechanism for bringing pressure to bear on governments — an institution whose prestige could usefully be exploited in local situations. Yet at the same time the 1940s concept of a world nature conservation 'movement' lent a certain ambivalence to IUPN. The choice of being either a non-governmental or an intergovernmental body was not seen as the real issue, nor the dichotomy itself as a valid one: both were welcome as members.

Several intergovernmental organisations at the global and regional levels have tackled various aspects of wildlife conservation. UNESCO's own involvement in the area was initially controversial, even after Huxley had given the organisation a determined push in that direction; and it could at times be somewhat disjointed, since programmes and policies had to be justified primarily on either educational, scientific or cultural grounds. Educational topics tended to be delegated by contract to IUCN. Though there were antecedents such as a focus on ecological problems of arid lands in the 1950s, UNESCO's major scientific programme in the area has been the large-scale Man and the Biosphere enterprise of the 1970s and the related work of its Division of Ecological Sciences. The organisation's goal of protecting cultural sites was blended successfully with IUCN's interest in habitat conservation in the 1972 World Heritage convention, and its 1978 Charter of Animal Rights touched on some facets of the problem. At the time of IUPN's establishment in 1948, FAO also had a commitment to wildlife by virtue of its agricultural and forestry work. This side developed considerably after 1959. Its Conference approved an expansion of wildlife management activities in that year, recommended that priority be accorded to this aspect, among others, of its forestry tasks in 1965, and in 1967 set up a new wildlife management unit.[40] The emphasis, that is, was on wildlife as a usable resource. Conservation was a utilitarian virtue. Thus the medium-term objective of FAO's work on 'forest, wildland and wildlife conservation' was described in 1975 as being 'to improve forest, wildland and wildlife conservation programmes by assisting national agencies to adopt and apply multiple-use development strategies ... and sustained utilitarian concepts within dynamic but comprehensive policies for natural resources conservation'.[41] Nature conservation as more traditionally conceived was unquestionably a function of UNEP from its establishment in 1973. It was set, however, within a larger environmental policy context. 'Conservation of nature, wildlife and genetic resources', that is, was only one priority area of the organisation.[42] UNEP's objectives with regard to the conservation of threatened species were defined in 1975 in these terms: '(a) to maintain the health of particular ecosystems, biomes or habitats, by preserving the minimum population size necessary for the survival of a given species; (b) to help ensure that conservation and management measures for endangered species, and the legislation on which such measures are based, take full account of [this]; (c) to support research activities designed to give an adequate basis for the right strategy to achieve these objectives.'[43]

The regional level of intergovernmental organisation has been increasingly involved in these kinds of matters, particularly in western Europe. The Council of Europe established a European Commmittee for the Conservation of Nature and Natural Resources in 1962, and a European Information Centre for Nature Conservation in 1967. A series of European Ministerial Conferences on the Environment has been organised on a triennial basis from the first in Vienna in 1973; wildlife conservation has been a regular agenda item. The Council's limited powers in relation to member governments, however, have restricted its potential role as an initiator of change. Its Committee of Ministers has passed a number of wildlife resolutions, for example on threatened birds, mammals and plants in Europe.[44] To promote its aims on a broader front, the Council has also developed an active publications programme and engaged in educational campaigns, notably on the question of European wetlands in 1976. In the late 1970s its conservation staff was concentrating on preparation of a draft convention on the protection of wildlife and habitats in Europe, which was first introduced to states in Berne in September 1979. The conservation interests of the European Community, by contrast, were somewhat slower to take off, primarily because of uncertainties as to its competence in such areas. Environmental attention focused at first on problems of pollution. In 1974, the Council of Ministers asked the Commission to begin work on an ecological classification and inventory of Community territory; a more specific emphasis emerged later on migratory bird issues, a topic discussed later in this book. This by no means exhausts the list of intergovernmental bodies. There are some unlikely candidates. NATO has supported conferences on threatened species research; COMECON's conservation of nature programme from the early 1970s has dealt with threats to ecosystems together with related questions such as atmospheric pollution.[45]

But the central intergovernmental actors, and the ones with which IUCN has been most closely involved, are FAO, UNESCO and UNEP. IUPN's partial dependence on UNESCO funding in the 1950s skewed its interests more in an educational direction. UNEP, two decades later, was a funding agency with more central ecological biases. Four categories of funding for wildlife and endangered species were developed: dissemination of information, training, research and the application of knowledge. The last embraced such activities as management and convention-making. Of the three other bodies, comparatively little went to UNESCO. FAO had an edge as a recipient in the training and application areas, IUCN/WWF in those of information and research. Thus in the three years 1974–6, FAO received in total nearly \$5.3 million from UNEP, and IUCN just over \$3.3 million;[46] but the union's 'application' capability was growing in the second half of the decade as a result of its treaty work, particularly the servicing of CITES. As at the NGO level, various co-operative links have sprouted. FAO and UNESCO both had active observers and liaisers with IUCN in the 1950s. Because of the formal consultative machinery maintained by intergovernmental organisations, relations could be more formally structured, as in IUCN's rise through UNESCO's non-governmental consultative hierarchy. FAO provided the union with its Secretary-General for a period in 1961–2. By the late 1970s something of an international conservation career network had emerged. Even leaving out national possibilities, it became feasible for the professional conservationist to slice a career into successive segments with a number of inter- and non-governmental bodies. The contrast with the late 1940s is striking. Organisations have also collaborated on projects, as in IUCN's participation in the MAB programme. An inventory of joint sponsorships of technical conferences over the years would be too lengthy to summarise.

But a second similarity with the NGO level is competition. There are no predetermined outcomes of encounters. Some guidelines exist. States deal with intergovernmental bodies, these in turn with non-governmental ones. Prudent NGOs keep an eye on intergovernmental actors, which are sometimes as ready to poach ideas as to ignore them. As well as enjoying easier access to states, intergovernmental organisations also have more administrative and financial resources to draw on. The element of hierarchy in the network, however, is rarely an adequate clue to its inner workings. Funding of IUCN by both UNESCO and UNEP, for example, has not been used as an overt instrument of power. It is not even clear that it affords either body greater access to union deliberations, since their overlapping functions would ensure this. The proportion of its funds that comes from such bodies, however, means that their views, most obviously in relation to specifically contracted tasks, have to be weighed carefully by IUCN. It is sometimes necessary to hint to restive NGO members that the proportion of union expenditure their fees account for may be smaller than they imagine, and that there are implications of such facts of life. More particularly, increases in membership fees, always a headache of an issue, followed on in 1979 at least partly from the insistence of external funding bodies that organisations supported should be able to cover their minimum core costs themselves.[47] All this still leaves considerable room for competitive manoeuvring. FAO and IUCN drew up alternative drafts of what became the 1968 convention on African wildlife conservation, and were unable to resolve their differences within the framework of a compromise text. A more intriguing instance is provided by the sequence of events that led to UNESCO's 1968 biosphere conference, itself a crucial forerunner of UNCHE in 1972. Following Coolidge's achievement of the Seattle national parks conference of 1962, Scott and others aired the idea of a comparable meeting on endangered species. The possibility was explored at IUCN's Nairobi Assembly in 1963. There it caught the imagination among others of US Interior Secretary Udall. A multi-NGO steering committee chaired by Scott drew up plans in 1965–6 for a 1968 intergovernmental conference on wildlife and ecosystem conservation. Lack of initial ECOSOC responsiveness to the IUCN proposal, however, left the field open for UNESCO's later notion of a more general conference on the rational use and conservation of the biosphere. UNESCO officials argued that a broadening of scope even beyond that which IUCN had envisaged was necessary if developing countries were to be persuaded of the virtues of conservation. There was some discussion of a 1949-type tandem arrangement; ICBP proposed a merging of the two projected conferences. But the momentum of the biosphere idea was too great. IUCN did take an active part in the Paris meetings in 1968, and there was a place in the resulting MAB programme for endangered species activity; but both clearly owed more to the groundwork done earlier in the IBP than to the post-Seattle species concept.

The 1970s were marked by more of a co-ordinating impulse. Partly this was a product of UNEP's establishment. One strategy was more effective co-operation among environmental NGOs, and stronger links between liaising bodies, such as the Environment Liaison Board, and UNEP.[48] An Ecosystem Conservation Group, comprising representatives of FAO, UNESCO, IUCN and UNEP, was established in 1975 and over the next year or so held three regular meetings, a working session on Africa and a special one on problems of marine conservation.[49] There were some teething problems, but the ECG developed into a useful forum for exchanges of views on nature conservation issues, reviews of the programmes of each member, and examinations of particular topics. Closer IUCN–UNEP relations evolved, UNEP officials for example participating in the work of IUCN's planning body of the late 1970s.[50] Other outcomes of funding discussions between the two at this time included provision for the union to launch a 'new generation' of *Red Data Book* volumes as part of its information dissemination role. The aspiration on the part of IUCN to be able to gear its conservation activity more to a longer term perspective dates back to the 1950s. Programming, for example in relation to the oceans, or in the form of the Conservation Quinquennium projected for the late 1960s, emerged much later. The term 'world conservation strategy' was being used in 1974–5 to describe a more comprehensive look at the future. In 1977 UNEP provided the union with funds to prepare a document bearing this title and having this function. An extensive consultative exercise followed. The WCS was planned from the start to perform a co-ordinating role itself: actions proposed would not be restricted to those habitually carried out by any particular body. The aim, further, was to produce a plan of attack that could be periodically revised in the light of changing conditions. Preparatory work on it ran into some snags at IUCN's Ashkhabad Assembly in 1978 and in exchanges with UNEP the following year. Some of the draft phrasing appeared too generalised and motherhood-oriented; insufficient stress was given to problems of the development process and broader questions of world population and resources; its provisions on education and implementation were thought weak; and the impact of pollution needed to be assessed more prominently.[51] More important, though, were the strengths of the WCS idea. Conservationists in the 1980s were to have at their disposal a coherent and patiently drawn up set of analyses, priorities and guidelines for conservation action on a world scale. There was, of course, no guarantee that all organisations would actually use this kind of signpost. But such problems have been intrinsic to the operations of the conservation network since the 1940s. They are not necessarily symptoms of failure.

Three case studies now rivet the ample sweep of this and previous chapters. They were not selected according to any criterion of success or accomplishment, though there are certainly achievements here worth noting. Each rather represents some long-standing concern of conservation groups. Indeed there are distant rumblings of a beginning of all of them in the late nineteenth century. Each further provides an opportunity to investigate at closer quarters the interrelationships between, as well as the impact of, several organisations. The different patterns of activity that seem to be characteristic of each of them will be discussed collectively in the concluding chapter.

# Part III

# Case Studies

# 7 Polar conservation

> This is the season of flowers, and behold! they have sprung up about us
> as if by magic: very beautiful ice-flowers, waxen white in the shadow,
> but radiant with prismatic colours where the sunrays light on their
> delicate petals.
>
> Excerpt from Scott's diary, Easter Sunday,
> 30 March 1902[1]

The sparseness, or absence of human settlement and exploitation in the
polar regions is the inevitable consequence of a harsh climate: but so too is
the fragility of their ecosystems. When contact between man and nature
was largely a matter of hunting by native peoples, or the occasional
scientific expedition, the latter fact was, if appreciated, only of academic
interest. Vulnerability was not among the most noticeable attributes of
areas where the visitor's attention had constantly to be turned to the
minutiae of survival. Mineral development, organised tourism,
intensification of fishing, even the emergence of scientific research stations
operating on a semi-permanent basis, have been a few of the more recent
factors that have had a discernible ecological effect in the Arctic and
Antarctic. In both regions, though, the minimal intrusion of traditional state
interests has to some extent facilitated the establishment of broader
international regimes for conservation of nature and natural resources. The
role played by the southern ocean in particular in world ecological
processes, moreover, gives these problems more than a merely local
significance. This first of three case studies deals in turn with conservation
issues in the Arctic and Antarctic regions, and the distinctive ways in which
international organisations have responded to the threats characteristic of
each.

*Exploration and science*

Discussion of international exploration in the polar regions was first introduced at a scientific conference held in Hamburg in 1879, out of which emerged an International Polar Commission.[2] The particular question of nature conservation was raised the following year, when the explorer Nordenskiöld called in Stockholm for the establishment of protected zones in the north, arguing in support of his proposal that these areas were in any case of no economic value.[3] International scientific work began in the 1880s. After conferences in Berne and St Petersburg, the First International Polar Year was declared in 1882–3 with eleven countries participating. Twelve stations were set up and manned in the Arctic and two in the Antarctic. At the fifth international conference in this series, in Munich in 1891, the Commission was dissolved and the results of the enterprise published. A fresh spurt came with the new century. In 1905, a group of explorers established in Mons an International Association for the Study of Polar Regions; in 1906 official delegates from fifteen states meeting in Brussels created a reconstituted International Polar Commission. Its objectives were to establish closer scientific relations between polar explorers, co-ordinate their scientific observations and methods, assess the scientific results of expeditions, and assist expeditions by indicating scientific problems. The Belgian Government gave funding the next year for an International Polar Institute in Brussels. This functioned essentially as a bibliographic and information centre. However, war largely dissolved interest in furthering international polar research.[4]

It revived in the 1920s with excitement at the potential of aircraft and other technical developments. More than a hundred countries took part in the Second International Polar Year of 1932–3. This concentrated on the Arctic and sub-Arctic regions and had an emphasis on meteorological research. It also resulted in the setting up of a small international bureau in Copenhagen to collect and disseminate research findings. Co-operation in the post-1945 period was thus founded on a solid basis of scientific work, specialised institutes and the growth of contacts between scientists in many nations. The Arctic Institute of North America was established at McGill University in 1945 as an information and bibliographic centre which also had the aims of encouraging research and promoting international co-operation in arctic science.[5]

The existence of this broader international polar network was crucial to the surfacing of interest in the polar regions, especially the Arctic, on the part of members of organisations such as IUPN and ICBP early in the 1950s. It was only gradually, however, that the nature of the problem came to be defined more precisely. Kenneth Bertrand summarised it briefly in 1974: 'About the only things that the Arctic and the Antarctic have in common are high latitude and low temperature, but [these] create a harsh environment that places all forms of life under severe stress. Even those native forms of life, which have adapted to the low temperatures and the alternate seasons of continuous night and continuous day, maintain a precarious balance that is easily upset.'[6] There are few places on earth, Dasmann commented in 1968 on Antarctica, 'where all of the species interacting within an ecosystem can be listed on the back of an envelope and where communities are so simplified that one can trace in detail all of the elements involved in the normally complex process of biotic succession'.[7] More particularly, this general condition of vulnerability could mean that sheer numbers were no clue to the degree of threat to a particular species. 'We are already wise enough to discard as a complete fallacy the argument that a species is in no danger because it is still common,' one scientist stated at a major 1962 conference on Antarctic biology; '... in a long-isolated realm of tenuous balance, where broods are small ... and the dangers of immaturity extravagant, the new interloper, Man, is the straw that can all too easily break the camel's back.'[8] By the 1970s, threats in varying degrees making an impact on the two environments were being well documented: the expansion of recreation and tourism; oil and gas exploration and development; growing interest, with population pressures on world resources, in exploitation of the marine life of the southern ocean; pollution, the presence of organochlorine pesticides in the Antarctic being detected and monitored at least from the mid-1960s; hunting threats to some species of wildlife; or the problems associated with scientific settlements established in areas typically having no subsoil leakage or rapid bacterial decomposition.

*Conservation of nature in the Arctic*

The Arctic had one advantage over the Antarctic as far as practical conservation measures were concerned: the presence of one species, the polar bear, whose status attracted wide international interest in the northern rim of states in the late 1960s and early 1970s. The treaty that resulted from these concerns, signed in Oslo in 1973, was a striking feather in IUCN's cap, and occupies a central place in this section. It has its origins in the first concerted attacks on the more general problem of Arctic conservation from the early 1950s.

Zoological and botanical publications had even earlier begun to draw attention to threats facing Arctic flora and fauna, and to relate these to wider policy issues. In the United States, for example, in 1951, careful administration of wildlife was advocated by one writer as the only practical method of land utilisation in the Arctic.[9] A small group of Soviet scientists was engaged in the collection of data on measures to protect Arctic mammals and birds in the USSR and in other countries.[10] Arguments were being put forward in Denmark in 1952–3 on the need for protected areas to be set aside in Greenland.[11] IUPN became a forum in which scientists from the Arctic nations could explore common problems and co-operative solutions. Its fourth General Assembly was convened in Copenhagen in 1954. This established a standing committee of the union to tackle problems connected with the protection of Arctic fauna. Denmark, Sweden, Canada, the United States, Norway and Finland were each represented by one member. One resolution of the Assembly noted the severe reduction in numbers of many Arctic and high boreal animals, and proposed measures for the better protection of some by the Swedish and Norwegian Governments: removal of the wolverine bounty for example. Finally, a resolution was passed which suggested that the countries concerned should consider co-operation with a view to preparing an international convention for the preservation of the marine mammals of the Arctic. This arose most immediately from data collected for the union's Survival Service by Petter on the status of polar bears, walruses and seals: 'owing to the animals' habits,' as the resolution note, 'the question is essentially an international one.'[12]

In relation to the polar bear, this issue later became a difficult technical one with important political implications. In the 1950s, though, the more pressing matter was to set international data collection on a more secure footing. Curry-Lindahl, a member of IUPN's Arctic fauna committee, wrote later that not much was achieved by 'this first attempt to focus international attention on Arctic problems of conservation'.[13] Some things did emerge, however, which had a longer term significance, even though paucity of funds tended to rule out meetings and necessitated exchanges of information and proposals for action being made primarily through correspondence. The polar bear became a central target for examination. Concern was expressed at the increasing capture of polar bear cubs for zoos and circuses (the unprecedented rise in public interest in the London Zoo that accompanied the appearance of the famous Brumas in 1950 was not an unmixed blessing), and bad treatment by trappers; the committee proposed that governments with Arctic territories should introduce or tighten regulations pertaining to the catch of young polar bears. Secondly, representations made to Scandinavian governments by Harroy on the basis of the 1954 Assembly resolutions, though having little obvious immediate effect, set a tentative precedent for the involvement of international conservation organisations in Arctic matters entering into relations between governments. One Danish scientist, Christian Vibe, was an important intermediary in this respect, being active both in Danish conservation circles and in the emerging IUPN Arctic framework. Denmark and Norway signed an agreement in July 1956 for the protection of north-east Greenland, under which shooting from aircraft was prohibited, and measures were introduced which afforded greater protection to birds and to other Arctic mammal species. Thirdly, the work of the Arctic fauna committee led directly to the participation by Soviet scientists in this area of IUCN's activities. This was one of the earliest instances of east-west co-operation in the field of environmental conservation. The Soviet Union had a large expanse of Arctic territory that would clearly need to be incorporated into the treaty area of any future conservation agreement that was to be even minimally effective. A Soviet decree of November 1956 further designated the polar bear as a completely protected species. Other species, such as walrus and wild reindeer, were given varying degrees of protection. The Soviet decision, which also included exceptions for local peoples using traditional hunting techniques, was increasingly cited in the late 1950s as the kind of norm of domestic legislation towards which states should be persuaded to move.

It was during this period that concern for the fate of the polar bear began to filter through to a wider public in the United States. In the spring of 1957, officials of the US Fish and Wildlife Service in Anchorage expressed alarm at the expansion taking place in the hunting of polar bear from aircraft. International co-operation for the further progress of research and management was recommended, and as a first step, information was sought from IUCN's committee on Arctic fauna.[14] Wildlife officials in Alaska were thus later receptive to the idea, pressed in particular by Soviet scientists working on Arctic conservation questions, of the convening of an international conference at which the requirements for the future Arctic regime could be examined in greater depth. This meeting finally took place at Fairbanks in September 1965. But by then the character of the problem, or the manner of its treatment, had altered. The polar bear had been elevated in the United States to the higher reaches of symbolic politics. Conservation groups assured the animal extensive publicity. Clues as to its status were snatched up by the news media — the high prices of skins at the Vancouver fur auctions for example.[15] Political and governmental leaders took up its cause. The Fairbanks meeting was formally proposed in February 1965 by Senator E. L. Bartlett, and supported by Interior Secretary Udall on the grounds that the polar bear range had contracted considerably since 1930, that data were not available on whether or not the animal was in fact rare, and finally that it was fitting to have such a meeting in International Co-operation Year.[16] In view of Soviet initiation of the moves that led to the meeting, the Fairbanks conference had a wider significance for east-west relations: the value of polar co-operation and the management and conservation of Arctic natural resources was stressed by President Johnson in a message to Bartlett that lent the prestige of his own office to the gathering.[17] With such a diversity of expectations directed towards it, and of people taking part in it, the conference not surprisingly edged towards the brink of becoming simply a talking-shop. But practical results did accrue.

It was already agreed that a primary obstacle to more effective polar bear protection was lack of information. There were various estimates available of polar bear numbers, rates of decrease, and of the degree of threat facing the species. It was precisely on this point that IUCN could be viewed as having a potentially more important role to play than it had done in the 1950s. This argument was put to the meeting by a Canadian scientist, C. R. Harington, who reviewed the union's *Red Data Book* work and urged that it be considered a clearing-house for information on polar bears. In its presentation to the conference, the Canadian delegation formally recommended that IUCN be approached with regard to the organisation and distribution of an international polar bear data sheet. Soviet scientists present, while sympathetic to this suggestion, at the same time had reservations about IUCN's judgment of the status of the species; they felt more particularly that deletion of the polar bear in 1961 from the IUCN list of animals thought to be in danger of extinction seemed premature. A related data question concerned the range of the animal. In the Soviet view, the polar bear was a monotype species. No national polar bear races or populations existed. Rather, 'all animals constitute a common resource of all nations having Arctic territories'. Any bear 'may sooner or later appear near the coast of Canada, Greenland, Spitzbergen, or Alaska'. Soviet management and conservation efforts, therefore, had been less effective than expected because bears continued to be harvested in other Arctic regions.[18] The issue had political implications. A regime dealing with discrete and localised races or populations would differ from one treating a migratory species; acceptance of the 'common resource' concept could imply, further, the need to establish a management authority with wider regulatory or licensing powers.

A Statement of Accord drawn up by Fairbanks delegates expressed some measure of consensus. Polar bears moved over large areas beyond national waters and could be 'considered as an international circumpolar resource'. It was the responsibility of each nation to take steps to conserve them, however, particularly in the case of cubs and mothers with cubs, and to continue research on the subject, each nation also having the authority to determine the character of its research activities. Countries should, though, 'give consideration to' the prompt exchange of information. Finally, IUCN ('or similar international organisation') was invited to receive and distribute information on polar bears. Future meetings of scientists and officials were recommended 'when urgent problems or new scientific information warrant international consideration'.[19]

The mechanism for the handling of longer term Arctic conservation questions was not, then, specified at Fairbanks. And while the principle of a degree of concerted effort was granted cautious recognition, agreement was not possible, or even attempted, in such a setting on an international collaborative research programme. Harington's proposal for data collecting within such a programme, however much leeway was left for individual nations, was taken further by him and a colleague, Charles Jonkel, after the Fairbanks meeting. The first requirement was seen to be the creation of a scientific forum of world polar bear specialists. A Polar Bear group of the SSC was duly established at a meeting of specialists funded by IUCN in January 1968.[20] S. M. Uspensky, the leading Soviet authority whose research had in large part paved the way for the 1956 decree, became its chairman; and the group comprised technical representatives from each Arctic nation. The goal of an international convention, on IUCN's table since the Copenhagen Assembly of 1954, was discussed. There was some disagreement, however, on approaches and timing. On the one hand, the Fairbanks meeting had generated extensive public and governmental interest in the United States which it might be timely to capitalise on by moving ahead speedily towards a convention. On the other, governments would not enter into an agreement until some crucial technical questions had first been answered and, in view of the novelty of the enterprise, a gradualist approach of small things first could be argued to be a better motto for the Group. The latter case on balance won the day. As defined later, the Group's objectives were: '(1) to expedite the collection of scientific data as a basis for future management and conservation; (2) to identify the scientific problems and geographical regions in which international research is desirable; (3) to determine research priorities and stimulate national action toward common goals; and (4) to serve as a general forum for exchange of ideas and information on this and other problems concerning high Arctic fauna.'[21] The process, that is, was to be strictly a technical one. The many conservation organisations, and individuals, interested in the polar bear but without recognised scientific competence should, it was felt, be excluded from it at that stage.

By the time of the Group's second meeting, in February 1970, the state of play was considerably more advanced. A long-planned conference on Arctic problems organised jointly by IUCN and IBP/CT was held in Edmonton late in 1969. It provided an occasion for Uspensky, Jonkel and others to reassess the polar bear situation. Oil exploration in the north, and native peoples' rights, were the key issues that dominated more general debate. Research needs for the polar bear and for other Arctic species of mammals and birds were pinpointed. The conference reaffirmed that 'in view of the proximity and interrelated resource management needs of circumpolar countries, management plans and associated research programmes demand strong efforts of international co-ordination'.[22] After the 1968 meeting, polar bear research was in fact already more international in character. The location of important denning areas was becoming known; and Canadian, Norwegian and United States scientists inaugurated a joint tagging programme. The very existence of the Polar Bear Group stimulated research indeed, if only by arming scientists with stronger arguments for funding from their own governments, a difficulty that was being met with particularly by Danish researchers. Several governments made moves to tighten their polar bear regulations. A federal-provincial Administrative Committee for Polar Bear Research and Management was initiated by Jonkel in July 1969. This was a significant development in view of Canada's position as the leading polar bear nation, and also the one with the most complex domestic administrative muddle. Seven governments shared competence to deal with polar bear questions; they were not accustomed to working closely together, and they differed widely in their management policies, from Manitoba which was closed to hunting and Quebec which was completely open.[23] Internal harmonisation was thus seen by Jonkel and other scientists in and out of government as a crucial step towards more productive talks at the international level. But, though the annual kill of bears was maintained at a steady rather than an increasing level during this period, other factors indicated a likely deterioration in the future. Economic development was emerging as a threat to habitats potentially more damaging than the direct impact of hunting. Inuit hunting by mechanised vehicles, and trophy hunting by aircraft off Alaska, were growing concerns. Wintering trappers in Spitzbergen still used set-gun techniques for hunting. Why should the USSR provide complete protection for the polar bear, Uspensky asked at the Group's 1970 meeting, if they were only producing a larger crop for neighbouring nations?[24]

The same meeting endorsed the Soviet view at Fairbanks that polar bear hunting should be banned internationally for a period of five years. After much discussion of tactics and timing within the SSC and IUCN Secretariat, the proposal was supported and transmitted to the governments concerned.

Burhenne also prepared for the second meeting an outline of alternative convention possibilities. Canada's federal-provincial committee called in 1971 for a treaty 'controlling [not prohibiting] the hunting of polar bear on the high seas'.[25] At the third meeting of the Group, in February 1972, it was generally acknowledged that the process of convention-building could be a long one, perhaps five or ten years. Some principles were nevertheless drawn up of a kind that might later be incorporated into the preamble of a treaty, for example that the polar bear constituted both a national and an international resource, and that the needs of local peoples had to be recognised. The last point, concerning Inuit and Indian hunting rights, was showing signs of becoming a thorny issue in Canada. As regards the first point, the majority of bears recovered in the tagging programme had been found in the general vicinity where they had been marked; this could have thrown into question the assumption of the creature's international status made at Fairbanks, but the evidence was thought not to preclude the possibility of it undertaking long-distance seasonal migrations. Finally, the Soviet delegation produced without warning its own draft of a protocol to provide in the interim for further protective measures. The Group asked IUCN to work on new drafts of the general principles and of a protocol banning polar bear hunting on the high seas.[26]

As in 1965, progress towards the intergovernmental conference in Oslo in November 1973 at which the Agreement was signed was marked by public clamour. It erupted quickly in Canada. In 1970, a speaker at a Royal Society symposium expressed regret at the lack of public will to put scientific knowledge of tundra animals into operation; in 1971 the federal-provincial polar bear committee saw a need for an official public relations campaign to counter 'the existing misconceptions and often unfounded concern for the survival of the various species'.[27] During 1973 the polar bear became a handy weapon in Opposition attacks on the minority Liberal government. John Diefenbaker, the former Prime Minister, said that MPs had been getting letters 'from all over this nation' about the 'survival of some of our most wonderful animals in the north'.[28] Other MPs accused the government of producing 'incorrect and deliberately evasive' polar bear kill statistics; criticised the advertising in Europe of the North West Territories hunting season; portrayed the polar bear as a symbol of the north and hence of the nation; proposed postponement of the Oslo meeting until Inuit concerns had been met satisfactorily; and vehemently denied ministers' claims that there was 'absolutely no danger of extinction' for the animal.[29] In the United States, too, the polar bear became, according to the head of that country's delegation to the Oslo conference, 'like the whale ... a symbol in the fight to stop the continuing destruction of man's own ecosystem'.[30]

Following mounting pressure from conservation lobbies and attention in the news media, both Houses of Congress in 1972 passed a resolution calling on President Nixon to negotiate a moratorium with other nations on the killing of polar bears in the Arctic.[31]

But this background noise probably had more of a stylistic than a substantive effect on the convention-making process itself. Some official American statements, for example, managed to convey the impression that it had been the United States that had cut a path to agreement through the obstructiveness of less high-minded nations. Resolution of the main issues was achieved for the most part before the conference. Congressional pressure confirmed, rather than created, the Administration's pursuit of an international accord. Wider public interest did, though, steer the wildlife biologists and other government specialists concerned in the direction of an early agreement; patiently waiting for research to produce further results was no longer a politically feasible precondition.

The draft prepared by IUCN was circulated to the five Arctic governments later in 1972, and a modified version used as the working paper of the Oslo meeting. Polar Bear Group members cleared up some of the remaining points during the course of IUCN's General Assembly in Banff in September 1972. The need to ban aircraft and certain other kinds of hunting, and to make especially strict provisions for cubs and mothers with cubs, were questions that found ready support among technical experts; more difficult issues were raised by the questions of native peoples' hunting rights, the co-ordination of national research programmes, and the phrasing of the principles of the agreement. The Canadian phrasing of the co-ordination problem, sensitive because of its implications for sovereignty in regions with strategic significance, was that each country could 'identify an area of management within which that participant would manage polar bear stocks in accordance with sound biological principles and beyond which ... the hunting of polar bear would be prohibited'.[32] A partial solution was provided in the preamble, which avoided the earlier language of national and international resources and stated simply that the polar bear was 'a significant resource of the Arctic Region which requires additional protection'. Article VII called on the Parties to conduct national research programmes. They 'shall as appropriate co-ordinate such research with research carried out by other Parties, consult with other Parties on the management of migrating polar bear populations, and exchange information on research and management programmes, research results and data on bears taken'. Among the exceptions listed in Article III was provision for the taking of polar bears by 'local people using traditional methods in the exercise of their traditional rights and in accordance with the laws of that Party' (and, more widely, 'wherever polar bears have or might have been subject to taking by traditional means by its nationals'). The core of the Agreement was Article 1, which prohibited the taking of polar bears by hunting, killing or capturing.[33] Bears could be taken only for *bona fide* scientific purposes, for conservation purposes, to prevent serious disturbance of the management of other living resources, and in the two circumstances just noted (Article III). Under Article IV the use of aircraft and large motorised vessels was prohibited (though not if this would be inconsistent with domestic laws). The Parties undertook to take 'appropriate action to protect the ecosystems of which polar bears are a part', and to manage populations 'in accordance with sound conservation practices based on the best available scientific data' (Article II). Two provisions reflected the signing of CITES earlier in the year. Article V prohibited the export, import and traffic in polar bears or their parts and products; and Article III(2) specified that skins and other items taken under the exceptions procedure for conservation purposes could not be made available for commercial purposes. Agreement was not possible, however, on two more specific points. Instead, an Annex to the official record took the form of a resolution on special protection measures. This requested, but, not being part of the accord imposed no obligation on, governments to take steps to provide a complete ban on hunting of female polar bears with cubs and of the cubs, and to prohibit hunting of polar bears in denning areas.

The exceptions and qualifications meant that the package was less watertight than some of the Soviet and Canadian scientists who had struggled long for its realisation would have preferred, but the successful conclusion of the polar bear agreement was justifiably regarded by IUCN as a substantial achievement. It entered into force in 1976 after ratification by Norway, Canada and the USSR. The Polar Bear Group stayed in existence (and resisted incorporation into a wider SSC bear grouping) as a mechanism for investigating continuing problems. Polar bears were occasionally reported in Iceland, for example, a country not party to the agreement. The group also recommended that IUCN approach the governments of states whose nationals might be engaged in harvesting bears or trading in their skins: nine countries, none of them signatories, were identified.[34] IUCN and WWF also became, as a result of the agreement, potential allies of northern native peoples. In 1974 Inuit communities urged them to continue their work of protecting Arctic animals on the grounds that 'these animals have been and still are the only means of subsistence for the Eskimo and Greenlandic peoples of hunters'.[35]

*Conservation of nature in the Antarctic*

Preservationist interest in the Antarctic land mass was born with the turn of the century. The great explorers of the age brought back accounts of the fauna of this distant and forbidding region and its surrounding waters and islands which excited the imagination of conservationists already flexing their muscles on issues nearer home. The RSPB in Britain urged protection of Antarctic penguins in 1905.[36] Ordinances to protect those in the vicinity of the Falkland Islands were issued in 1909 and 1914.[37] But more general conservationist arguments often had little credibility in the vast expanses of the southern oceans. The government of New Zealand refused in 1925 to designate the Auckland Islands, a group to the south of South Island, as a protected reserve on the grounds that their annual rental as a sheep run (£40) was a more important consideration.[38] During the 1920s and 1930s, ICBP kept an occasional watch on Antarctic bird preservation problems. Representatives from New Zealand associations took part early in the activities of the organisation, though domestic concerns tended to take precedence over glances southward. Concrete results sometimes stemmed from pressures by groups, as in the establishment by Argentina of a reserve on the Isla de los Estados, south of Tierra del Fuego, an area which included several species of penguins.[39] But for practical reasons, interest in Antarctica and its neighbouring waters on the part of international wildlife protection bodies was necessarily marginal.

This pattern remained essentially unaltered until the signing of the Antarctica Treaty in 1959. The scientific advisory machinery set up as part of the Antarctica arrangements opened up new possibilities of access for organisations like IUCN. The wider provisions of the Treaty need not detain us here.[40] Scientific co-operation was channelled through the Special (later Scientific) Committee on Antarctic Research (SCAR), established by ICSU in 1958 to assist in framing programmes of circumpolar scope and significance, and designated the scientific advisory body to signatory governments. Countries party to the treaty were represented on the Committee by technical delegates. A Working Group on Biology (WGB) was one of a series set up in 1958.

It was through this Group that there emerged in 1964 the makings of a first nature conservation regime for Antarctica. Concern for the flora and fauna of the region was expressed before the treaty conference, notably at SCAR's third meeting in Canberra in the spring on 1959. WGB members proceeded to identify research needs in antarctic biology. In 1961 a set of recommendations was drawn up on the conservation of nature. It was proposed that all land and fresh water, including fast ice and ice shelves, and all coastal waters south of latitude 60° South, should be recognised internationally as a nature reserve; further, that important or vulnerable species and habitats should be given special protection. WGB shortly afterwards urged the listing of species and areas requiring such protection.[41] Conservation requirements were assessed in 1962 at a major symposium on antarctic biology organised in Paris by SCAR.[42] Finally, at the third meeting of the treaty powers, in Brussels in 1964, delegates recommended approval and implementation of the 'Agreed Measures for the Conservation of Antarctic Fauna and Flora'. These provided for the prohibition of 'the killing, wounding, capturing or molesting of any native mammal or bird' without a permit. Criteria were listed for the taking of animals by authorised persons. Specially Protected Species could be designated (Article VI), as could Specially Protected Areas (Article VIII). Provision was also made for the control of harmful interference with the living conditions of animals, for example by vehicles (Article VII).[43]

The existence of this framework of scientific co-operation to aid the Antarctica treaty powers widened the range of organisations that could be actively interested in the conservation problems of the region. Contact could be made through the SCAR national committees. Robert Carrick, for example, WGB Secretary, presented a paper on Antarctic conservation to the Seattle national parks conference in 1962. Discussion of the question led to passage of a resolution calling for more positive measures to prevent the exploitation of the marine life on which the antarctic ecosystem depended.[44] The advent of the treaty also served to reawaken ICBP interest in the continent and its surrounding waters. At its 1958 and 1960 Conferences, the threat posed by increased human contact was noted. Specific dangers to fauna came from releasing sled dogs, the introduction of exotic species, discharge of oil, and interference by crews and personnel. The generality of the 1959 treaty was criticised, and the need for adequate reserves emphasised. ICBP's Conference of 1962 concluded, on this issue, that there was an urgent need for scientists to survey and define requirements for conservation in the sub-Antarctic region, and for governments to embark on a concerted programme of study and management of natural resources.[45] The Agreed Measures themselves were widely welcomed both for their comprehensiveness and for their pioneering coverage of the fauna of a very large region of the earth.[46]

The 1964 framework thus set the pattern for the decade. Areas and species were officially designated as being in need of special protection under the terms of the Measures. WGB drew up more specific criteria for such decisions in 1966, proposed that information on the status of species and the taking of animals under permit be exchanged, and drew up interim guidelines for the conservation of fauna and flora. A joint WGB–IBP study of the protection requirements of oceanic islands was undertaken. Improvements were made in the machinery. In 1968 WGB established a conservation subcommittee to survey existing and potential Specially Protected Areas, and various modifications were made of procedures, for example on the definition of an 'authorised person'.[47]

But a change of tone began to be evident from the later 1960s. The growth of knowledge and the expansion of human activity in the region were rapidly outdating the 1964 Measures. These reflected, one writer argued in 1971, the spirit of the period before the International Geophysical Year (the programme out of which the 1959 treaty arose), 'when the continent was still distant, isolated, and little known'.[48] Two factors were increasingly seizing the attention of SCAR scientists. As early as 1960, the Committee had drawn up plans for a leaflet on preservation of wildlife to be drafted and circulated to all persons landing in Antarctica. In Tokyo in 1970 the consultative meeting of the treaty nations stated that tourists could have 'lasting and harmful effects on scientific programmes, on the Antarctic environment, particularly in Specially Protected Areas, and on historic momuments'. Delegates recommended that governments ensure that tourists did not engage in activity contrary to the principles and purposes of the treaty. The vulnerability of the antarctic ecosystem to human interference was stressed: the region derived much of its scientific importance from its uncontaminated and undisturbed condition. A second threat was posed by rising interest in the unexploited natural resources of the area. In the mid-1960s, Japanese and Soviet scientists carried out experimental krill-cropping programmes. The ecological significance of any move to regularise fishing of this small but protein-rich crustacean lay in its position in the southern ocean food web, particularly as the diet of baleen whales. The question was examined in depth at SCAR's ninth meeting in 1966. Inadequate implementation of the 1964 system seemed to indicate, moreover, that it would not be able to withstand such pressures. SCAR questioned the representativeness of Specially Protected Areas designated up to the early 1970s. Samples of all major antarctic land and freshwater ecological systems, it argued, should be included in the series, together with areas with unique complexes of species and those which were the type locality or only known habitat.[49] Moreover, not all recommendations of SCAR or of meetings of the treaty powers themselves had led to approval and the passage of implementing legislation and regulations by each government.

The Antarctic, in other words, was not only becoming better known, it was being approached as a resource-rich area. In this altered economic environment, conservation requirements changed. The 1959 treaty, by which competing territorial claims had been at least temporarily set aside, was a potential casualty. Technological change was rapid. Even in the early 1970s one writer could conclude that krill harvesting on an economic scale was still a 'fairly remote possibility';[50] by the late 1970s, argument centred rather on the figure that was economically and ecologically appropriate as an annual quota. Exploration for oil, gas and minerals, not economically or technologically feasible at the beginning of the decade, could realistically be planned at its end. A SCAR report of 1976 indicated the probable existence of mineral deposits in Antarctica comparable with those of other fragments of the old Gondwana supercontinent. Offshore operations, it concluded, were most likely to attract commercial interest in the foreseeable future.[51]

These developments of the second half of the 1970s caused conservation bodies to seek out their own resources of antarctic expertise. ICBP's interest was a continuing one. That of IUCN came more slowly, though at least one staff member in the 1960s had explored the area.[52] Development of an independent capability to tackle such questions was dictated by their growing urgency in the face of a possible 1980s scramble for resources; by doubts that the environmental impact of oil exploration in particular was being adequately assessed — SCAR in the mid-1970s tended towards the view that oil spills would be a threat to seabirds, but that in general the effect of release of oil was likely to be localised; and by the climate of scientific uncertainty that surrounded the size, annual production rate, character and effect on whale populations of the regularised depletion of the krill resource. The Sierra Club embarked in 1976 on a multidisciplinary study of the ecological implications of antarctic development; the International Institute for Environment and Development (IIDE) in the same year began an investigation of the legal and political problems of alternative resource exploitation regimes in the region. The latter project was linked with IUCN's own southern ocean work in 1978, and the union supported research directed towards a model of the southern ocean ecosystem that could be used to predict the impact of increased human incursions.[53] Indeed, extra-treaty scientific and legal studies of this kind multiplied, particularly in the United States, during this period. They met difficulties, however, when attempts were made to inject findings into the Antarctica treaty policy process.

At their meetings in Wellington in 1972 and Oslo in 1975 the treaty powers expressed concern that the unique antarctic environment should be protected.[54] Related progress was made in the signing in London in 1972 of a Convention for the Conservation of Antarctic Seals. It was increasingly clear, though, that both krill and mineral regimes would be required. In a series of meetings from London in the autumn of 1977 to Canberra in 1980 representatives of the treaty governments engaged in a lengthy convention-making process in relation to marine living resources. A measure of consensus was reached. An ecosystem approach was adopted — itself a break with the single-species thinking behind traditional fisheries regimes — and agreement reached on the principle (argued not to be self-contradictory) that exploitation of krill should not be allowed to threaten whale populations. It was planned to set a low initial krill quota so that the effects of sustained catches could be monitored. Extension of the convention north of the treaty limit of 60° South also seemed essential in view of the ranges of the species concerned, as did inclusion of non-treaty powers as signatories if the regime were to be an effective one. Interim guidelines were also drawn up in the hope that the pre-ratification phase could be made subject to regulation.[55] Several problems arose. Questions of enforcement were difficult to resolve; there was a background of disagreement between Soviet and United States scientists, for example, on quotas (though some earlier estimates of the annual krill catch being larger than that of all other world fisheries combined had been discarded); the convention also posed issues of competence and sovereignty, and of decision-making on quotas and other matters. Also it had to be co-ordinated with other conventions. Apart from those on fisheries and whaling, CITES covered several marine species, and an unsuccessful last-minute effort was made by a group of the leading krill-taking nations to exclude crustacea and other marine species from the 1979 Bonn convention, moves having failed earlier to remove the polar regions entirely from its scope.

For the most part, though, bodies like IUCN were onlookers. Even FAO, which had a recognised expertise in relation both to whales and fisheries, found obstacles in the way of intervention. The importance of these developments to conservation organisations was demonstrated at the union's 1978 Assembly, a resolution of which identified a number of principles which the convention should recognise, and called for steps such as the creation of Specially Protected Areas where no commercial taking of krill would be permitted, and the inauguration of an International Decade of Southern Ocean Research.[56] In contrast to Arctic conservation issues earlier in the decade, however, IUCN's capacity to translate such thoughts into action was severely constrained by the more exclusive nature of the Antarctic intergovernmental machinery.

# 8 East African wildlife

> The sky has no limit
> birds fly free
> animals get fat
> in the bush by His grace.
> Shaaban Robert, *Utendi wa Adili*[1]

Colonial explorers found the savannahs of east Africa to be spectacularly rich in wildlife. Anxiety about the fate of various species, particularly the larger mammals, was voiced at least as early as the 1890s. They became, together with areas thought fit to become national parks on the United States model, items on the agendas of the colonial powers in the period before the First World War. In the conventions of 1900 and 1933, the British Government took the lead in drawing together other European states with territorial possessions on the continent as a whole in efforts to preserve certain areas and species from threats posed by hunting, poaching and encroachment on habitat by other forms of land use. Changing political structures in Africa from the late 1950s brought in their wake different problems and approaches. Attempts to impose solutions from the metropole, difficult enough in the colonial era, were not viable in a milieu of newly independent nations often acutely sensitive to outside interference, especially perhaps from those conservation groups in western countries that seemed less able to adapt to new political realities and priorities. East African countries, though, particularly Kenya, were in a better position than other developing nations to implement protectionist measures: the wildlife resource was increasingly incorporated into definitions of national identity and, by attracting tourists, came to play a central role in economic development. The aim of this second case study is to examine the part played by international conservation organisations in this process.

*Ecology and colonialism*

A brief glimpse at history must come first. One factor in what Helge Kjekshus has called the ecological crisis of Africa in the 1890s[2] was hunting.

The extent and intensity of the activity make up a formidable record. Rival claims to hunting records kept alive a competitive momentum: according to one compilation of statistics published in 1932, the most successful elephant hunter had a total of 1011 animals to his credit, one particularly good day alone yielding nineteen; the best safari produced 14,780 pounds of ivory;[3] more than 1440 elephants, and over 1000 rhinos, were claimed by another hunter in a book published in 1953,[4] but the technique used, taking pot shots from a moving train, would probably have excluded him from the stricter code of his earlier peers.

By the early 1900s there was mounting evidence that animal populations were declining. One writer in 1910 described British East Africa as 'the most wonderful shooting country in the world, not only in regard to the large number of different species obtainable, their gameness, and value as trophies, but also as to its healthfulness and easiness of reach'. However, there was 'no question that the enormous herds of game ... are quickly diminishing before the advancing army of settlers, hunters and naturalists, who now yearly visit the country.... the big game there is rapidly being shot off'.[5] He estimated that about 150–200 shooting parties were then visiting British East Africa annually, to take about 10,000 animals. The solution, he argued, was wider support for and further extension of the game laws, but others differed. For some hunters, diminishing numbers were a signal to move in quickly before game completely disappeared. The reformed hunter then made his appearance and a stream of books and articles dealt with the fascination and superior virtues of attacking wild animals with cameras rather than rifles.[6] Hunters were also keen to combat the growing criticisms of 'sentimentalists': a force of opinion to be reckoned with in Britain in the early 1900s, and one held to be ignorant of the hardships, principles and what later would have been called the ecological value of the hunting fraternity.[7]

While hunters were visible and satisfying targets for preservationist wrath, other factors had a long-term significance for deterioration of habitats and declines of species. The disappearance of wild animals on the east African savannahs has frequently been attributed to the intensive exploitation of land for agriculture and pastoralism, and the loss of grass cover and soils that has resulted.[8] The relative importance of different causal factors, however, is difficult to assess, especially for earlier historical periods. Research in the Amboseli Game Reserve in Kenya in the early 1970s, for example, suggested that degradation of vegetation there was due not to overgrazing and trampling by Masai cattle, but rather to a number of ecological circumstances associated with general climatic changes, notably a steady rising of the watertable and a corresponding increase in salinity.[9]

The numbers of wild animals were also officially controlled for two main reasons in the colonial period. The first was the need to protect agriculture from pests. Elephants periodically stampeded on newly planted tea; monkeys devastated some maize plots in western Kenya; cotton development was virtually destroyed in parts of Uganda by giraffe trampling.[10] Secondly, and more controversially, the protection of human populations and domesticated stock from disease was held to necessitate elimination of wild animals acting as potential hosts for trypanasome parasites. Colonial tsetse fly operations at times aroused heated public debate in Britain because of the sheer numbers involved. In Southern Rhodesia, for example, a total of 321,518 animals were killed in the period 1924–45.[11] But it has never been fully possible to separate technical analyses of the causal factors at work from larger political considerations. At their worst, exchanges between Europeans and Africans in the 1960s and 1970s could degenerate into slanging matches: western conservationists condemning the inadequate policies and enforcement of laws of African governments, or maintaining that the cause of wildlife preservation would be bound to be badly served in cultures where the same term, *nyama*, referred both to meat on the table and to creatures in the wild; Africans focusing on the colonial heritage left by hunting, zoo collecting, the trophy market, and the neglect of human welfare entailed by the excessive fondness of colonisers for unspoilt nature.

Preservation of nature was indeed one aspect of the imperial order. In 1897, Lord Salisbury approached the German Government with a view to prohibiting the small-ivory export trade from east Africa. An estimated two-thirds of game lived in British colonial territories, and the government was under pressure both from preservationist groups and from hunters concerned about the future availability of game. Proposals for wildlife protection, covering the ivory trade, fishing, skins and trophies, the institution of closed seasons, and other matters, were contained in a Note circulated to other governments in 1899. A conference of the six colonial powers concerned met in London the following spring, resulting in a convention on the preservation of African fauna.[12] Though it was never set in operation, a number of its provisions in practice were implemented by some countries.

Renewed publicity was given to African questions in the 1920s by British and, increasingly, by United States groups. Issues were aired at the International Congress for the Protection of Nature held in Paris in 1931. The British Government responded to the alarm being expressed particularly by the SPFE, and summoned a new intergovernmental conference for 1933. The preamble of the convention that emerged affirmed that 'the natural fauna and flora of certain parts of the world, and in particular of Africa, are in danger, in present conditions, of extinction or permanent injury'. Preservation could best be achieved by the constitution of national parks and various categories of reserves, the institution of regulations covering areas outside such reserves, the regulation of the traffic in trophies, and the prohibition of certain methods of hunting, killing and capturing fauna. Article 3 committed the parties to 'explore forthwith the possibility of establishing in their territories national parks and strict natural reserves'. Consultation in the case of a national park being established contiguous to another territory was provided for under Article 6. The use of motor vehicles and aircraft, and methods such as the surrounding of animals by fire, for hunting were prohibited by Article 10. The convention recognised four types of protected area in terms of hunting policy. Article 8 extended protection to species 'of special urgency and importance'. These were listed in an Annex. Species of Class A were to be protected as completely as possible; for those in Class B a special hunting licence was required to be issued by game authorities.[13] A Protocol provided in addition for later meetings, and a second conference was held in London in 1938.[14]

The 1933 convention, together with that of 1940 for wildlife preservation in the Americas, was generally viewed by conservationists at the time of the founding of IUPN in 1948 as, at the least, a useful step forward that with appropriate revisions could be made the basis of a more effective and lasting regime. Critics identified several weaknesses, however: the lack of obligation on the part of the colonial powers to institute measures; uncertainties, more particularly, as regards the provisions for preserving (and reviewing the accuracy of lists of) threatened species; the absence of any permanent machinery, other than infrequent meetings of the signatories; the considerable diversity that existed as between the policies of different governments, or in the degree to which regulations were in practice enforced; and the difficult question, on which preservationists often disagreed, of native hunting rights. In retrospect, also, this and other nature preservation developments of the colonial period were open to the charge that later difficulties were being stored up by the gulf that was created between the concerns of Africans and those of conservationists. Efforts to protect animals for reasons meaningless to the indigenous population, one writer has argued, produced a resentment against wildlife. 'Wildlife did not represent a resource to the local people; protection of it was, in effect, foisted upon them.'[15] The convention itself did have some value. The SPFE, by drawing up data on threatened African species,[16] initiated the practice of non-governmental organisations playing a technical advisory role in relation to the making of international conventions dealing with wildlife; some progress towards conservation goals was made as British, French and Belgian officials became increasingly aware of each others' shortcomings or accomplishments; and recognition was given to the idea that wildlife preservation could be an appropriate subject for negotiation between governments.

*International organisation and African wildlife*

Colonial possessions meant that in the late 1940s reservoirs of expertise on African conservation questions existed in several European countries. Of the leading individuals active in international developments at that time, for example, Huxley, Coolidge, Harroy, Fraser Darling and Monod all had had a close interest in the continent's wildlife. IUPN's first technical symposium, held at Fontainebleau in 1948, included meetings on game protection, national parks and reserves, and the status of international conventions in relation to African requirements. At Lake Success the following year, Africa remained a dominant topic, particularly in view of the failed groundnut scheme. Harroy had hoped that this could be studied more thoroughly by the union; discussions were held with officials of the Overseas Food Corporation and Colonial Office in London, but financial constraints prevented the organisation taking this possibility further. A number of factors were held to be contributing to the vanishing of game herds in Africa. Participants criticised extermination of game as a method of combating trypanosomiasis. The supply of firearms to natives and the increase in the value of game meat that had followed a colonial ruling entitling workers to a certain daily protein ration were among other causes of diminishing stocks of wildlife identified at the meeting. The British Government was urged to convene a meeting of signatories of the 1933 convention.[17]

The convention was not thought, however, to be free of imperfections. This view emerged clearly in assessments of the early 1950s. The urgency of the situation was stressed. At IUPN's 1950 Assembly, French delegates introduced a resolution on the 'grave dangers' threatening natural life in tropical Africa, drawing attention particularly to monoculture.[18] Harroy's own official and scientific contacts in Belgium and in francophone Africa were instrumental in the convening of a major conference on African issues at Bukavu in the Belgian Congo in 1953. Though the British Government had turned down suggestions for a meeting of the parties to the 1933 convention, official representatives attended this more exploratory one, organised by the Belgian government. Harroy circulated the results of a survey of African conservation policies based on replies from colonial authorities. A wide range of issues was tackled but a central conclusion was that a new convention was required. The protection of nature in Africa involved 'much more than the protection of fauna and flora by the means defined in the 1933 Convention.... the vital problem of protecting the human environment in Africa cannot be solved solely by the creation of nature reserves and the protection of certain species, rare or threatened with extinction'. Governments were accordingly asked to consider preparation of another convention 'which would establish the broader elements of a general policy of nature conservation in Africa ... with the object of ensuring the conservation of natural vegetation cover, soil, water and natural resources, primarily in the interest of the populations of Africa'.[19] Several specific changes were proposed: the creation of a Class C to include species needing protection only in certain specified areas; the shifting of some species between Classes, for example the gorilla from B to A; and an article giving the department of wildlife in the government of each party an official status.

The Bukavu meeting came at a time when it was reasonable to anticipate political continuity in Africa. Later in the 1950s this was no longer the case. The prospect of independence for many of the colonial territories in Africa set back these preparatory moves towards an international convention: the parties involved would be different, as might well be their priorities and objectives in relation to conservation issues.

IUCN continued, though, to act as a forum for exchanges of views on African problems. In 1957 Monod proposed that a list should be compiled of animals permitted to be hunted, and that there should be a complete prohibition of hunting of all others, in a new convention.[20] Attention was increasingly turned to east Africa. Talbot and other United States conservationists took their concerns over the Serengeti region of Tanganyika direct to the British Colonial Secretary. Noel Simon, representing an African Game Management Committee established by the union, held talks with the Governor of the colony, Sir Richard Turnbull, about this and related problems. At the root of this unease lay two divergent concerns: first, that future African leaders would give scant regard to the preservation of their countries' wild fauna and flora; second, a view that was expressed more vocally by American groups, that the British authorities were doing too little by way of preparation for independence as far as wildlife was concerned and, more generally, that the British in east Africa placed insufficient trust in the capacity of Africans to manage their natural resources. By the time of IUCN's 1960 Assembly in Warsaw, Africa had emerged as the central problem overshadowing all else. The SSC carried out a major black rhino survey in 1959–60 following an initiative of Mervin Cowie, Director of the Royal National Parks of Kenya.[21] Then, at the Arusha conference in 1961, the centrepiece of IUCN's African Special Project (ASP), delegates, including many from African countries, concluded that 'the accelerated rate of destruction of wild fauna, flora and habitat in Africa — without adequate regard to its value as a continuing economic and cultural resource — was the most urgent conservation problem of the present time'. The resource included the 'finest and most varied large animal populations remaining on earth', and its destruction 'would be a biological and cultural catastrophe'.[22]

The most important longer term consequence of Arusha and the ASP was to set in motion again the idea of a conservation treaty for the continent. The more immediate results contributed to this end, but were also of value in themselves. Thus the Programme, the aim of which was defined as informing and influencing public opinion in Africa, dealt with the full gamut of conservation problems: water, soils and vegetation as well as wildlife. In this it followed the direction taken by Bukavu in 1953. Secondly, these developments added considerably to the upswelling of public, scientific and governmental interest in African conservation questions that characterised the early and middle 1960s. Prime Minister Nyerere's Arusha Manifesto stressed the importance of wildlife conservation both in itself and as a source of future livelihood,[23] and was given wide publicity by conservation organisations. The World Wildlife Fund was formed in London in 1961 in an atmosphere of public and media concern sparked off largely by Huxley. Thirdly, the African focus was associated with organisational changes and a newfound vitality on the part of IUCN. A new *Bulletin* series was inaugurated; two successive Secretaries-General, Gerald Watterson from FAO, and Sir Hugh Elliott from an administrative career in Tanganyika, brought their own experience to bear on the union's handling of African questions; the headquarters of the organisation moved from Brussels to Morges in Switzerland. The transition was symbolic. At the Warsaw Assembly, Cowie argued that if the union's headquarters were 'in a country whose government had no possessions or territories in Africa, it would show that the Union was really an international body and enhance its standing in Africa'.[24] Finally, the IUCN emphasis on education, training and the informing of African public opinion of this period took concrete form in a number of ways later in the decade. In 1963 a College of African Wildlife Management was established at Mweka in Tanganyika, following the government's declared goal of complete Africanisation of the game service by 1966, and a francophone equivalent later at Garoua in Cameroon.[25]

The College was initially established with a starting grant of funds from a United States body, the African Wildlife Leadership Foundation, and was later given assistance by UNDP and FAO. It is this pattern of collaboration between a variety of non-governmental and intergovernmental actors, and of a certain competitiveness between them, which has been typical of the external environment of African states in the 1960s and 1970s. Both the Bukavu and Arusha conferences, for instance, flowed from active and constructive co-operation between IUCN and CCTA, the francophone body with conservation interests primarily in the west of Africa; the detailed investigations of African states' conservation requirements that were the main task of the ASP were sponsored jointly by FAO and IUCN; and UNESCO was an active background participant in these developments, contracting IUCN, for example, to produce a primary and secondary school conservation textbook for use in the Sahel region.[26]

There was some jostling for the honour of drafting the proposed convention itself. Arusha made a few suggestions. The need for a list of natural habitats and areas was recognised; the conference also supported a proposal that the concept of 'strict nature reserve', as defined in the 1933 convention, be applied wherever possible. Governments were urged to integrate wildlife management with land use and development plans, and to consider IUCN as the organisation responsible for advising governments on how best to proceed with these tasks.[27] The difficulty was that FAO, while actively collaborating with IUCN in the early 1960s on the ASP, also had somewhat different interests of its own to pursue in the emerging political framework of Africa. In 1960, the organisation had set up a small working party — which existed in name only, said its critics in other bodies — tasked among other things to draft an African convention for the conservation and utilisation of wildlife. At Dar es Salaam early in 1963, CCTA approved at its eighteenth session a draft of an African Charter for the Protection and Conservation of Nature, based on the recommendations of a scientific advisory meeting in Kenya the year before. The language very much reflected the thesis of the ASP, that conservation practices based on ecological knowledge were in the best interests of all African countries, and the Charter was endorsed by IUCN's General Assembly in Nairobi that September.[28] This momentum was kept up by a conference on conservation research and training organised the next year in Lagos by UNESCO and the UN Economic Commission for Africa. The meeting, which included delegates from twenty-eight African countries, formally called for revision and modernisation of the 1933 convention, and recommended that the new OAU be invited 'to entrust the preparation of a preliminary draft to the IUCN assisted by UNESCO and FAO'.[29]

A request to this effect was duly forwarded to IUCN by the OAU Secretariat through UNESCO, and the union's Legislation Commission began work on the draft. Burhenne and his colleagues prepared this for a meeting of African officials and specialists and representatives of the intergovernmental organisations interested in Morges in December 1965; a second version was sent to the OAU a year later for circulation among its member states.

During 1965, however, FAO decided to put in an alternative bid. It had a long history of involvement in economic aspects of wildlife conservation in Africa. There was some feeling also that IUCN in its preparatory work was not paying due regard to wildlife as a resource to be exploited, that it was not sufficiently sensitive to criticisms and inputs from outside, and that its inexperience in convention drafting compared with that of FAO made for tardiness and error. An early draft was drawn up quickly and distributed to member states early in 1966, and a session of the organisation's 1960 working party held at Fort Lamy, Chad, in February 1967 to finalise it. The formula reached here, in which IUCN felt obliged to acquiesce, was approval of the FAO draft, the union's role being restricted to assistance to be given by the SSC in the preparation of the lists of protected species to be annexed to the convention.[30]

Thus by the spring of 1967 two different drafts of the proposed convention, each enjoying a considerable measure of support from African nations, were in an advanced stage of preparation. That by IUCN was eventually accepted by the OAU as the basis for the convention adopted at its Fifth Assembly of Heads of State and Government in Algiers in September 1968. But friction between IUCN and FAO was a seemingly unavoidable by-product. The quite reasonable differences that had marked the approaches of the two organisations to the question of establishing a legal regime for the conservation and utilisation of natural resources in Africa became identified with conflicts of personalities; relations deteriorated almost to vanishing point until new people on both sides in the early 1970s were able to patch lines of communication together again. At Kinshasa in September 1967, the OAU summit insisted that only one convention was required. The following February, its ministerial body turned down further consideration of either FAO's Fort Lamy draft, or of a compromise hammered out in January 1968 in Rome between FAO, IUCN and UNESCO which consisted essentially of the two drafts being placed one after the other in a single document. The IUCN framework, which had CCTA support, became the draft approved by the meeting, and, after further comments from OAU member states, was finally signed in September.[31]

The convention entered into force in October 1969 following ratification by four states (Upper Volta, Swaziland, Kenya and Ghana), and represents a significant step in the history of efforts to conserve the natural resources of the continent. The 'fundamental principle' of the convention sprang from the Bukavu-Arusha line of argument: the contracting states undertook to adopt measures necessary 'to ensure conservation, utilisation and development of soil, water, flora and faunal resources in accordance with scientific principles and with due regard to the best interests of the people' (Article II).[32] Soil and water conservation in land-use planning were dealt with in Articles IV and V, and the protection of flora and fauna in Articles VI and VII. Encouragement was given, for example, to the establishment of botanical gardens to perpetuate plant species of particular interest and the setting aside of forest reserves and conservation areas, and attention drawn to the need to control bush fires, overgrazing and other problems. The criteria for plant conservation went beyond the economic factors traditionally given weight in FAO to include species or communities 'threatened and/or of special scientific or aesthetic value'. The phrasing of Article VII reflected more the FAO view: parties were to 'manage wildlife populations inside designated areas according to the objectives of such areas and also manage exploitable wildlife populations outside such areas for an optimum sustainable yield, compatible with and complementary to other land uses'. In line with the concerns of MAR, AQUA and other projects earlier in the decade, aquatic environments were singled out for consideration in Article VII(1)(b). Particular methods of hunting liable to cause mass destruction of wild animals were listed and prohibited. It was recognised as 'important and urgent to accord a special protection to those animal and plant species that are threatened with extinction, or which may become so, and to the habitat necessary to their survival'. Where such a species was represented in the territory of only one party, it had a 'particular responsibility for its protection'. Following 1933 practice, two lists of species were attached: Class A for those to be totally protected throughout the territory of the parties, and Class B for those which could be hunted or otherwise taken by special authorisation. Article IX, which provided for regulation of the trade in specimens and trophies, also stemmed from earlier conventions (a trade regulation clause had been inserted into the 1900 convention) but more importantly arose from, and gave added vigour to, IUCN attempts in the 1960s to precipitate an endangered species trade agreement.

Other provisions echoed earlier developments. Conservation areas, variously defined, were to be maintained, extended and added to (Article X). The emphasis on research, education and training of the ASP was confirmed in Articles XII and XIII. Following IUCN's growing developmentalism after the UNESCO and UN General Assembly resolutions of 1962, Article XIV stated that 'in the formulation of all development plans, full consideration shall be given to ecological, as well as to economic and social factors'. One Bukavu recommendation emerged as Article XVI, which called for a single agency in each state empowered to deal with all matters covered by the convention. One provision built on that of 1933 for consultation between contiguous national park authorities in neighbouring states, to urge co-operation whenever necessary to give effect to the provisions of the convention and, anticipating an important theme of UNEP in the 1970s, whenever a national measure was likely to affect the natural resources of another state (Article XVII).

Its acknowledgment of the development needs of African states was one of the document's strengths. This had been central to the FAO approach. IUCN's own moves towards definitions of conservation more embracing than wildlife preservation were also given particular encouragement by Soviet scientists active in the affairs of the union.[33] But even as drafted, the convention had certain weaknesses. The exceptions clause modified the vigour of the main provisions: these were not to affect the responsibilities of the signatories in relation to their paramount interests, *force majeure*, and the defence of human life, nor to prevent states enacting contrary measures in time of famine, for the protection of human health, and in defence of property. Some of the most difficult and delicate questions proved impossible to resolve satisfactorily, such as the manner in which customary rights were to be reconciled by national legislation with the provisions of the convention (Article XI). Others were couched more as aspirations than commitments, such as the call in Article XIV for due weight to be given to ecological factors in development planning. The provisions were not implemented uniformly. The extent to which protected areas were created or adequately maintained tended to rest more on the availability of external funding; while this could not be spelled out in the convention itself, it was a factor widely recognised at the time of its signature, and had been affirmed unequivocally by Nyerere at Arusha in 1961 and by Kenyatta at Nairobi in 1963. Some articles constituted guidelines for the framing of national legislation; Kenya, for example, worked gradually towards centralisation of its administrative machinery for conservation during the 1970s. Therefore the African convention of 1968 did not usher in a new conservation regime, but neither can the neglect and abuses to which western critics pointed in the 1970s be taken as evidence of its failure to initiate change. Developments in the period since are complex. The processes by which international organisations, both of a governmental and a non-governmental character, have played a part in shaping the conservation policies of African states will be examined in the next section of this chapter by focusing on one particular country.

## Wildlife and economic development in Kenya

No African country can be considered typical. But Kenya does have special attributes that need to be mentioned at the outset. The richness of the wildlife resources of the nation, in terms both of variety and of biomass, would have been sufficient in itself to stimulate keen interest on the part of western conservationists. The fact that the resource was perceived to be threatened early in the 1960s by decolonisation — whether the blame was laid primarily at the door of future African leaders or of the British colonial authorities — served to confirm this external preoccupation with Kenyan wildlife management policies. Further, the links that the country maintained after independence with Britain and with other Commonwealth and western nations made for a degree of openness and access that did not obtain universally in Africa. British, United States and West German organisations have been active together with international bodies in the development and conservation of wildlife in Kenya, and the character of the resource attracted broader intergovernmental attention. First, greater use, it was argued, could be made of wildlife as a source of protein; wider conservation goals would thereby be promoted since wild ungulates leave their habitat in good condition compared to the depredations from overgrazing inflicted by domestic livestock.[34] Second, what was eventually the more crucial consideration, wild animals were clearly a key to revenue from tourism. Kenya was thus in a position to lure foreign aid directly or indirectly related to wildlife on the grounds that there would be sound economic returns from the investment.

Internal debate on the colony's wildlife gathered force in the mid-1950s. Game officials were quick to defend their record: 'Whatever pessimistic views may be held by some people, the prospects for the survival of the wonderful wild life in the Colony are bright.'[35] The report of a Game Policy Committee set up in 1956 attributed some failures to the lack of power to control human activities of those officials entrusted with wildlife conservation.[36] Financial constraints, however, were put forward by the authorities as the main reason for not more thoroughly implementing some of the more far-reaching recommendations of the 1956 Committee. But the major official document that emerged from this process of re-evaluation, a sessional paper of 1959 on *A Game Policy for Kenya*, did place a central stress on the need to preserve wildlife. Game was 'the most important tourist attraction in the country' and the tourist industry was 'of considerable economic importance'. Further, game had 'an aesthetic and cultural value'; its preservation was 'a duty which the government and people of Kenya owe to posterity and the world'.[37]

The independence struggle disrupted this process. Criticism of the authorities voiced in the late 1950s gave way to a more pervasive sense of alarm. Diminution of the British presence in some areas in 1960–1 had some immediate consequences. In the Aberdares and parts of the Mount Kenya slopes, farms had left pasture as a protective buffer between forest and sown crops. The spread of agricultural smallholdings right to the forest edge, combined with lack of funds for game-proof fences or ditches and disappearance of the traditional Honorary Game Warden system, was leading, Game Department officials warned, to marked increases in raiding and poaching.[38] In general, though, game officials took steps where possible to quieten the more extravagant fears being expressed in the British community. This was not easy in the circumstances of the time. Some wardens in 1961 reported the killing of elephant 'out of sheer bloody-mindedness aroused by nationalist politics'. Under an independent government, one was quoted as saying, game would be 'just "meat on the hoof" unless something is done.... People who were savages sixty years ago can have no feeling for the preservation of game'.[39] These kinds of fears for the future, however expressed, were basic ingredients in the debate in Britain in 1960–1 on Africa's wildlife and the transition to independence. In the United States, on the other hand, there was more of an inclination on the part of conservation groups to locate the root causes of the problem in colonial mismanagement of the resource, and more particularly in the separation of wildlife protection from the lives of Africans. The presumption of an irreplaceable British role in relation to wildlife was also criticised by the leaders of the nationalist movement. Jomo Kenyatta placed special emphasis on wildlife in a 1961 interview. 'It is very important that we should preserve our game.... It is a great asset, economically and otherwise, and we must protect and ensure the survival of the animals we have ... they are part and parcel of the prosperity of our country and in fact of Africa in general.'[40] This view was developed by him at IUCN's Assembly in Nairobi in the autumn of 1963 and given more publicity than would have been possible two or three years earlier.[41]

Conserving this 'great asset' in an independent Kenya has been a task shared by a variety of actors. The policy-making as well as the implementing process has included domestic and external conservation groups, various agencies of government, and a number of intergovernmental organisations with interests primarily either in wildlife-related matters or in more general issues of economic development.

At the first and more relatively straightforward level, several non-governmental organisations have played an important role in helping to finance national park maintenance, research and training, and educational activity. Two western zoological societies have been among the leading institutions here. The New York Zoological Society's interest in east Africa arose in 1955 in the context of broader United States fears for the future of the Serengeti. A regional survey of possible sites for national parks and reserves was supported over the next few years. Typical kinds of assistance in Kenya since include provision of equipment for the Masai Mara Game Reserve in 1968, and purchase of an anti-poaching aeroplane in 1964. Ecological research has been financed; for example on primates in the early 1960s, the black rhino in Tsavo in 1967, the effects of pesticides in Lake Naivasha in 1970, and on the Tana River red colobus and mangabey in 1973. In several such cases aid has been channelled through local bodies. The educational and training function of the NYZS has emerged in projects such as collaboration in 1963–4 in the trial use of film in conservation education, and support in 1959 and 1969 for Kenyan officials to undertake further study abroad.[42] Tanzania has been a major focus of interest for the Frankfurt Zoological Society that has spilled over into Kenya, largely through funds raised by Bernhard Grzimek in his *Hilfe für die bedrohte Tierwelt* campaigns. On balance most funding support has gone into provision of equipment, particularly in Tsavo: for fire breaks in 1963; the maintenance of Mzima Springs in 1969 in the wake of problems caused by growing tourist pressure; replacement of an anti-poaching vehicle, supply of radio equipment, and assistance towards replacement of an aeroplane used in border supervision work, in 1970–1; and support in 1973–5 for an anti-poaching team to deal with pressures on Tsavo arising from an increase in the price of ivory. The effects of pollutants in the Rift Valley lakes, particularly with reference to flamingo populations, were researched with Society funding in the early 1970s. Assistance has also been extended to local bodies such as the Wildlife Clubs of Kenya and the East African Wild Life Society for educational and information work.[43]

This is more than an external presence. A gradation of different kinds of organisations gives the network a mixed Kenyan and international character. The African Wildlife Leadership Foundation, for example, has an active role from its Nairobi office and has had a record since its founding in 1963 of good relations with government. There has been a consistent emphasis on the training of officials aimed ultimately at fully Kenyan administration of parks and reserves. AWLF has also funded educational and anti-poaching programmes in Kenya, and field research by graduate students on such questions as drought and game-ranching.[44] Similarly WWF, having funded more than thirty educational, research and park-maintenance projects in the 1960s, approved the setting up of a Kenya National Appeal in 1973 with President Kenyatta as patron.[45] This was later actively involved in the controversies surrounding the management of Kenyan wildlife, sometimes from a perspective critical of certain aspects of government policy in the country. Inside Kenya, organisations like the Wildlife Clubs of Kenya, with a largely secondary school membership, the Wildlife Society of Kenya, and the East African Wildlife Society have played a major part in the creation of an internal constituency for wildlife conservation. The last body, originally in 1961 straddling Tanzania, Kenya and Uganda, has its own internationally spread membership, and as well as supporting programmes in Kenya has taken on a significant external information role through its more technical *East African Wildlife Journal*.

The policy significance of conservation bodies is a function of the importance of the wildlife resource in Kenyan economic development. At least three different facets of the problem are involved: tourism, the role of wildlife in rural development, and its place in more general ecological problems such as conservation of soils, water and vegetation. The economic significance of wildlife has long been emphasised both inside Kenya[46] and outside by, among others, FAO and the World Bank. FAO's East African Livestock Survey of the mid-1960s pointed to wildlife as 'a vast potential revenue earner and source of food for the local population'. A joint wildlife management programme with the Kenya Game Department in the first half of the 1970s investigated the potential of the resource in integrated patterns of land use.[47] But it is the first aspect, the tourist industry, that has stimulated most attention to wildlife issues. As one senior Kenyan official said in 1978, 'Kenya's wildlife is the base upon which the tourism industry depends'.[48] An IBRD mission reported in 1963 on the need for additional wildlife protection measures in the development of the middle-income tourist trade. A greatly expanded infrastructure investment programme in existing and new reserves and parks was prominent among the recommendations of a subsequent mission in 1975. World Bank and UNDP assistance to Kenya has reflected these kinds of conclusions, and the importance of the tourism-wildlife link was underlined in Kenya's development plans for the periods 1970–4 and 1974–8.[49]

The development requirements of an important sector of the economy thus created a degree of dependence on foreign conservation expertise. However, such dependence had clearly to be controlled. First, it was vital for Kenya that the basis be laid for an autonomous management capability in the future. Secondly, not all of the many, and often strident, voices of western environmentalism could be given equal consideration. The mid-1970s saw a rising tide of external criticism of Kenyan policies. Wildlife was allegedly being depleted through neglect, failure to control poaching, and corruption. Such attacks often ignored the demand side of the equation. As Kenyan officials pointed out, the fact that such lucrative markets existed for ivory or rhino horn in the west, the Arab world and Asia could easily undermine anti-poaching efforts. 'Who are these so-called expert planners or conservationists that want to impose their will on us?... It is the same propagandists that have encouraged poaching of our wildlife resources that now turn round and shout that Kenya is allowing the extermination of her wildlife.'[50] It was the comparatively small number of conservation bodies that had forged long-standing and constructive relations with Kenyan institutions that were able to play the appropriate kind of partnership role: AWLF was one, and the New York Zoological Society, which in the late 1970s supported and staffed a small planning unit in the Kenyan Ministry of Tourism and Wildlife, another. Even traditionally good relations could be marred by occasional sourness or friction. FAO at times had consultants who seemed too ready to make extrapolations to Kenya from the North American experience, and IUCN its experts who seemed unwilling to temper their concern for threatened species of wildlife with a commitment to the welfare of humans.

One of the lasting contributions of conservation bodies has thus been their role in facilitating the emergence of an African conservation view. Kenyan officials effectively pressed in 1973 for a stronger CITES draft; the presence of a number of African delegations intent on securing a more comprehensive outcome was a major factor shaping the character of the migratory species convention that came out of the Bonn conference in 1979. The problem of involving rural communities at the village level in the conservation and utilisation of the wildlife resources of African countries remains. But the size and vigour of the internal Kenyan conservation lobby, in the context for example of the 1978 trophy ban,[51] indicates clearly that the desire to conserve wild fauna and flora on the continent is not one restricted to outsiders. Whether it could continue to respond effectively to intensifying pressures on wildlife habitats, arising for example from the changing character of the tourist industry, had still to be tested.

# 9 Migratory bird protection

If ever I saw anything like actual migration, it was last Michaelmas-day. I was travelling, and out early in the morning: at first there was a vast fog; but, by the time that I was got seven or eight miles from home towards the coast, the sun broke out into a delicate warm day. We were then on a large heath or common, and I could discern, as the mist began to break away, great numbers of swallows clustering on the stunted shrubs and bushes, as if they had roosted there all night. As soon as the air became clear and pleasant they all were on the wing at once; and, by a placid and easy flight, proceeded on southward towards the sea: after this I did not see any more flocks, only now and then a straggler.

Gilbert White, *The Natural History of Selborne*, letter of 28 February 1769[1]

Bird politics are a function of the migratory nature of many species, and of the fascination which they have long held for man. The first characteristic means that many bird protection issues cannot be localised. Concerns traverse national frontiers. Groups in one country are drawn to seeking policy solutions in the internal land-use affairs of other states. Organisational networks can in favourable conditions spread with relative ease across borders. The fact, secondly, that 'of all living things no other class of animals has such immediate appeal', as Roger Tory Peterson has put it,[2] has given rise to energetic conservation groups quick to seek legislative and regulatory measures to advance the protection of birds, and as often zealous in the defence of their own territory within broader environmental movements. Particular threats, such as oil damage of seabirds, have been instrumental in drawing wider attention to more fundamental environmental questions. Endeavours to construct international conventions of general applicability are one topic of this chapter; it ends by examining moves to bring about a migratory bird protection regime within the framework of European Community institutions. The pioneering North American developments that followed the signature in 1916 of the Anglo-American treaty form too big and separate a subject to be handled here.

*Migration and politics*

The disappearance of many birds in winter intrigued western man at least from the time of the Greeks. Many of Gilbert White's observations in eighteenth-century Hampshire were devoted to resolving the issue of whether birds migrated or simply hid from view in hibernation sites. The fact of migration having been established, the navigation systems and the sheer distances involved have proved to be questions equally as fascinating. 'It is not long', R. E. Moreau has written, 'since there was talk of the Skagerak (a mere ditch) as a potential barrier to migration.... [Then] I regarded the non-stop crossing of the Sahara (say 1600 km), often with the addition of the Mediterranean, as a commonplace achievement of those migrants which winter in tropical Africa. Now we are faced with the problem of those birds which migrate from Soviet Asia to the tropics — say 6000 km from the neighbourhood of Tomsk to that of Khartum.'[3] While research continues — that on migration routes and the ranges of birds is an essential tool of conservation — enough was understood of the habits of birds from at least the latter part of the nineteenth century to provoke agitation by protectionist organisations, particularly in the United States and Britain. Organisations such as ICBP from the early 1920s gradually developed the idea of migratory waterfowl constituting a resource shared by the European nations. 'No nation', a 1939 ICBP meeting in Vienna concluded, 'has in principle any absolute property right in the migratory duck which come to her. She receives them, so to speak, on the basis of a sort of entail. She has no moral right to decimate them regardless of the interests of other nations. It is the bounden duty of each nation to see that her entail is not broken.'[4] The background of nineteenth-century pressure group activity which led to the signing in 1902 of an international bird protection convention was discussed in an earlier chapter. This identified in a Schedule various 'birds useful to agriculture', especially insect-eaters. These were to be 'unconditionally protected by a prohibition forbidding them to be killed in any way whatsoever, as well as the destruction of their nests, eggs and broods' (Article 1). Birds noxious to agriculture were, by definition and by Article 9, exempt from this prohibition. One provision, that in Article 3 forbidding methods of wholesale capture or destruction of birds, was to have echoes in European bird conservation politics in the 1970s.[5]

*The route of international conventions*

Efforts to secure revision of the 1902 convention were being made almost as soon as it had been signed. Criticism grew with the opportunities for contact between national groups created by the existence of the ICBP from 1922. Classification of birds into two categories, useful or noxious, appeared taxonomically inappropriate and grossly inadequate as the conceptual foundation for a conservation regime. The slow process of change culminated in a new convention in Paris in 1950. A second convention with which we shall be concerned in this section was that signed at Ramsar, in Iran, in 1971. While this dealt with wetlands designated as being of international importance, its genesis lay primarily in the international agitation of the 1950s and 1960s for the more effective protection of migratory waterfowl.

The agreement of 1950 was more ambitious in that it went far beyond migratory bird protection questions. In this respect its descent from that of 1902 and its intellectual debt to the earlier convention are, ironically, among its salient features. Demands for revision of the 1902 treaty were voiced as early as the Luxembourg meeting of ICBP in 1925.[6] The topic became a recurrent motif of international ornithological congresses of the interwar years. It was an issue that dominated ICBP's sixth meeting in Brussels in 1935. Each National Section was asked to suggest modifications to the convention, and the proposals varied in their radicalness. Scandinavian groups tended towards the view that an entirely new convention was needed — and indeed put forward a draft for one — and that tinkering would leave the objectionable principles of the original intact. Agreement on the form that revisions might take was reached at ICBP's European continental section meeting held in Vienna in 1937. National groups began to bring the proposals to the attention of governments, but the coming of war checked a bourgeoning momentum which was being directed increasingly towards the convening of an intergovernmental conference. The Vienna package was dusted off in London in 1947 at the first post-war meeting of the section, and the main outlines and much of the detail of the convention draft then took shape at a meeting of ICBP experts in Brussels later that year. The text that emerged in July 1948 from detailed examination by European section delegates meeting in Paris was forwarded to the French government by the French National Section of ICBP, and the intergovernmental conference was finally held there in October 1950.[7] Official representatives of thirteen European countries took part; Bulgaria sent a delegate, but the cold war division of the continent effectively barred the way to the wider geographical scope of the convention anticipated in the late 1930s.

Protection of migratory species nestled within a grander structure in the resulting International Convention for the Protection of Birds. The preamble noted 'the danger of extermination threatening certain species of birds' and 'the decrease in numbers of other species, particularly of migratory birds'. As was seen in an earlier chapter, endangered birds were a growing concern of ICBP after the Lake Success conference of the year before. A decisive break with the 1902 ethos was also realised with the assertion that 'from the point of view of science, the protection of nature and the economy of each country, all birds ought, in principle, to be protected'. This controversial core later became an obstacle to signature and ratification by governments whose protection and hunting laws started out from fundamentally different premises. Article 2 accorded protection more specifically to 'all birds, at least during the breeding season, and in addition migratory birds during their return to their nesting-places' and to 'species which are threatened with extinction or which are of scientific interest, throughout the year'. Trade in birds killed or captured in contravention of the provisions of the convention was prohibited under Article 3, and the parties further undertook to regulate the trade in protected species under Article 9. Eggs and nests were protected by Article 4. Article 5 aimed at the prohibition of various methods of taking birds, including snares, poisoned bait, fishing tackle for catching aquatic birds, automatic guns, and 'all other methods for wholesale capture or destruction of birds'. The rights of unrestricted shooting and netting were to be regulated throughout the year. Other threats to birds were identified in Article 10: oil and other pollutants of water, lighthouses, electric cables, insecticides and poisons. The parties undertook to study and adopt measures to prevent the destruction of birds by such means (and also to 'endeavour to educate children and public opinion to appreciate the necessity for preserving and protecting birds'). Habitat conservation was the theme of Article 11. Encouragement was given to 'the creation of aquatic and land reserves, of appropriate size and situation, where birds can nest and rear their young in safety and where migratory birds may likewise rest and find their food in peace'. Several exceptions were provided for. These included species that were a menace to agriculture (a tenacious residue of the 1902 convention), the taking of birds in the interests of science or education, and the rearing of game birds. However, 'no measure may be taken in any country that might lead to the total destruction of the indigenous or migratory species' concerned.[8]

High expectations were raised by the Paris convention of 1950, particularly in view of the comparative speed with which the preparatory moves had gone ahead after 1947. But there followed a slow, at times virtually stationary, process of ratification. It did not come into force until 1963.[9] British officials put forward in defence the principle that it was not government policy to ratify international conventions until such time as national legislation enabled all obligations imposed by them to be met in full; ICBP's British section argued that the differences between the obligations of the Paris convention and those of British domestic law (the key statute a few years later was the Bird Protection Act of 1954) were not sufficiently great to warrant continued aloofness. In some countries hunters' organisations mounted successful campaigns against signature or ratification. Objections were raised by French groups concerning the clauses prohibiting spring shooting and automatic weapons. Similar arguments appeared in West Germany, Austria, Ireland and Italy. The annual destruction of migratory birds in Italy in particular constituted a central target for attack by bird preservation bodies. Hungarian conservationists, for example, maintained that ratification of the 1950 convention would be of no great help unless the southern European countries also took this step. Norwegian officials took exception to the principle that all birds should be protected. The principle of the Norwegian Game Act was precisely the opposite: namely, that all species could be shot within the open season, apart from some which were specifically protected. The issue was raised in Nordic Council discussions, and opposition to the 1950 principle described later as 'very strong'.[10]

Conservation organisations made sporadic efforts during the 1950s and 1960s to secure wider recognition for the treaty. The problem was reviewed at length at ICBP's conference in Cambridge in 1966; at the same time the General Assembly of IUCN being held in Lucerne expressed concern at the difficulties being encountered in gaining wider support for the convention.[11] By the middle and later 1960s, however, a rather different set of obstacles had emerged. Environmentalism and the greater sense of urgency that surrounded assessments of the position of threatened birds brought a measure of criticism of the convention's inadequacies. In particular, the Council of Europe in 1968 tentatively pressed the virtues of the convention in exchanges with member governments; but a significant share of the responses talked in terms of its revision. A detailed critique was drawn up in a report of 1976. The exceptions clauses were thought to seriously impair the effectiveness of the convention. Migratory species were held to be inadequately protected; conservation of biotopes, though dealt with briefly in the convention, was considered rudimentary. The absence of lists of protected species further reduced its attractiveness as a conservation document — as did the fact that after over a quarter of a century so few countries had in fact ratified it. On the other hand, some strong points were acknowledged. The trade provisions of Articles 3 and 9 stood out as progressive developments in a period when international attention centred on CITES, and the detailed listing in Article 5 of banned methods of killing or capture of birds likewise assumed greater significance in the context of moves in western Europe in the mid-1970s towards the more effective regional regulation of the hunting of migratory birds.[12]

The Paris convention of 1950 therefore failed to bring about much discernible change in the international protection of birds. While in the 1950s and 1960s it enjoyed considerably more support from ornithologists than its predecessor of 1902 ever had, its theoretical and practical failings had by the 1970s made it more of a historical relic than a workable way forward. The wetlands convention of 1971 had more immediate impact. It too was the product of a lengthy gestation at the non-governmental level.

Migratory waterfowl were the subject of sustained international preservationist interest from early in the 1930s. A conference called by the British government in 1927 recommended a shortening of the open season, and further investigation of migration patterns by ringing.[13] ICBP's British Section became the centre of the information-gathering network that emerged during the following decade. This development paralleled official measures in Britain that had international overtones. An Act for the protection of wild duck and geese was passed by Parliament in 1939, and two major reports were published in 1940–1 by the British Wildfowl Inquiry Committee.[14] It was agreed at the London meeting in 1947 of ICBP's European section that the British section of ICBP should logically be the body through which information and policy recommendations from different European countries should be correlated; the accumulated findings of the wildfowl committee had already made it abundantly clear that co-operation between European countries was essential if these species were to be adequately protected in the future.[15] Shortly afterwards, ICBP's interest in the area was further consolidated with the establishment of an International Wildfowl Research Institute to work under its auspices. Intended primarily as an information centre, its tasks were at first concentrated on the correlation of information from ringing and counts of resident and migratory species in various European countries. A particular watch was kept on species reported to be threatened in some areas, notably Grey Lag, Brent, Barnacle and Bean Geese. Close links were maintained from 1951 with CIC, particularly through its Migratory Game Birds Commission, following overtures from ICBP personnel the year before. And it was at this time, in 1950–1, that ICBP began seriously to examine the possibility of establishing a system of European reserves on migration routes similar to that under process of creation in North America.

But good data was a precondition. Organisation of the counts of European migratory waterfowl species was handed over to the Wildfowl Trust in Britain in 1954.[16] By 1958 there was a growing body of support for the reserve system idea.[17] The Dutch section of ICBP in particular took up the cause at the Council's meeting in Helsinki that year. A resolution noted the danger of extinction of some migratory species because of loss of habitat, particularly by the intensive drainage of marshland. Prompting by IWRB (the designation that the wildfowl research body had adopted) persuaded ICBP to set up an international committee of specialists to advise on the creation of a system of European refuges, and in addition to ask each country to collaborate in establishing such reserves at appropriate points along migration routes. Support in principle was also extended by IUCN, and by CIC's game birds commission at its meeting in Vienna in 1959.[18]

This line of activity now coincided fruitfully with emerging ecological interest on the part of IUCN and other bodies in wetlands. The background to this interest was examined in an earlier chapter. And since migratory bird protection was increasingly defined as meaning habitat conservation, organisations like IWRB were widening the scope of their assault on the issue. Threats to the marismas of Guadelquivir provided the immediate policy context in which the two convergent perspectives could be neatly blended. Max Nicholson, head of the Nature Conservancy in Britain, then set in motion a sequence of events that culminated in the wetlands treaty just under a decade later by proposing, at a meeting of IWRB's Executive Board in Belgrade in September 1962, that an 'exploratory meeting on European wildfowl conservation' be held the following year, and that it be organised jointly by IWRB and the Nature Conservancy.[19] Discussion of the proposed European refuge network was a focal point of the MAR conference in November. Delegates emphasised the importance of wetlands as habitats, the need for wetland reserves, and the requirement of more data on wildfowl wintering in Mediterranean countries. But the crucial resolution was one which called on IUCN to compile a list of European and North African 'wetlands of international importance' as a foundation for an international convention on wetlands.[20] A draft list drawn up by IUCN through its ecology commission was circulated to individuals and organisations for comment in 1963, and an initial listing was published two years later.[21]

The conference proposed by Nicholson took place at St Andrews in October 1963 and representatives from organisations in seventeen countries participated. The prospects for improved co-operation between European nations on wildfowl conservation were evaluated. A target date of 1966 was set for the establishment of a network of refuges, and both the Council of Europe (for which Harroy, while working on IUCN's national parks list for the UN, was acting as chairman of an advisory expert committee) and IUCN were urged to seek the agreement of governments towards this goal.

Particular data gaps were identified for southern Europe, and the conference called on IWRB to organise wildfowl counts for the countries in this region.[22] The proposals were endorsed by ICBP's European section in June 1964, and by CIC, whose General Assembly in the Hague a few weeks earlier reiterated the urgent requirement of a network of reserves, and reaffirmed that IUCN's MAR list of wetlands should be taken by governments as a basis for such a system. That an international convention on wetlands was needed was also underlined by CIC at its Arles Assembly in 1965.[23] This step was by then well under way. After the St Andrews meeting, IWRB circulated eight draft points of a possible convention to organisations and officials in thirty-five countries. A second European wildfowl conservation meeting was convened by the Dutch government at Noordwijk aan Zee in May 1966, where convention-building was a central theme. As early as 1964 IWRB's Executive Board had decided that this projected second meeting should concentrate on devising practical measures to implement the MAR wetlands list. The Noordwijk conference among other things called on the Netherlands to explore the possibility of drafting a wetlands convention with reference especially to the MAR list.[24]

A small group of officials of the Dutch Ministry of Cultural Affairs, Recreation and Social Welfare was particularly active in collaborating with IWRB, in preparation both for this meeting and for the projected convention. Further consultation with the Dutch foreign ministry resulted in a draft being circulated for comment to other governments and to interested organisations. This was assessed by IWRB's Executive Board in Morges in November 1967.[25] Wetlands, their progressive deterioration in Europe and the consequences for birdlife in particular of this, were rapidly becoming a focal point of conservationists' fears at this time. An important technical meeting on problems of wetlands conservation was held in Turkey in October 1967, an upshot in part of earlier recommendations from the Noordwijk and other conferences that the scope of the MAR enterprise should be extended into western Asia and the Middle East.[26] Also in the autumn of 1967, plans were being finalised for a third meeting in the St Andrews–Noordwijk series which, on the initiative of Soviet representatives to IWRB, was to be held in Leningrad. The vital need for Soviet participation in these developments followed logically from waterfowl migration routes. Tentative contacts between IWRB and Soviet wildlife biologists had been opened up in the 1950s, but it was not until the Noordwijk meeting that serious co-operation on problems of common concern could be initiated. A few weeks before the Leningrad meeting, however, Soviet military forces intervened in Czechoslovakia. The event was sudden, and the consequences for the conference devastating: apart from one scientist whose research in the field had kept him isolated from news sources, no western representatives turned up. IWRB helped later to prepare a formal summary report of the proceedings and, the tension of the moment having begun to ease, Leningrad duly assumed its place in the prehistory of Ramsar, in particular for its advocacy of an acceleration of the convention-making process.[27]

Delay was indeed already a source of annoyance for some environmental groups. IWRB acknowledged that the wetlands convention was taking its time, but cited that of Paris in 1950 as a salutory experience that indicated the wisdom of proceeding cautiously and ensuring, so far as was possible, prior agreement on contentious issues among the parties.[28] After Leningrad, the Dutch draft was joined by a Soviet competitor that ate less deeply into national sovereignty. The two could not be reconciled satisfactorily by IWRB, but officials of the Bureau acted as intermediaries in the precipitation of a revised Dutch 'Draft for a Convention on Wetlands as Wildfowl Habitat'. This was the working document for a small technical meeting held at Espoo in Finland in March 1970: the Finns had previously been engaged with CIC in the preparation of a set of international wildfowl hunting regulations, and the location reflected both this background and the need to meet the Soviet Union half-way, geographically as well as metaphorically.

The draft finally produced at Espoo by national experts and representatives of the main non-governmental organisations involved — notably IWRB, CIC, ICBP and IUCN — went straight to the intergovernmental conference at Ramsar early in 1971. Iran had been the leading state in the region to respond positively to IWRB and IUCN moves in the middle and later 1960s to add western Asia to the conservationist interest in European wetlands. The main provisions of the convention can be summarised briefly. Article 1 put forward a definition of wetlands, and of waterfowl[29] as birds ecologically dependent on them. The main provision, the origins of which were in the MAR conference of 1962, was also the one that had given rise to some of the most difficult sticking points in the preparatory phases. Under Article 2, the parties were to designate 'suitable wetlands' within their territories for inclusion in a 'List of Wetlands of International Importance'. Criteria were listed in broad terms. The wetlands should be selected 'on account of their international significance in terms of ecology, botany, zoology, limnology or hydrology'. But birds were crucial: 'in the first instance wetlands of international importance to waterfowl at any season should be included'. Since this already entailed some intrusion into sovereignty, further inventories of responsibilities were omitted. Each party would simply 'consider its international responsibilities' for conservation, management and wise use of migratory stocks of waterfowl, and, by Article 4, take steps such as the establishment of nature reserves on wetlands, the encouragement of research, and the promotion of training. As in the African convention of 1968, consultation in the case of wetlands extending across the territories of more than one party was provided for under Article 5. Following a Dutch proposal, IUCN assumed continuing secretariat duties, defined primarily in terms of the convening and organising of periodic advisory conferences of the parties, and of the maintenance of the proposed wetlands List (Articles 6 and 8). This last duty included receiving information from the parties concerning changes in their wetlands listings, or in the ecological character of particular wetlands.[30]

The Ramsar convention was the first of a batch of conservation treaties arrived at in the 1970s. It did not, however, finally come into force until December 1975. There were then still only eight parties, and a further eight signatories. IUCN and ICBP appeals, for example on the basis of the economic importance of estuary-dependent fish, were making heavy weather of it. A variety of criticisms arose. First, the convention was held to have neglected the crucial question of migratory air corridors, and the related need of harmonising hunting laws along migration routes through different countries. Second, its emphasis on avifauna, some conservationists argued, was ecologically too restrictive. A list of broader criteria was agreed upon at a later conference in Heiligenhafen in 1974.[31] Third, the focus on importance to the international community as a criterion for identifying wetlands to be conserved was held to make the potential scope of the convention unnecessarily narrow. Finally, several conservation groups expressed objections to the limited provisions for enforcement. The West German delegation, for example, abstained at Banff in 1972 in a vote on an IUCN General Assembly resolution calling for wider adherence to Ramsar on these grounds.[32] The weak point in such reservations lay in the fact that the convention had probably gone as far to the limits of the possible as it could if there was still to be reasonable assurance that states would sign and ratify the document. It was clear before the conference that states 'would not accept a convention that infringed their sovereign rights to deal with their own natural resources. It was therefore out of the question to draw up a convention prohibiting absolutely change in the ecological status of wetlands, backed by mandatory sanctions.'[33]

*Migratory birds in western Europe*

European Community institutions provided conservation groups with a useful way of avoiding tackling sovereignty head-on. While problems of migratory birds in western Europe were old concerns with bodies like ICBP, it was only in the 1970s that a concerted effort directed at Brussels made a significant dent in government policies.

The issue emerged into a conflict between north and south. Conservationists in Britain, the Netherlands and West Germany targeted their attacks on several areas — south-west France and Malta for example — but reserved their major assault forces for the Italians. Of the four chief migration routes for European birds, two went respectively down the Italian peninsula and through Sardinia. Around two million *cacciatori* annually killed an estimated 166 million migratory birds, with a heavy concentration in the northern third of Italy.[34] Recreational and culinary habits are difficult to change. Small birds, whether roasted on skewers for sale in *rosticcerie* or hunted at weekends for the family table, constituted either a greatly appreciated delicacy or else a supplementary protein source; exchanges between protectionists and defenders of traditional ways were invariably sharp.[35] One problem for ICBP in the 1960s was that this issue did not relate directly to its endangered species emphasis; indeed only four west European species were sufficiently rare to warrant *Red Data Book* listings.[36] The 1950 convention's provision for the outlawing of methods of mass destruction of birds, however, formed one basis from which to approach the question. The European and world meetings of ICBP in 1964 and 1966, for example, called urgently for a prohibition of the use of nylon mist nets for catching birds.[37]

An important precursor of action by the EC was the involvement from 1967 of the Council of Europe in bird protection questions. In October of that year, its Committee of Ministers passed a resolution on birds in need of special protection in Europe; various species were listed 'by way of example'. A more generally couched resolution on disappearing wildlife at the same time recommended the creation of areas for the complete protection of mammals and migratory birds.[38] The following year some effort was made to secure wider support for the 1950 Paris convention, but the Council met with little positive response from member governments. More adequate data were seen by it, therefore, as a preliminary to action. ICBP's National Sections took part in the gathering of information on threatened European birds that led eventually to the Council's publishing a report on this subject in 1974.[39] Work on this report, and repercussions from the EC's stirrings in this direction, produced further steps. A resolution of the Committee of Ministers of October 1973 recommended that governments reinforce measures for the protection of avifauna and habitats, especially with regard to endangered species already identified by consultants, and that they give 'special attention to the migratory species'. The organisation's Parliamentary Assembly was receptive to overtures from bird protection groups. A 1976 report expressed 'alarm at the continual slaughter of migratory birds' and proposed measures such as the creation of a network of stopping places on migration routes and harmonisation of hunting regulations across western Europe.[40] The Council's work then centred on preparation of a more general migratory species convention, and the European nature protection convention eventually opened for signature in Berne in September 1979.

If, as the Council of Europe's parliamentarians tended to argue, the restricted membership of the EC limited its utility as a promoter of conservation measures, it was also true that Community rules lent greater force to the decisions of its policy-making organs. ICBP's conference in the Netherlands in 1970 dwelt at length on the migratory bird problem. Delegates argued that the EEC should draw up rules for the protection of these birds. The French government was urged to prohibit the taking of small migratory birds in Aquitaine during their autumn migration, and the Maltese to halt their indiscriminate destruction on the island. Finally, the conference proposed that ICBP National Sections in EEC member countries approach their governments with a view to the Community's openly examining the Italian question.[41] This was only one of the organisations pursuing the matter. During the early 1970s several groups with Communitywide links sought to exert pressure on EC bodies. They were assisted in this by the Commission's own wish to extend its newly achieved environmental competence into nature conservation areas. The RSPB in Britain played an important co-ordinating role in relation both to established organisations and the various groups that were set up, for example in West Germany, specifically to combat the mass destruction of migratory birds. The Frankfurt Zoological Society engaged in poster campaigns in major Italian cities, carried out research on member-state legislation and on the ecological effects of songbird hunting, gave evidence to the Commission on this aspect of the question, and produced an influential report on threatened bird species in Europe.[42] The network extended into Italy, where ICBP had an active National Section. Italian nature protection organisations were themselves paying more attention to the problem. A group originally founded in 1965 on British initiative, the Lega Italiana per la Protezione degli Uccelli, was seeking parliamentary action to secure the prohibition of certain methods of capture or killing, and wider public appreciation of the value of birds.[43]

In all, this activity was directed at each of the three main Community institutions: the Commission, Council of Ministers and European Parliament. Groups were able to obtain the tabling by sympathetic members of parliamentary questions; petitions were presented in 1974 and 1976; and the Parliament's Committee on Public Health and Environment produced a detailed report early in 1975 which urged among other things that the Community accord greater priority to the protection of migratory birds. The Commission and Council were, more importantly, by then already handling the issue. The environmental programme adopted by the Council in 1973 included items dealing with migratory birds in the context of the broader protection of wild fauna. The Commission was required to study national regulations with a view to possible harmonisation.[44] There were some interesting extra-Community precedents, such as the 1970 Benelux convention on the protection of birds which was moving the three governments concerned in this direction. An extensive consultative process involving organisations such as ICBP, RSPB and the Frankfurt Zoological Society culminated in December 1976 in the Commission's publishing the draft of a directive on bird conservation. A few days earlier, the Council had approved the Community's second environmental programme; this included proposals for measures to harmonise certain aspects of hunting.[45]

The draft directive, modified in mid-1977 after further exchanges,[46] was generally welcomed with a few reservations by ICBP and other bird conservation organisations. It provided, among other things, for the listing of species in Annexes, the first of which covered those in need of special protection (sixty-two being identified initially). Certain methods of mass destruction of birds were specifically prohibited and there was provision for the protection of game birds, while the sale of living or dead birds was to be restricted to Annex III species in the hunting season. The importance of the protection of habitats was recognised, but various derogations were to be allowed, in order to prevent damage to agriculture for example, to protect indigenous fauna and flora, or in the interests of scientific research. It was a full two years, however, before member governments were able to reach agreement on its approval by the Council of Ministers. The French and Italian governments made known their reservations with respect to the list of banned hunting methods, and France in particular took a strong position on the Community's responsibilities in the field of habitat protection. Agreement was not possible at a Council meeting in December 1977. Annex III presented obstacles. The Commission had proposed to include six species here that could be marketed: France objected strenuously to expanding this list, while Denmark, the Federal Republic of Germany and

Britain argued that all species that could be hunted should be allowed to be marketed.[47] Discussions in 1978 through the Committee of Permanent Representatives were unable to resolve the deadlock. Apart from the marketing issue, the French government also raised in particular two species, skylarks and ortolans, which it insisted its hunters should be allowed to continue to shoot. The objection to this on the part of other Council members was that it could lead to the unintentional killing of other rarer species because of difficulties of identification. ICBP urged that a way be found to bridge the remaining few differences.[48]

The Council of Ministers finally adopted the directive in December 1978. The list of twenty-six marketable species was substantially longer than that in the Commission's original proposal, and went a long way towards meeting French demands (though the Commission undertook to investigate some to see if such trade was likely to have a serious adverse effect on populations). On the other sticking point in the negotiations, ortolans were protected: but French and Italian hunters were still allowed to take skylarks — the 'sacrifice' of this species conservation groups reluctantly accepted as the price that had to be paid to secure adoption of the directive.

# Part IV

# Conclusions

# 10 Wildlife conservation and world politics

> If you want to live and thrive
> Let a spider run alive.
> Children's saying cited by the Opies[1]

The process of conserving nature involves inherently political questions. These are often neglected. Misunderstandings of the essence of politics are partly to blame. Politics is regarded as a term synonymous with the dirty tricks of the craft of persuasion. Science speaks with the voice of truth: all else is either commonsense or wilful obscurantism. Like the curate's egg, this conviction is good in parts. Politicians are no angels. But oversimplifying the character of political processes, and disdaining to treat larger questions, can do conservation a disservice. Karl Deutsch has suggested that the fault is present in much environmental writing. 'Many articles on the management of the environment seem to ignore politics. They appear to deal almost entirely with ecology, technology, resources and sometimes culture. Political processes and institutions are rarely mentioned directly and even more rarely analysed in detail. And yet, the substance of politics — decisions and commands, compliance and enforcement, demands and support, opposition or resistance, the allocation of values, costs and burdens — all this is inescapably implied in almost every ecosocial problem.'[2] For the conservationist to argue that nature is apolitical can be a useful strategy. For him actually to believe this is a recipe for ineffectiveness.

Misconceptions operate in the reverse direction. An image of amateurishness and nuttiness still clings to would-be defenders of the wild. The reasons for saving wild animals and protecting wild areas seem clear enough to outsiders. Such things appear morally unobjectionable, like motherhood. And some people prefer to spend their leisure time outside cities. There is a huge gap, in other words, between the perceptions of the problem shared by conservationists and their fellow-travellers on the one hand, and those of even generally well-informed citizens of western countries who have not taken an interest in these questions on the other. Some advantages accrue to low-priority issues. The support of political leaders can sometimes be obtained with relatively little effort, as in the case of congressional and presidential support in the United States for international polar bear conservation in the early 1970s. Agencies of government comparatively low in the bureaucratic hierarchy may enjoy a certain freedom of manoeuvre denied to others that are larger and ostensibly more powerful. But there are costs too. So long as the reasons for conservation of nature are inadequately understood, a sense of urgency cannot be communicated. One dilemma has traditionally been that since an appreciation of the notion of ecological process is difficult for the non-specialist to grasp and sustain, the task of educating has begun with species: and that this then risks exposing the raw nerve that will sooner or later protest that people matter more than animals. The charge can be deflected to some extent by restating ecological truisms. Man is part of nature. All things are connected. Tampering with one part of a dynamic and complex system can have unforeseen and possibly disastrous consequences for other parts. Interconnectedness, though, is a tough thesis to put across unless the links are clear in principle and seem unequivocally tied to important issues, as perhaps with the place of krill in the antarctic food web.

Relating wildlife issues to human needs is therefore not easy. The success of conservation organisations has been in large measure a function of their ability to argue persuasively in wider political arenas about the significance of these relationships. The temptation to dismiss such questions has sometimes been strong. Creating or extending a national park could be urged by a group without too much thought being given to the families that might have to be displaced in the process; uplifting whole villages and relocating them elsewhere has been put forward as a solution to the habitat needs of threatened species in developing countries. Traditional practices can serve conservation goals, but they can also conflict with more specific objectives being pursued by conservation organisations. Among the Héta Indians in South America the skins of jaguars and ocelots are valued for their use in curing illness.[3] Yet these are among the species on which much conservationist attention has focused, particularly in relation to issues of international trade and the fur industry. Such questions can be accommodated, as in the case of Inuit hunting of polar bear in the 1973 convention, as part of the rights of native peoples that need to be acknowledged and that have marginal impact on the status of threatened species. The sociological and anthropological data on which such judgments have to be made, however, have not usually been prominent among the resources of international conservation bodies. Similarly, ecologically sound programmes can themselves have unanticipated repercussions. The introduction of vegetation or trees to check desertification or prevent soil erosion, slippage or flooding can increase the incidence of allergic disease in some populations; Kuwaitis, particularly women, appear from recent medical research to be especially vulnerable to some allergens such as prosopis trees and Bermuda grass.[4]

The point is not that conservation of nature starts out from ethically suspect premises, nor that its consequences are inevitably damaging to human interests at some point. Wildlife conservation advocates were foremost among those drawing attention in the 1940s and 1950s to broader questions of the global balance between human population, resources and the natural environment. The need is rather the twofold one of greater knowledge of the interplay between human society and natural processes, and of a greater readiness on the part of conservation organisations to stray from the more narrowly scientific pathway. Perception of an anti-developmental bias on their part has been at times a major constraint on their capacity to tackle conservation problems in Africa, Asia or Latin America. Many organisations have been slow to come to terms with development needs, possibly because the North American and European experiences of widespread destruction of species and natural habitats seemed to point out a clear lesson for those countries where processes of industrialisation and intensive agricultural development were in their infancy. For organisations within the United Nations system, standards of respectability can be as finely drawn as in the Victorian drawing-room. IUCN has not been the only organisation to discover that lack of the appropriate developmental credentials can provoke a sharp rebuke or a polite rebuff. While efforts were made at least from the early 1960s to integrate conservation concerns with wider development perspectives, the union's comparative neglect of New International Economic Order debates in the 1970s, or of changing notions of economic and social development such as the 'common heritage' concept, and some of the difficulties it encountered in trying to hammer out its World Conservation Strategy, indicated that the learning process had still not been completed.

International conservation bodies face a number of other constraints. The magnitude of the problem of enforcement has had at times an almost numbing effect on their approaches to programme planning. Lack of resources of personnel and equipment at the local level, especially in developing countries, has persuaded several of the NGOs active in east Africa to target a substantial part of their funding at support for anti-poaching teams. That he will refrain from helping to kill elephant is not a realistic expectation of a villager, given the incentives to the contrary. One official in a remote area of Zaire reported in 1974 that poaching was practised 'avec le complicité tout justement de ces mêmes villageois sur qui nous devrions compter pour avoir renseignements précis. Car, le premier geste de ces chasseurs irréguliers, quand ils arrivent dans une localité, est d'abattre un ou deux éléphants et d'en distribuer la viande aux villageois pour ainsi s'assurer de leur mutisme'.[5] Even in countries where administrative personnel are not so thinly spread the circumventing of hunting regulations can be commonplace, and the steady encroachment of economic activity on designated protected areas insidious. While the signing and even the ratification by states of international conventions does not of itself guarantee that conservation measures will be enforced at the local level, one consequence of CITES in this respect has been the use made of its provisions by conservation groups in Britain, West Germany and other countries to have traders in endangered species and their products brought to court. A related aspect of the problem is that there may be no single government agency with primary responsibilities for wildlife conservation matters in a country. In view of the many areas of land-use policy that the subject touches on, indeed, this tends to be the normal state of administrative affairs. Improving this situation was one of the objectives behind the 1968 convention on the conservation of African fauna and flora; similarly, bringing greater co-ordination into play in Canada among the various levels of government and official bodies with polar bear management roles was an essential step on the way to the 1973 agreement of the Arctic nations.

The gap between the worsening condition of the world's natural environment and the capabilities of conservation bodies to deal effectively with these issues has often made resources, particularly financial resources, appear a more pressing and debilitating constraint. This was the chief consideration that led to the founding in 1961 of WWF, and one that lent particular significance to the existence of UNEP in the following decade. The capacity of funds to generate action can be exaggerated by the impoverished, though. In an area like nature conservation, and especially to the extent that it is grounded in the science of ecology, holistic thinking can stretch definitions of the subject matter into many fields both of human activity and of scientific research. Enforced frugality concentrates minds. Or, of course, it can batter them into passivity, which tended on balance to be the danger facing IUCN in the 1950s. Three results followed directly from financial strain. The fundamental task of data gathering on threatened species and habitats could not forge ahead with the vigour that deteriorating environmental conditions demanded; the union's advisory commissions could not be organised and co-ordinated effectively from a headquarters well staffed with skilled professionals; and few projects could be funded. Where external funding was more readily available, as from UNESCO on conservation education topics, the upshot could be a dependency that in practice compelled a reshuffling of the organisation's priorities. WWF has for its part generally coped well with the stresses of success. Some of the older complaints about IUCN from the days when funding was on a far more precarious basis have persisted, however, and these will be taken up shortly.

Prescriptions based on ecological analyses must at some point confront the reality of the nation-state in the international system. The Ramsar convention on wetlands, for example, was criticised by some conservationists for its lack of teeth; but it had to accommodate objections from governments that some of the earlier proposals would have eroded sovereignty to an unacceptable degree. The 1950 Paris convention on bird protection, on the other hand, was a closer reflection of conservationist opinion at the time, and hence ran into opposition from several countries. The principle that wildlife forms part of the natural resources of states, and that states have primary responsibility for its management and conservation, has been a crucial one in the international legal enterprises of the 1970s. Whether to engage in principled attack from outside or to aim for compromised influence from inside is a classic political dilemma that has also left its mark on conservation bodies, and that has been accentuated in the case of IUCN by that organisation's hybrid membership and by its twin commitments to both action and scientific repute. Both strategies were present in treatments by various NGOs of the problems of east African wildlife in the 1960s and 1970s. The heat of encounters over the annual Newfoundland seal cull was largely a function of the perceived identification of external conservation organisations — whether from abroad or from other parts of Canada — with urban values of softness and affluence. And while the argument that a particular species in a country may be threatened with extinction — there being no other populations of the creature in other parts of the world — can on the face of it be a powerful appeal for national action, the apparent whimsy of zoological taxonomy can throw a spanner into the political works. An interesting colouring here, or an unusual tuft of hair there, do not seem to be attributes worth making too many sacrifices for.

These kinds of constraints have made the appropriate organisational structure of conservation bodies a perennial topic of debate. Two international organisation models existed in the 1940s: the intergovernmental 1913 Consultative Commission on the one hand, and the non-governmental IOPN of the 1930s on the other. Partly on the basis of prompting from UNESCO, an extended version of the latter seemed not only the more practicable in the circumstances, but also the more suited to the requirements of world conservation. The mixed institutional format that resulted, particularly as more states or governmental agencies took out membership, has had both strengths and weaknesses. The former arise chiefly from the facility it lends to the union's performing a distinctive combination of roles in world society. These will be summarised in a moment. The hybrid character of IUCN is an advantage too to the extent, first, that conservationists in different countries share perceptions of their being participants in a movement the boundaries of which transcend conventional distinctions between governmental and non-governmental actors; second, less clearly the case, that such conceptions are founded upon realistic appraisals of the changing character of international relations. On the other hand, the search for a quasi-intergovernmental legitimacy seems to have added at times to inner dissensions. The intergovernmental level may seem seductive only because remote; conservationists less entranced by its potential have bucked at some of the costs. The presence of both state and non-state members also saddled the union with endless constitutional debate about the voting powers of different categories of members in sessions of its General Assembly, rumbling beneath the surface of which could often be found conflicting notions of intraorganisational democracy.

While IUCN has thus altered in various ways since 1948, it is probably not useful to try to divide its history into discrete phases. Identification of supposed fresh starts, in the past or immediate future, has been part of the mythology of international conservation since the beginning of the century and, as such, has played an important morale-building role. But continuities and gradual change are as likely to impress the more dispassionate observer. A number of roles of international conservation bodies can accordingly be discerned, though clearly these do not come complete in a neat package at the time an organisation is established. Nor can all of them necessarily be performed by all actors. The funding of various research, training, educational or management projects, for example, is an option available to relatively few. The ability to fund has often been the key to autonomy and visibility inside the conservation network and in the field, particularly in developing countries. Second, while IUPN in the early 1950s learned to fight shy of overt attempts to influence governments, this possibility surfaced again later, for example through WWF's high-level contacts or those environmental NGOs that had established close working relations with the Kenyan government. Third, one organ of IUCN has developed a significant advisory role in relation to the drafting of conservation legislation by states, while the union generally has been an important source of change in international law through its preparation of draft conventions. Through the provision of secretariat facilities, for example in relation to CITES, it has also been central to processes of implementation, monitoring and evaluations of changing requirements.

A more intangible set of functions centres on the genesis and spread of knowledge about threatened species and habitats. The gathering of basic facts on these subjects by IUCN, sometimes in league with other organisations as in the IBP and MAB programme, is its main claim to a clearly identifiable expertise in the world community, and its key, therefore, to legitimacy and influence. While its own publications have tended to have a somewhat restricted and more technical audience, its Assemblies and scientific meetings of various kinds have constituted, like WWF Congresses, forums for the initiating and exploring of conservation ideas. CITES had its origins in discussions at the Arusha conference in 1961; the Seattle national parks conference of 1962 later set in motion the 1965 planning for a threatened species conference which, as taken over by UNESCO, took shape as the 1968 biosphere conference and thus paved the way directly for UNCHE in 1972. The fact that such a body as IUCN exists has sometimes been a useful weapon in the hands of local groups endeavouring to bring pressure on governments. Even if the union itself takes no steps — a recurrent issue of the 1950s and 1960s was the extent to which it should involve itself in local situations — its prestige is a usable commodity, and its declarations on threatened species and habitats are potential ammunition. IUCN's linking function has accordingly been central. In the 1940s, the few nationally based organisations that did exist were scattered; even the presence of an international union in the 1950s did not necessarily create working connections, given financial constraints and the state of communications technologies. The process of network formation and development is thus a continuing one. Membership disputes, for example over hunters' organisations, have provided test cases for defining the boundaries of this network; IUCN has not by any means comprised all world conservation actors.

While IUCN can therefore claim with some justification that its praises have gone unsung, its comparative lack of political visibility has remained something of a check on its capacity to exercise leadership. As its first Secretary-General has commented, it has not evolved into an Amnesty International of the environment.[6] Within the conservation network, three kinds of factors have set restraints. A traditional one has been meagre resources and, perhaps more important, the atmosphere of uncertainty and caution produced by lack of guarantees for the future. Secondly, some constraints have been self-imposed. Cultivation of standing in what could, as some encounters with IUBS showed, be an unsympathetic international scientific community, and of acceptability within an already competitive world of intergovernmental organisations, was seen as a goal that necessitated a curbing of impulsiveness and bluntness. The more public role of WWF after 1961 served to confirm the union's occupying just such a niche, though rising pressure from environmental NGOs in the middle and later 1970s set up countervailing forces in the opposite direction. Thirdly, various characteristics of the conservation network make it a milieu not conducive to leadership roles of a kind that IUCN has, ironically, been criticised for not playing. Disagreements can be rife, conflict endemic. The nature of the subject may itself be a factor. Threatened species of wildlife seem to be more than usually adept at bringing to the surface the prima donna quality latent in any expert. Competitiveness is also an upshot of the sheer numbers of organisations involved at the non-governmental level. This in turn is in part a function of the sense of urgency attached to the problem: by a process of ecological succession, new groups arise to challenge or by-pass the alleged failings of older ones. In the late 1970s, WWF had for some already taken its place among the old guard of established organisations with origins lost deep in an imperial antiquity.

But this argument cannot be pushed too far. Interactor relations are also marked by co-operation. There is a co-ordination reflex. While this has been more evident in the 1970s, the development of constructive working relations between organisations going far beyond *modi vivendi* has long been a characteristic of the network, as the links in the 1930s between IOPN, ICBP and national bodies such as the ACIWLP amply demonstrated. Viewed from this perspective, indeed, there is some merit in the proliferation of organisations. As Fred Bergsten has noted, the history of international organisation shows that it is 'unwise to pursue co-ordination by locating functionally separate issues under a single institutional roof'.[7] Conservation of nature, on the face of it a neat bundle of technical questions, in practice comprises many different and arguably separate kinds of issues. Indeed one proponent of the 'virtues of chaos' has argued that pluralism and the fragmentation of responsibility among various organisations in a given functional area disperses initiative and releases energies; a state of 'organised disorganisation', another writer has suggested, may be necessary to cope with the unexpected.[8] The solutions to the problems posed by the number and diversity of conservation bodies would seem to lie, then, not so much in institutional amalgamation or the creation of yet more umbrella groupings, as in the unspectacular tending of day-to-day relations: purposiveness within a larger framework of *ad hoccery*, perhaps, rather than vice versa.

A more balanced conclusion, of course, is that both are needed. Certainly the trend in world conservation over the last decade or so has been more in the direction of concerted effort and the pursuit of longer term goals. This still leaves the criticism that IUCN has been slow to exploit opportunities to lead public opinion more generally in the direction of greater appreciation of the human costs of a rapidly deteriorating world natural environment. There are some problems with such calls. They can overlook the complexity of political processes. Publics can blow hot and cold on issues, especially on questions as immediately appealing to some as the saving of wild animals and wilderness areas. Informed or politically attentive publics can be ignored, in part because of a certain tendency on the part of specialists in the area to think in terms only of two basic kinds of writing, the scientific and the popular — the latter often polemical, derivative and oversimplified, and the former generally ignoring related questions that arise in the social sciences or humanities. There is the further obstacle that general statements of environmental problems, while having impact in the Stockholm atmosphere of the early 1970s, could appear dully repetitive declarations of the obvious only a few years later. Hence another dilemma. Since nature conservation is an issue that still has something of an old-fashioned aura clinging to it, an organisation like IUCN has had to emphasise all the more strongly that its roots lie in ecology; but since the resulting amalgam of concerns can then look indistinguishable from those voiced by any environmental group, the crucial attribute of distinctiveness can be blurred.

International conservation organisations, though, have in fact moved substantially away from being merely noises off in a general environmentalist clamour. Some have become integrated into policy processes at the national and international levels. A central nucleus of conservation actors, embracing both intergovernmental and non-governmental organisations on the one hand, and both traditional conservationist and developmental perspectives on the other, has emerged as a structural underpinning of these processes. But as the contrast between the Arctic and Antarctic cases indicated, there is not necessarily any concomitant uniformity in the manner in which world conservation questions are tackled. More particularly, it seems clear that, in this functional area at least, the state is not by any means being supplanted by the varied kinds of international actors that have come into existence over the last hundred years or so. Indeed it is the vitality of the national level that is increasingly evident. The taking of initiatives by state agencies, for example in relation to the trails that led to CITES and the Ramsar convention, can be an important determining factor in the successful take-off or premature crash-landing of ideas. The development of bilateral or multilateral environmental treaties has gone on in parallel to the activities of international organisations, and not necessarily been dependent upon them. Enthusiasm, in both its Greek and eighteenth-century senses, seems to be an irreplaceable energy source for world conservation, and one that is located primarily at national and local levels. Bodies such as IUCN/WWF thus have a multiplicity of roles: as actors, coaches, directors, producers, audience and auditorium — and, perhaps, as embryonic institutions of representative government for the other species of the planet.

# Bibliography

Anuchin, D. N., *Okhrana Pamyatnikov Prirody* (Moscow, 1914).

Baer, J. G., 'Aperçu historique de la protection de la nature', *Biol. Cons.*, 1(1), 1968, 7–11.

Berwick, E. J. M., 'The IUCN', *Biol. Cons.*, 1(3), 1969, 191–9.

Bougault, E., *La Protection des Animaux et le Droit International* (Bordeaux, 1937).

Bourlière, F., 'The Evolution of the Concept of Nature Protection', IUCN *Bull.*, 10 (1964), 1–2, 6.

Brouwer, G. A., *De Organisatie van de Natuurbescherming in de Verschillende Landen* (Amsterdam, 1931).

Buchinger, Maria, 'International cooperation in natural areas preservation', *BioScience*, 18 (1968), 388–92.

Budowski, G., 'The current state of world conservation', *Nature and Resources*, 9(1), 1973, 19–23.

Chichvarin, V. A., *Okhrana Prirody i Mezhdunarodnye Otnosheniia* (Moscow, 1970).

Colinvaux, P., *Why Big Fierce Animals are Rare: An Ecologist's Perspective* (Princeton University Press, 1979).

Coolidge, H. J., 'Advances in international conservation', *Science*, 120(3123), 1954, 742–4.

—— 'An outline of the origins and growth of the IUCN SSC', *Trans. N. Am. Wildl. Nat. Res. Conf.* 33 (1968), 407–17.

Curry-Lindahl, K., *Let Them Live: A World Wide Survey of Animals Threatened with Extinction* (New York: Morrow, 1972).

—— *Conservation for Survival: An Ecological Strategy* (New York: Morrow, 1972).

—— 'Background and development of international conservation organisations and their role in the future', *Env. Cons.*, 5(3), 1978, 163–9.

Dasmann, R. F., *Planet in Peril: Man and the Biosphere Today* (Harmondsworth: Penguin, 1972).

——, J. P. Milton and P. H. Freeman, *Ecological Principles for Economic Development* (New York: Wiley, 1973).

de Klemm, C., *Conservation et Amenagement du Milieu: Aspects Juridiques et Institutionnels Internationaux* (IUCN, 1969).

—— 'Species and habitat preservation: an international task', *Env. Policy and Law*, 1(1), 1975, 10–15.

Derschied, J.-M., 'La protection de la nature dans le monde', *Terre et Vie*, 1 (1931), 45–53.

de Vos, A., *Africa, the Devastated Continent?* (The Hague: Junk, 1975).

Dorst, J., *Avant que Nature Meure* (Neuchâtel: Delachaux et Niestlé, 1965).

—— 'Die Entwicklung des modernen Naturschutzgedankens', *Zool. Anzeiger*, 28 (1965), 213–31.

Drury, W. H., 'Rare species', *Biol. Cons.*, 6(3), 1974, 162–9.

Fitter, R. S. R., *The Penitent Butchers* (London: Collins, 1978).

Fraser Darling, F., 'Conservation and Ecological Theory', *J. Ecol.*, 52 (1964), 39–45.

—— 'Impacts of man on the biosphere', *Unasylva*, 22 (1968), 3–13.

Friends of the Earth International, 'World wildlife strategies', *FOE Link* (June 1979).

Goodwin, H. A. and J. M., *List of Mammals which have become Extinct or are Possibly Extinct since 1600* (IUCN, 1973).

Graham, E. H., 'A world network of research reserves', *New Scientist* (14 October 1965), 127–9.

Guruswamy, Lakshman, 'Eco-legal conspection and the New World Economic Order', *Earth Law J.*, 2(1), 1976, 23–42.

Harroy, J.-P., 'L'UICN: origine et constitution', *Biol. Cons.*, 1(2), 1969, 106–10.

Hayden, S. S., *The International Protection of Wild Life* (New York: Columbia University Press, 1942).

Heim, R., *Destruction et Protection de la Nature* (Paris: Armand Colin, 1952).

Herman, O., *The International Convention for the Protection of Birds ...* (Budapest: V. Hornyánszky, 1907).

Hudson, R., *Threatened Birds of Europe* (London: Macmillan, 1975).

Johnson, B., 'International environmental conservation', *Ambio*, 5(2), 1976, 55–65.

Jonkel, C., 'The Roles of International Groups in Wildlife Research and Management', *Proc. XIII Cong. Game Biologists* (Atlanta, 1977), 25–9.

Kiss, A., *Survey of Current Developments in International Environmental Law* (IUCN, 1976).

Linear, M., 'The economics of wildlife,' *Ceres*, 3(3), 1970, 51–4.

Lucas, G. Ll. and Synge, A. H. M., 'The IUCN Threatened Plants Committee and its work throughout the world', *Env. Cons.*, 4(3), 1977, 179–87.

Maldague, M., *Problématique de la Crise de l'Environnement* (Université Laval, 1973).

Mallinson, J., *The Shadow of Extinction: Europe's Threatened Wild Animals* (London: Macmillan, 1978).

Melville, R., 'Plant conservation and the Red Book', *Biol. Cons.*, 2(3), 1970, 185–8.

Meyer, R. L. 'Travaux préparatoires for the UNESCO World Heritage Convention', *Earth Law J.*, 2(1), 1976, 45–79.

Munro, D. A., 'The thirty years of IUCN', *Nature and Resources*, XIV(2), 1978, 14–19.

Myers, N., 'An expanded approach to the problem of disappearing species', *Science*, 193 (1976), 198–202.

—— 'Disappearing legacy', *Nature Canada*, October 1978, 41–54.

Navid, D. B., 'Draft International Convention on the Conservation of Migratory Species of Wild Fauna', *Env. Policy and Law*, 2(3), 1976, 116–19.

Nicholson, E. M., *The Environmental Revolution: A Guide for the New Masters of the Earth* (New York: McGraw-Hill, 1970).

O'Riordan, T., 'The Third American Conservation Movement', *J. Amer. Studies* (1971), 155–71.

Osborn, F., *Our Plundered Planet* (Boston: Little, Brown, 1948).

Passmore, J., *Man's Responsibility for Nature: Ecological Problems and Western Traditions* (New York: Scribner's, 1974).

Poore, D., 'Conservation and development', *Env. Cons.*, 2(4), 1975, 243–6.

—— 'IUCN: a dynamic strategy', *Env. Cons.*, 4(3), 1977, 119–20.

Quinet, Dr, *Protection Internationale des Oiseaux: Notes Critiques sur le Concordat de Paris de 1895* (Bruxelles: Vanbuggenhoudt, 1898).

Ratcliffe, R. A., 'Thoughts towards a philosophy of nature conservation', *Biol. Cons.*, 9(1), 1976, 45–54.

Regenstein, L., *The Politics of Extinction: The Shocking Story of the World's Endangered Wildlife* (New York: Macmillan, 1975).

Reiger, G., 'The world shepherds its wildlife', *Int. Wildl.*, 3(4), 1973, 4–13.

Ribaut, J.-P., 'Conservation de la nature et recherche scientifique', *Mém. Soc. Vaudoise des Sciences Naturelles*, No. 90. Vol. 14 (1968), 233–58.

Robinson, N. A., 'Migratory bird species conventions', *Earth Law J.*, 2(IV), 1976, 415–22.

Russell, C., 'Environment and development,' *Biol. Cons.*, 7(3), 1975, 227–34.

Sachs, I., 'Ecodevelopment', *Ceres*, 7(1), 1974, 8–12.

Sasson, A., *Développement et Environnement: Faits et Perspectives dans les Pays Industrialisés et en voie de Développement* (Paris: Mouton, 1974).

Singh, N., 'A world charter for nature', *Env. Policy and Law*, 3(1), 1977, 24–6.

Strong, M. F., 'The international community and the environment', *Env. Cons.*, 4(3), 1977, 165–72.

Talbot, L. M., *A Look at Threatened Species* (FPS, 1960).

Train, R., 'Convention for the protection of the world cultural and natural heritage', *Nature and Resources*, 9(1), 1973, 2–7.

UICN, 'Conservation de la flore et de la faune', in *Ressources Naturelles de l'Asie Tropicale Humide* (UNESCO, 1974), pp. 427–46.

UNEP, 'Register of International Conventions and Protocols in the Field of the Environment', Doc. UNEP/GC/Info./5 (7 February 1977).

Vincent, J., 'List of birds either known or thought to have become extinct since 1600', IUCN *Bull.*, 16 (1965), Suppl.

Vollmar, F., 'The WWF in the 1970s', *Biol. Cons.*, 3(2), 1971, 85–7.

Walter, I., 'Environmental management and the International Economic Order', in F. Bergsten (ed.), *The Future of the International Economic Order: An Agenda for Research* (Heath, 1973), Ch. 9.

Ward, B. and Dubos, R., *Only One Earth: The Care and Maintenance of a Small Planet* (London: Deutsch, 1972).

Ziswiler, V., *Extinct and Vanishing Animals: A Biology of Extinction and Survival* (New York: Springer-Verlag, 1967).

# Notes

## Preface

1 J.-P. Harroy, 'La conservation mondiale, 1948–1978: célébration et évaluation' (mimeo., 1978), p. 1.
2 S. S. Hayden, *The International Protection of Wild Life* (New York: Columbia University Press, 1942).
3 V. A. Chichvarin, *Okhrana Prirody i Mezhdunarodnye Otnosheniia* (Moscow 1970).
4 R. F. Dasmann, *Environmental Conservation*, 3rd edn (New York: Wiley, 1972), p. 431.

## Chapter 1  The changing character of international organisation

1 Dien Zuh-wing, in ICBP *Bull.*, VIII (1962), p. 45.
2 W. F. Lothian, *A History of Canada's National Parks*, Vol. I (Ottawa: Parks Canada, 1976), p. 12.
3 The literature on these subjects is vast and cannot be summarised here. For two recent surveys and discussions, see R. W. Mansbach *et al.*, *The Web of World Politics: Non-state Actors in the Global System* (Englewood Cliffs: Prentice Hall, 1976); Charles Pentland, 'International Organizations', in J. N. Rosenau *et al.* (eds), *World Politics* (New York: Free Press, 1976), pp. 624–59.
4 E. H. Carr, *The Twenty Years' Crisis* (New York: Harper and Row, 1964).
5 R. F. Hopkins, 'The international role of "domestic" bureaucracy', *International Organisation*, 30(3), 1976, 406.
6 D. P. Forsyth, 'The Red Cross as transnational movement: conserving and changing the nation-state system', *International Organisation*, 30(4), 1976, 607–30.
7 As the last body indicates, national as well as various categories of international bodies can fulfil these kinds of roles.
8 See in particular the chapter by A. J. N. Judge in A. J. R. Groom and P. Taylor (eds), *International Organization: A Conceptual Approach* (London: Pinter, 1978). The term 'international organisation' has been used in the present study to cover a number of institutions of different types.
9 See T. A. Hockin, 'Adversary politics and some functions of the Canadian House of Commons', in R. Schultz *et al.* (eds), *The Canadian Political Process* 3rd edn (Toronto: Holt, Rinehart and Winston, 1979), pp. 325–6. It is not, of course, being suggested that the two kinds of bodies are equivalent in their roles or power.

NOTES    189

*Chapter 2    Conserving nature: issues and perspectives*

1  W. H. Auden: *A Selection by the Author* (Harmondsworth: Penguin, 1958), p. 169.
2  Management of Natural Resources in Africa: Traditional Strategies and Modern Decision-Making (UNESCO: MAB Technical Notes, 9, 1978), p. 81.
3  E. Leach, *Lévi-Strauss* (London: Fontana/Collins, 1970), p. 40.
4  G. Soutar, *Nature in Greek Poetry* (London: Milford, 1939), p. 8.
5  *Sir Gawain and the Green Knight*, trans. B. Stone (Harmondsworth: Penguin, 1959), p. 54; *Beowulf*, trans. E. Morgan (University of California Press, 1966), p. 39.
6  Joan Barclay Lloyd, *African Animals in Renaissance Literature and Art* (Oxford: Clarendon Press, 1971), pp. 17, 119.
7  Pratapaditya Pal, *The Arts of Nepal*, Part II (Leiden: E. J. Brill, 1978), p. 105.
8  Margaret Atwood, *Survival: A Thematic Guide to Canadian Literature* (Toronto: Anansi, 1972), p. 73.
9  W. G. Hoskins, *The Making of the English Landscape* (Harmondsworth: Pelican, 1970), p. 139.
10  G. M. Trevelyan, *Illustrated English Social History*, Vol. 3 (Harmondswoth: Pelican, 1964), p. 196.
11  H. R. Fairclough, *Love of Nature among the Greeks and Romans* (New York: Longmans, Green, 1930), p. 4.
12  R. Williams, *The Country and the City* (Oxford University Press, 1973), pp. 124–5, 128, 287.
13  Gilbert White, *The Natural History of Selborne*, ed. R. Mabey (Harmondsworth: Penguin, 1977), pp. 103–4.
14  Charles Dickens, *The Posthumous Papers of the Pickwick Club* (London: Hazell, Watson and Viney, n.d.), p. 11.
15  E. Warming, *Oecology of Plants: An Introduction to the Study of Plant Communities* (Oxford: Clarendon Press, 1909), pp. 368–9.
16  See e.g. A. E. Roland and E. C. Smith, *The Flora of Nova Scotia* (Halifax: Nova Scotia Museum, 1969), p. 5.
17  See the survey cited by Desmond Morris, *Manwatching: A Field Guide to Human Behaviour* (London: Cape, 1977), p. 265.
18  H. A. and J. M. Goodwin, *List of mammals which have become extinct or are possibly extinct since 1600* (IUCN, 1973).
19  V. H. Cahalane, in *Yosemite Nature Notes*, XXVI (5), 1947, p. 67.
20  *The IUCN Plant Red Data Book*, comp. G. Lucas and H. Synge (IUCN, 1978), p. 3.
21  D. Western, *An aerial method of monitoring large mammals and their environment*, Kenya Game Dept. and UNDP/FAO: Project KEN: 71/526, Doc. 9 (1976).
22  Charles Darwin, *The Origin of Species* (New York: Literary Classics, n.d.), pp. 46–7.
23  J.-P. Ribaut, 'Conservation de la nature et recherche scientifique', *Mém. Soc. Vaudoise des Sciences Naturelles*, No. 90, Vol. 14 (1968). 238–9.
24  IUPN, *Proc. 2nd sess. Gen. Ass.* (1950), p. 25.
25  V. Ziswiler, *Extinct and Vanishing Animals: A Biology of Extinction and Survival* (New York: Springer-Verlag, 1967), Chs 1, 2.

26  R. van der Woude and A. Van Wijngaarden, *Animals in Danger: A Study of Certain Mammal Species Threatened with Extinction in Europe* (Council of Europe, 1969), p. 10.

27  J. Heslop-Harrison, 'The plant kingdom: an exhaustible resource?', *Trans. Bot. Soc. Edinburgh*, 42 (1973–4), 5.

28  P. Palmgren, 'Notes on the spiders of some vanishing habitats in the surroundings of Helsingfors', *Mem. Soc. Pro Fauna et Flora Fennica*, 53 (1), 1977, 39–42.

29  T. Harrisson, 'Notes on marine turtles: 18', *The Sarawak Museum Journal*, xv (30–1), 1967, 430.

30  M. Nicholson, *The Environmental Revolution: A Guide for the New Masters of the Earth* (New York: McGraw-Hill, 1970), pp. 308–35.

31  Cited by J. Rodman, 'The liberation of nature?', *Inquiry*, 20 (1), 1977, 115.

32  Soutar, op. cit., p. 6n.

33  Cited by Singer, *Animal Liberation* (London: Paladin, 1977), p. 26.

34  P. Singer, op. cit.

35  Ramanlal C. Shah, *Lord Mahavir and Jainism* (Mombasa: Shree Jain Shvetamber Deravasi Sangh, n.d.), pp. 9–11.

36  J. Harry *et al.*, 'Conservation: An upper-middle class social movement', *Journal of Leisure Research*, 1 (1969), 246–54.

37  *The Times*, 25 September 1978.

38  Morris, op. cit., p. 266.

39  O. S. Kolbasov, 'Leninskiye idei ob okhrane prirody', *Priroda* (1958), 41–4.

40  Preface to Chichvarin, op. cit., p. 3.

41  Cheng Tso-hsin, *Zhongguo Niaolei Fenbu Minglu*, 2nd edn (Peking: Science Press, 1976), p. xii.

42  A. Wierzbicki, 'Czlowiek a środowisko naturalne w Stanach Zjednoczonych Ameryki Pn.', *Sylwan*, cxxi (9), 1977, 17–41.

43  'UNSCCUR, Final Report (Pt. I)', Doc. NSC D. 819 (n.d.), p. 13.

44  T. U. Keil, article in *Naturwissenschaften* republished in *Universitas*, 20 (2), 1978, 145.

45  A. G. Bannikov and B. N. Bogdanov, 'Conservation as a long term development tool', in IUCN, *Papers and Proc. 12th Tech. Mtg.* (1972), p. 125.

46  Sir Peter Scott, conversation with the author, May 1978.

47  F. G. A. Smit, 'A new bird-flea from Peru', *Zool. J. Linnaen Soc.*, 62 (1978), 189–92; Jun-ichi Aoki, 'A new species of oribatid mite found in the middle of Tokyo', *Bull. Nat. Sci. Mus. Tokyo*, 17 (4), 1974, 283–5.

48  E. Wilson, 'The nature of human nature', *New Scientist*, 5 October 1978, p. 22.

49  *India News*, 22 June 1972, pp. 2–3.

50  L. J. Lundqvist, *Environmental Policies in Canada, Sweden and the U.S.* (Sage Prof. Paper, 1974), pp. 6, 22.

51  UNEP/GC/31, 11 February 1975.

52  UNEP/GC/60, 21 January 1976, p. 24.

Chapter 3    Origins and evolution

1  C. Sachs, *The Wellsprings of Music*, ed. J. Kunst (New York: McGraw-Hill, 1965), p. 33.
2  Hoskins, op. cit., p. 138.
3  O. Lattimore, in *Pacific Affairs*, 50 (3), 1977, 428.
4  G. P. Dementiev, 'La protection de la nature en URSS', *Terre et Vie* (1957), 305–17.
5  M Maršákova-Němejcová and Š. Mihálik, 'Vývoj Chráněných Území v ČSSR', *Československá Ochrana Prírody*, 16 (1976), 1.
6  W. A. Baillie-Grohman, 'The chamois', in C. Phillipps-Wolley (ed.), *Big Game Shooting*, Vol. II (London: Longmans, Green, 1894), p. 77.
7  O. Herman, *The International Convention for the Protection of Birds....* (Budapest: Victor Hornyánszky, 1907), p. 32.
8  L. R. Brightwell, *The Zoo Story* (London: Museum Press, 1952), pp. 39–41.
9  House of Commons, *Report from the Select Committee on Wild Birds Protection*, 23 July 1873, App. 5.
10  Herman, loc. cit.
11  *Feathers and Pacts* (RSPB, n.d.), p. 26.
12  Phyllis Barclay-Smith, 'The British contribution to bird protection', *Ibis*, 101, 1959, 115–22.
13  Herman, op. cit., p. 33.
14  Dr Quinet, *Protection internationale des oiseaux: notes critiques sur le concordat de Paris* (Bruxelles: Vanbuggenhoudt, 1898), pp. 6–9.
15  Herman, op. cit., pp. 126–37; Phyllis Barclay-Smith, in ICBP *Bull.*, x (1967), pp. 118–9.
16  See *Congrès International pour l'étude et la protection des oiseaux* (Luxembourg, 1925), p. 25.
17  'Noch einmal ein Chocolat-Taler', *Schweizer-Naturschutz*, XIII (1947), 1.
18  E. Larsson and R. Bollvik, *Vi och vår natur: natur- och miljövård i Sverige*, 3rd edn (Stockholm: LTs Förlag, 1976), p. 294; and *Sveriges Natur* (1910), 21.
19  V. Nielsen, 'Om vaern om vore omgivelser', *Nordisk Administrativt Tidsskrift*, 56, 1975, 137–53.
20  Zbigniew Kawecki, 'Stulecie nowoczesnej ochrony przyrody w Polsce', *Przeglad Zoologiczny*, XII (3), 1968, 249 ff.
21  D. N. Anuchin, *Okhrana Pamyatnikov Prirody* (Moscow, 1914), pp. 6 ff.
22  R. S. R. Fitter, *The Penitent Butchers* (London: Collins, 1978).
23  Anuchin, op. cit., pp. 4–6.
24  *Congrès International pour la Protection des Paysages* (Paris, 1909), Compte Rendu.
25  *Conférence International pour la Protection de la Nature* (Berne, 1913), Proc.-Verb., pp. 23 ff.
26  Ibid., pp. 187–91.
27  J. Büttikofer, in *International Conference for the Protection of Nature* (Brunnen, 1947), Proc., pp. 132–3; *Conference for the International Protection of Nature* (Basle, 1946), pp. 61–2.
28  ICBP, *Bull.* (1927), pp. 3, 18. An international committee for bird protection had been set up in 1910 at the 5th International Ornithological Congress in Berlin, but the two developments were not directly related. See G. A. Brouwer,

*De Organisatie van de Natuurbescherming in de Verschillende Landen* (Amsterdam, 1931), p. 43.
29 ICBP, *2nd Bull.* (1929), p. 7.
30 See further his *Adventures in Bird Protection* (New York: Appleton-Century, 1937).
31 ICBP, *2nd Bull.* (1929), p. 4.
32 *International Conference on the Protection of Migratory Waterfowl* (London, 1927), Report.
33 On its history see J. H. Koeman, 'De Nederlandse Commissie voor Internationale Natuurbescherming haar verleden en toekomst' (Amsterdam, 1975, mimeo.).
34 IOPN, *Report for the Years 1940–46*, pp. 8–10.
35 IOPN, *The IOPN* (1936), pp. 9–10.
36 IOPN, *Synoptic Summary of the Principal Legislative Measures concerning the Protection of Birds* (1932); and the summary by Tienhoven in *2e Congrès International pour la Protection de la Nature* (Paris, 1931), pp. 133–8.
37 H. C. Carey, 'Saving the animal life of Africa,' *J. of Mammalogy*, 7 (2), 1926, 77–85.
38 H. J. Coolidge, Jr., 'Brief History of the Formation of the ACIWLP', *Yearbook of the Boone and Crockett Club* (1930).
39 G. M. Allen, *Extinct and Vanishing Mammals of the Western Hemisphere* (ACIWLP, 1942); F. Harper, *Extinct and Vanishing Mammals of the Old World* (ACIWLP, 1945).
40 IOPN, *Report for the Years 1940–46*, p. 12.
41 See reports by Col. A. H. W. Haywood and Maj. R. W. G. Hingston respectively at *J. of the SPFE*, Pt. 16 (Sept. 1932), 27 ff.; Pt. 18 (Jan. 1933), 32 ff.; Pt. 12 (1930), 21–57.
42 *2e Congrès International pour la Protection de la Nature* (Paris, 1931), pp. 106–8, 330–2.
43 Marquis of Dufferin, in *FO. 2nd Int. Conf. for the Preservation of the Fauna and Flora of Africa* (London, 1938), Doc. PFF 38, p. 2.
44 *FO. Int. Conf. for the Preservation of the Fauna and Flora of Africa* (London, 1933), Doc. PFF 7.
45 *The London Convention for the Protection of African Fauna and Flora* (ACIWLP, 1935).
46 Hayden, op. cit., pp. 62 ff.
47 Brouwer, op. cit., p. 38.
48 Hayden, op. cit., pp. 67–89.
49 IOPN, *Report for the Years 1940–46*.
50 ICBP *Bull.*, vi (1952), p. 48.
51 *Brunnen Conf.*, p. 50.
52 *Basle Conf.*, p. 42 (italics added).
53 Ibid., pp. 14–15.
54 J. Huxley, *Memories II* (New York: Harper and Row, 1973), p. 127.
55 Ibid., pp. 34, 50–1.
56 'UNSCCUR. Mem. from Chairman to members of NRC Co. on UNESCO' (mimeo., n.d.), p. 11; and 'UNSCCUR, Final Report (Pt. I)', Doc. NSC D. 819 (n.d.), p. 63.
57 Ibid., pp. 64–5.

58 Cited at 'UNSCCUR. Mem. from Chairman to members of NRC Co. on UNESCO' (n.d.), pp. 8–9.
59 Doc. IOPN/C/8, *Brunnen Conf.*, p. 146.
60 Letter to Dr Westermann, cited ibid., p. 147.
61 'Explanatory "hierarchical" list of international scientific organisations', UNESCO/Cons./Exec./2e sess./27 (1947), pp. 1–2.
62 'Chronological List of NYZS Conservation Achievements' (mimeo., 1974), pp. 17–18.
63 Doc. IOPN/C/5.
64 *Brunnen Conf.*, pp. 149–50.
65 Ibid., pp. 149–50, 152–63, 169, 188, 199–200. At the suggestion of an IUBS delegate the term 'Union' was used in preference to 'Organisation' to express better what was planned, and also to avoid the new body having the same initials as the existing IOPN (ibid., p. 183).
66 UNESCO, Exec. Bd., Programme Co., 4th sess., EX/4CP/3 (1948), p. 15.
67 *IUPN: Established at Fontainebleau, 5 October 1948* (Brussels, 1948), p. 4. The statutes are at pp. 16 ff.
68 H. J. Coolidge, Jr., 'The birth of a Union', *National Parks* (1949), p. 2.
69 'Minutes of the Natural Sciences Panel of the US National Commission for UNESCO, 27 September 1948', mimeo., pp. 6–7.
70 UNESCO, Gen. Conf., 3rd sess., Programme and Budget Commission, Subcommission of Natural Sciences, 3C/PROG/5.4 (1948), p. 2.

*Chapter 4   Scientific development : knowledge and its uses*

1 A. A. Milne, *The House at Pooh Corner* (London: Methuen, 1928), p. 63.
2 IOPN, *Report for the Years 1940–46*, pp. 1–2.
3 IUPN, *Proc. 3rd sess. Gen. Ass.* (1952), pp. 44–5.
4 IUCN, *Proc. 9th sess. Gen. Ass.* (1966), pp. 125–6.
5 H. J. Coolidge, Jr., 'The growth and development of international interest in safeguarding endangered species ...', *Proc. XV Int. Cong. of Zoology* (London, 1958), p. 58.
6 C. Elton, *The Ecology of Invasions by Animals and Plants* (London: Methuen, 1958).
7 IUBS, *Proc. XIV sess. Gen. Ass.* (1961), p. 22.
8 A. MacFadyen, 'Some thoughts on the behaviour of ecologists', *J. of Ecol.*, 63 (2), 1975, 388–9.
9 Harper, op. cit.; Allen, op. cit.
10 IOPN, *Report for the Years 1940–46*, pp. 30 ff.
11 UNESCO, *Int. Tech. Conf. on the Protection of Nature* (1949), Doc. UNESCO/IUPN/Conf. 2/15, pp. vii–ix (hereafter cited as *Lake Success Conf.*).
12 Ibid., pp. 499 ff.; pp. 504–15.
13 *Lake Success Conf.*, pp. 25, 129 ff., 177 ff.
14 IUPN *Bull.*, II (4), 1953, p. 2.
15 IUPN, *Proc. 4th sess. Gen. Ass.* (1954), p. 43.
16 L. M. Talbot, *A Look at Threatened Species* ... (FPS, 1960), pp. 5–6, 10, 13–94.
17 On the last, see reports by Grimwood, *Oryx*, VI (6), 1962, 308–34; VII (5), 1964, 223–6.

18 IUCN, *Proc. 7th sess. Gen. Ass.* (1960), p. 76.
19 IUCN, *Proc. 8th sess. Gen. Ass.* (1963), p. 113.
20 *Mammalia, Red Data Book 1* (IUCN, 1966).
21 E.g. WWF, *The Launching of a New Ark: 1st Report of the WWF*, 1961–64, pp. 155 ff.
22 J. Fisher, N. Simon and J. Vincent (eds), *Wildlife in Danger* (London: Collins, 1969).
23 IUPN, *Proc. 4th sess. Gen. Ass.* (1954), p. 59.
24 IUCN, *Proc. 9th sess. Gen. Ass.* (1966), p. 80.
25 E.g. *Rote Liste der gefährdeten Tiere und Pflanzen in der Bundesrepublik Deutschland* (Greven: Kilda Verlag, 1978).
26 ICBP *Bull.*, XI (1971), pp. 147–8.
27 IUCN *Bull.*, 9(6), 1978, p. 29.
28 IUCN, *Proc. 8th sess. Gen. Ass.* (1963), p. 113.
29 IUCN *Bull.*, IX (1–2), 1960, p. 3.
30 *The Behaviour of Ungulates and its Relation to Management*, Symp., Univ. of Calgary (1971), (IUCN, 1974), p. 11; and *Wolves. Proc. 1st Mtg. of Wolf Specialists and of 1st Int. Conf. on the Conservation of the Wolf*, Stockholm (1973), (IUCN, 1976), pp. 12–13.
31 *Lake Success Conf.*, pp. 135–7.
32 ICBP *Bull.*, VI (1952), p. 21.
33 IUPN, *Proc. 3rd sess. Gen. Ass.* (1952), pp. 52–3.
34 J. C. Greenway, *Extinct and Vanishing Birds of the World* (ACIWLP, 1958).
35 J. L. Peters, *Check List of Birds of the World*, 10 vols. (Harvard University Press, 1931–64).
36 IUCN, *Proc. 5th sess. Gen. Ass.* (1956), pp. 88, 92–3; ICBP *Bull.*, VII (1958), pp. 16, 37–40, 131.
37 ICBP *Bull.*, VIII (1962), pp. 72–6, and IX (1963), pp. 78–80.
38 IUCN *Bull.*, 16 (1965), Suppl.
39 Vincent, at ICBP *Bull.*, X (1967), pp. 82 ff.
40 IUCN *Bull.*, VI (5), 1957, p. 2.
41 See n. 22 above, comments by R. R. Miller on p. 339.
42 *Lake Success Conf.*, pp. 137, 139, 185.
43 IUPN, *Proc. 2nd sess. Gen. Ass.* (1950), pp. 26–7, 49; *3rd sess.* (1952), pp. 53–5.
44 *Angiospermae, Red Data Book 5*, comp. R. Melville (IUCN, 1970–1).
45 G. Ll. Lucas and A. H. M. Synge, 'The IUCN Threatened Plants Committee and its work throughout the world', *Env. Cons.*, 4(3), 1977, 179–87; and IUCN, *Proc. 13th sess. Gen. Ass.* (1977), pp. 18, 79.
46 G. Ll. Lucas and A. H. M. Synge, 'Threatened Higher Plants', IUCN Doc. GA.78/10 Add. 5, p. 7.
47 IUCN, *Proc. 5th sess. Gen. Ass.* (1956), pp. 82–5.
48 IWRB *Newsl.*, 11 (1961), p. 35.
49 IUCN *Bull.*, 3 (1962), pp. 1–2.
50 IWRB *Newsl.*, 12 (1961).
51 *Project MAR.... Proc. Conf. Les Sainte-Maries-de-la-mer* (1962), (IUCN, 1962), pp. 26 ff.; and *List of European and North African Wetlands of International Importance* (IUCN, 1965), pp. 10–12.
52 *Proc. Tech. Mtg. on Wetland Conservation*, Ankara-Bursa-Istanbul (1967), (IUCN, 1968), pp. 3, 265.

53 IUCN, *Proc. 9th sess. Gen. Ass.* (1966), p. 60; *10th sess.*, pp. 95–7. See also H. Luther and J. Rzoska, *Project Aqua: A Source Book of Inland Waters Proposed for Conservation*, ICBP Handbook, 21 (Oxford: Blackwell, 1971).
54 IUBS, *Proc. XIV sess. Gen. Ass.* (1961), pp. 22–4.
55 E. B. Worthington, 'The Relationships between IUCN and IBP/CT', IUCN *Bull.*, 17 (1965), pp. 1–2.
56 *Proc. Conf. on Productivity and Cons. in Northern Circumpolar Lands* (Edmonton, 1969).
57 MAB, *Exp. Panel on Project 8, Final Report* (UNESCO: MAB rept. series, 12, 1973), pp. 5–6, 18–19, 38–43.
58 R. F. Dasmann, 'Towards a system for classifying natural regions of the world and their representation by national parks and reserves', *Biol. Cons.*, 4 (4), 1972, 247–55; and his *Classification and Use of Protected Natural and Cultural Areas* (IUCN, 1973).
59 M. D. F. Udvardy, *A Classification of the Biogeographic Provinces of the World* (IUCN, 1975); G. Carleton Ray, *A Preliminary Classification of Coastal and Marine Environments* (IUCN, 1975).
60 Ibid., p. 5; *International Classification and Mapping of Vegetation* (UNESCO: Ecol. and Cons. Series, 6, 1973); *A Working System for Classification of World Vegetation* (IUCN, 1973).
61 MAB, Int. Co-ordinating Council, 5th sess. (1977), (UNESCO: MAB rept. series, 46, 1977), p. 35.
62 *Lake Success Conf.*, p. 165, Doc. UNESCO/IUPN/Conf. 2/IV/1.
63 G. Atkinson Willes, 'The importance to wildfowl of the reservoirs in England and Wales', *J. Brit. Waterworks Ass.*, 43(1961), 151–4.
64 IUCN, *Proc. 5th sess. Gen. Ass.* (1956), p. 113.
65 IUCN, *Proc. 7th sess. Gen. Ass.* (1960), p. 43.
66 *1st Wld. Conf on Nat. Parks* (Seattle, 1962), Washington, DC: Nat. Parks Service, Dept. of the Interior (1962), p. 381.
67 The origins of these can be traced to discussions at IUCN's 1960 General Assembly.
68 IUCN, *Proc. 11th sess. Gen. Ass.* (1972), p. 247.
69 IUCN, *Proc. 9th sess. Gen. Ass.* (1966), p. 45.
70 *MAR Conf.*, p. 55.
71 IUCN *Bull.*, 8(4), 1977, pp. 23, 25.
72 R. Dasmann, J. P. Milton and P. H. Freeman, *Ecological Principles for Economic Development* (New York: Wiley, 1973). See further M. T. Farvar and J. P. Milton, (eds), *The Careless Technology: Ecology and International Development* (New York: Doubleday, 1972).
73 IUCN *Bull.*, 3(10), 1972.

*Chapter 5    Political development: constraints and influence*

1 J. J. Rousseau, *Oeuvres Complètes*, I (Paris: Editions Gallimard, 1959), pp. 1135–6.
2 IUCN, *Proc. 7th sess. Gen. Ass.* (1960), p. 66.
3 IUCN, *Proc. 8th sess. Gen. Ass.* (1963), p. 42.

4 IUCN *Bull.*, 10(1), 1979, p. 1.

5 IUPN, *Proc. 2nd sess. Gen. Ass.* (1950), pp. 49, 63; *3rd sess.* (1952), p. 38; *4th sess.* (1954), pp. 27, 34.

6 IUCN, *Proc. 5th sess. Gen. Ass.* (1956), p. 34.

7 IUCN, *Proc. 9th sess. Gen. Ass.* (1966), p. 94.

8 IUCN *Bull.*, iv (1), 1955; 6 (1963), p. 4.

9 WWF, *The Ark under Way: 2nd Report of the WWF, 1965–67*, p. 47.

10 WWF, *Yearbook 1974–5*, pp. 52–3.

11 IUCN, *Proc. 10th sess. Gen. Ass.* (1969), p. 121.

12 M. Coe and K. Curry-Lindahl, 'Ecology of a mountain: 1st Rept. on Liberian Nimba', *Oryx*, viii (3), 1965, 177–84.

13 See reports by Grimwood at *Oryx*, vi (6), 1962, 308–34; vii (5), 1964, 223–5.

14 WWF, *2nd Report, 1965–67*, pp. 7, 46, 49.

15 WWF, *Yearbook 1974–75*, p. 44.

16 WWF, *Yearbooks* for 1973–4, pp. 176–7; 1971–2, p. 85; 1969, p. 143.

17 WWF, *Yearbook 1974–75*, p. 23.

18 Published by Elsevier.

19 Cited at IUCN, *Proc. 7th sess. Gen. Ass.* (1960), p. 96.

20 Ibid., p. 71.

21 *1st Wld. Conf. on Nat. Parks* (Seattle, 1962), Washington, DC: Nat. Parks Service, Dept. of the Interior (1962), pp. 376, 380, 384.

22 IUCN, *Proc. 10th sess. Gen. Ass.* (1969), pp. 22, 156.

23 IUCN *Bull.*, 3(11), 1972, pp. 51–2, Suppl.

24 Brussels, 1951.

25 IUCN, *Proc. 7th sess. Gen. Ass.* (1960), pp. 40–1.

26 IUCN, *Proc. 11th sess. Gen. Ass.* (1972), pp. 15, 102, 149–52; and *An International Environmental Law Information System* (Bonn: E. Schmidt Verlag, n.d.).

27 See e.g. A. Kiss, *Survey of Current Developments in International Environmental Law* (IUCN, 1976).

28 IUCN *Bull.*, 5(2), 1974, p. 6; 5(3), p. 10.

29 IUCN, Environmental Law Centre, *1976 Annual Rept.*, App. II, pp. 21 ff.; IUCN, 'Activities in the Law and Policy Field.... 1977–78' (mimeo., 1978), pp. 11–13.

30 IUCN, *Proc. 8th sess. Gen. Ass.* (1963), p. 136; *9th sess.* (1966), p. 165.

31 Ibid., p. 119.

32 *Project Tiger: A Planning Proposal for Preservation of Tiger ... in India* (New Delhi: Indian Bd. for Wild Life, 1972), p. 11; WWF, *Yearbook 1974–5*, pp. 185–6.

33 *Lake Success Conf.*, pp. 151–8, 187.

34 IUPN, *Proc. 3rd sess. Gen. Ass.* (1952), pp. 60–1; *4th sess.* (1954), pp. 42–3.

35 IUCN *Bull.*, 8(10), 1977, p. 59; 9(10–11), 1978, p. 58.

36 IUPN, *Proc. 3d sess. Gen. Ass.* (1952), p. 24.

37 IUCN, *Proc. 7th sess. Gen. Ass.* (1960), p. 154.

38 IUCN, *Proc. 8th sess. Gen. Ass.* (1963), p. 130.

39 IUCN, *Proc. 10th sess. Gen. Ass.* (1969), pp. 54, 109, 121–2, 158.

40 See further A. W. Reitze, Jr., *Environmental Planning: Law of Land and Resources* (Washington, DC: North American International, 1974), section Ten-13.

41 IUCN *Bull.*, 4(3), 1973, p. 10.
42 'Chronological List of NYZS Conservation Achievements' (mimeo., 1974), pp. 52–4.
43 Indeed, close contacts maintained between US conservationists and Kenyan officials were an important background factor in the development of the convention.
44 A copy of the text is at IUCN *Bull.*, 4(3), 1973, Suppl.
45 CITES, *2nd Mtg. Conf. of the Parties* (1979), Doc. 2.5, p. 3; TRAFFIC *Bull.*, 1(5), 1979, p. 1.
46 CITES, *Proc. Special Wkg. Sess., Conf. of the Parties* (1977), pp. 3–4; *Proc. 1st Mtg. Conf. of the Parties* (1976), Docs. 1.1–3, pp. 31–5.
47 IUCN, *Proc. 12th sess. Gen. Ass.* (1975), p. 117; *13th sess.* (1977), p. 80.
48 Ibid. *13th sess.*, p. 81; D. B. Navid, 'Draft international convention on the conservation of migratory species of wild fauna', *Env. Policy and Law*, 2(3), 1976, 116–9.
49 Text at *Env. Policy and Law*, 5, 1979, 156–60; IUCN *Bull.*, 11(1–2), 1980, Suppl.
50 IUCN, *Proc. 5th sess. Gen. Ass.* (1956), p. 63.
51 'UNSCCUR, Final Report (Pt. I),' Doc. NSC D. 819 (n.d.), p. 71.
52 IUPN, *Proc. 3d sess. Gen. Ass.* (1952), p. 36.
53 IUCN, *Proc. 7th sess. Gen. Ass.* (1960), p. 67.
54 *Lake Success Conf.*, pp. 29–63, 179, 181.
55 IUPN, *Proc. 2nd sess. Gen. Ass.* (1950), p. 65.
56 IUCN, *Proc. 9th sess. Gen. Ass.* (1966), p. 144.
57 H. J. Coolidge, Jr., 'The growth and development of international interest in safeguarding endangered species ...', *Proc. XV Int. Cong. of Zoology* (London, 1958), pp. 58–9.
58 IUPN, *Activity ... from its establishment to 1 Jan., 1950*, p. 4.
59 IUPN *Bull.*, 1(1), 1952, p. 1; IUCN *Bull.*, 9(7–8), 1978, p. 35.
60 Published as the first in a projected *Pro Natura* series, 1954.
61 Fisher *et al.*, op. cit.
62 IUCN, *Proc. 5th sess. Gen. Ass.* (1956), p. 33.
63 (IUCN, 1976), p. 13.
64 MAB, International Co-ordinating Council, 4th sess. (1975) (MAB Rept. 38), p. 21.

*Chapter 6    Network development : policy-making in a complex milieu*

1 IUCN, *Yearbook 1973*, pp. 30–1.
2 IOPN, *Report for the Years 1949 and 1950.*
3 *Lake Success Conf.*, pp. 559 ff.
4 IUPN, *Proc. 2nd sess. Gen. Ass.* (1950), p. 46; ICBP *Bull.*, VI (1952), p. 17.
5 IUPN, *Proc. 3d sess. Gen. Ass.* (1952), p. 53.
6 On the background to this work see Phyllis Barclay-Smith, op. cit., pp. 121–2.
7 ICBP *Bull.*, 4 (1935), p. 14.
8 ICBP *Bull.*, XII (1975), p. 63; ICBP, *The President's Letter*, 42 (1977), pp. 5–6.
9 E. Hindle, 'International Wildfowl Conservation, 1936–61', IWRB *Newsl.*, 12 (1961), pp. 3–12; ICBP *Bull.*, VII (1958), p. 47; G. V. T. Matthews, 'The IWRB', *Wildfowl*, 20 (1969), 94–7.

10 IUCN *Bull.*, 9(7–8), 1978, p. 47.
11 Victor Stolan, a journalist, wrote to Huxley and started the process. See WWF, *The Launching of a New Ark : 1st Rept. of the WWF, 1961–64*, pp. 26–8, 31–2.
12 IUCN *Bull.*, 2 (1961), p. 2.
13 Figures from IUCN, *Annual Reports*.
14 WWF, *1st Report*, p. 46.
15 IUCN *Bull.*, 3(12), 1972, pp. 55–6.
16 IUCN *Bull.*, 8(12), 1977, pp. 72–3; 9(7–8), 1978, p. 36.
17 *World Directory of Environmental Organisations*, 2d edn (Sierra Club, 1976).
18 IUPN *Bull.*, II(6), 1953, p. 1.
19 Sierra Club, Off. of Int. Env. Affs., 'International Program' (n.d.)
20 For a recent critical view, see W. Jordan and S. Ormrod, *The Last Great Wild Beast Show* (London: Constable, 1978).
21 Jeremy Mallinson, Letter to the author, November 1978.
22 NYZS, 'Chronological List of NYZS Conservation Achievements' (mimeo., n.d.)
23 This work is discussed later in Chapter 8.
24 IUPN, *Proc. 2nd sess. Gen. Ass.* (1950), Annex II, p. 57.
25 G. P. Dementiev, in *Cons. of Natural Resources and the Establishment of Reserves in the USSR*, transl. Nat. Sci. Foundn. (Washington, DC, 1960), p. 7.
26 IUCN *Bull.*, 10(9), 1979, p. 92.
27 IUCN, *Proc. 12th sess. Gen. Ass.* (1975), p. 244.
28 Africa figures here exclude South Africa. Source: IUCN, *Membership List, 30 June 1976* (mimeo.).
29 IUPN, *Proc. 4th sess. Gen. Ass.* (1954), p. 27.
30 IUCN, *Statutes 1963; Statutes 1972; Statutes as adopted by the 13th (Extr.) Gen. Ass.... 1977; Statutes as revised by the 14th sess. Gen. Ass.... 1978.*
31 IUCN, *Proc. 13th sess. Gen. Ass.* (1977), pp. 164–5.
32 IUCN, *Proc. 5th sess. Gen. Ass.* (1956), p. 62.
33 IUCN, *Proc. 11th sess. Gen. Ass.* (1972), p. 275.
34 At the 13th N. Am. Wildl. Conf., St Louis, March 1948; see *Lake Success Conf.*, pp. 133, 486.
35 IUPN, *Proc. 3rd sess. Gen. Ass.* (1952), p. 32; *10th sess.* (1969), p. 10; *Bull.*, 9 (10–11), 1978, p. 61.
36 IUCN, *Proc. 7th sess. Gen. Ass.* (1960), p. 94.
37 IUCN, *Proc. 10th sess. Gen. Ass.* (1969), p. 54.
38 *Maclean's*, 29 October 1979, p. 44b.
39 Coolidge, at IUCN, Doc. GA.11.Conf.5.
40 FAO, CONF. (1959), 10th, par. 264; (1965), 13th, par. 196; (1967), 14th, par. 385.
41 FAO, CONF. (1975), 18th sess., Doc. C 75/3, p. 171. On the organisational structure, see Docs. C 75/3, Annex, pp. 437 ff.; C 77/3.
42 UNEP/PROG/3, pp. 100–22.
43 UNEP/GC/31, p. 20. On institutional arrangements, see further UNEP/GC/75, p. 11.
44 Council of Europe, Co. of Mins., Res. (67)24, (73)31, (77)6, (77)7.
45 *Conservation of Nature in the Soviet Union* (Moscow: Ministry of Agriculture, 1972), p. 31.
46 Adapted from UNEP/GC/60, Table 4, p. 29.

47 IUCN *Bull.*, 9(5), 1978, p. 25.
48 UNEP/GC/53, Decision 46 (iii); UNEP/GC/77, pp. 1–3; NGO Env. Liaison Bd., *Rept. on UNEP Proj. RB-0303-75-01* (1976).
49 UNEP/GC/Info./4, 17 February 1977.
50 The Programme Planning Advisory Group. See IUCN *Bull.*, 10(4), 1979, p. 26.
51 IUCN *Bull.*, 10(11), 1978, p. 64.

*Chapter 7    Polar conservation*

1 Elspeth Huxley, *Scott of the Antarctic* (New York: Athenaeum, 1978), p. 72.
2 B. Roberts, 'International organisation for Polar exploration', *Polar Record*, 5 (1949), 332.
3 Cited by Büttikofer, *Brunnen Conf.*, p. 131.
4 Roberts, op. cit., pp. 332–4.
5 P. D. Baird, 'The Arctic Institute of North America', *Polar Record*, 8 (1956), 22–3.
6 In G. S. Schatz (ed.), *Science, Technology, and Sovereignty in the Polar Regions* (New York: Lexington Books, 1974), p. 15.
7 R. F. Dasmann, 'Conservation in the Antarctic', *Ant. J. of the US*, III (1), 1968, 1, 3.
8 R. C. Murphy, 'Conservation of the Antarctic fauna', in *Biologie Antarctique. Symp. organisé par le SCAR, 1962* (Paris: Hermann, 1964), pp. 574–5.
9 A. E. Porsild, 'Land use in the Arctic', *Proc. 2nd Alaska Sci. Conf.* (1951), pp. 75–80.
10 S. M. Uspensky and L. K. Shaposhnikov, 'Okhrana zhivotnogo mira arktiki', *Priroda*, 6 (1957), 29–34.
11 C. Vibe, 'Vilde dyrs forhold til mennesket i arktiske egne', *Grønland*, 3 (1953), 119–20.
12 IUPN, *Proc. 4th sess. Gen. Ass.* (1954), pp. 48, 63.
13 K. Curry-Lindahl, 'Conservation of Arctic fauna and its habitats', *Polar Record*, 17 (1974), 245.
14 IUCN *Bull.*, VII (1958), p. 2.
15 *New York Times*, 6 June 1965; R. Murphy, ibid., 28 March 1965.
16 *New York Times*, 11 July 1965; *Cong. Rec.*, 89th Cong., 1st sess., 13 July 1965, Vol. III, No. 126, Senate.
17 *Proc. 1st Int. Mtg. on the Polar Bear* (Fairbanks, 1965), p. 6.
18 Ibid., pp. 13, 15, 40, 42, 58.
19 Ibid., p. 66.
20 See the report by the group's secretary, R. A. Cooley, in IUCN *Bull.*, 2(7), 1968, pp. 54–6.
21 IUCN *Bull.*, 2(17), 1970, p. 149.
22 *Proc. Conf. on Productivity and Cons. in Northern Circumpolar Lands* (Edmonton, 1969), pp. 32–6.
23 C. Jonkel, 'Some comments on polar bear management', *Biol. Cons.*, 2(2), 1970, 115–9.
24 IUCN *Bull.*, 2(17), 1970, pp. 149–51.
25 A. H. Macpherson, in *Trans. 35th Fed.-Prov. Wildlife Conf.* (Toronto, 1971), p. 17.

26 *Proc. 3d Wkg. Mtg., Polar Bear Spec. Gp.* (Morges, 1972), pp. 6–15.
27 W. O. Pruitt, Jr., in *Trans. Royal Society of Canada*, 4th series, VII (1970), p. 21; Macpherson, loc. cit.
28 *Hansard*, H. of Commons, 29th Parlt., 1st sess., Vol. VIII, p. 8122 (26 November 1973).
29 Ibid., II, p. 1217, 1353; III, p. 3076; VII, p. 7626; VIII, p. 8122.
30 *Conf. to prepare an Agreement on the Cons. of Polar Bears* (Oslo, 1973), Final Act and Summary Record, p. 33.
31 *New York Times*, 11 October 1972; 16 February 1972.
32 *Oslo Conf.*, p. 26.
33 The term 'taking' was open to varied interpretation; see e.g. 'An Analysis of the Canadian Explanatory Declaration' (n.d.)
34 *Proc. 5th Wkg. Mtg., Polar Bear Spec. Gp.* (St. Prex, 1974), pp. 8–9, 20, 22.
35 IUCN *Bull.*, 7(5), 1976, p. 25.
36 *Birds Notes and News*, 10 (1905), pp. 65–7; 11 (1905), pp. 81–3, 90–1.
37 *Falkland Islands Gazette*, Vol. 19, No. 11 (1909), pp. 164–5.
38 The islands were, however, declared a reserve in 1934. See H. Barraclough Fell, 'The fauna of New Zealand', *Nature*, 147/3722 (1941), pp. 253–4.
39 *Bull. of the ICBP* (1927), p. 7; ICBP *Bull.*, VI (1952), pp. 110–12, 181–2.
40 *Conf. on Antarctica ... The Antarctica Treaty, Washington, 1 December 1959*, Treaty Series No. 97, Cmd. 1535 (1961).
41 G. de Quetteville Robin, 'Formes de mesures suggérés pour encourager la conservation de la nature dans l'Antarctique', *Terr. des Terres Australes et Antarctiques Françaises*, 17 (1961), 36–50. For a summary of the 1960s meetings of SCAR, see G. Llano, 'Antarctic conservation', in *Proc. Coll. on Conservation Problems in the Antarctic* (Blacksburg, 1971), pp. 3 ff.
42 See n. 8 above.
43 Cmd. 2822 (1965).
44 *Seattle Conf.*, pp. 281–6.
45 ICBP *Bull.*, VIII (1962), pp. 17, 31–2; IX (1963), pp. 39–40.
46 B. Roberts, in *Phil. Trans. Royal Soc.*, B. 279 (1977), p. 100; D. Anderson (of the Foreign Office), in *Polar Record*, 14 (1968), 25.
47 SCAR *Bull.*, 19 (Jan. 1965); Cmds. 3404, 3993.
48 Llano, op. cit., p. 3.
49 Cmds. 4698, 5502.
50 R. Perry, *The Polar Worlds* (New York: Taplinger, 1973), p. 285.
51 SCAR *Bull.*, 57 (Sept. 1977), pp. 209–13.
52 See Dasmann, op. cit. in n. 7 above.
53 IUCN *Bull.*, 9(4), 1978, p. 23.
54 Cmd. 5502; SCAR *Bull.*, 53 (May 1976), p. 125.
55 IUCN *Bull.*, 10(4), 1979, p. 25.
56 IUCN, 14th sess. Gen. Ass. (1978), *Resolutions*, p. 5.

*Chapter 8 East African wildlife*

1 L. Harries, *Swahili Poetry* (Oxford: Clarendon Press, 1962), p. 161.
2 Helge Kjekshus, *Ecology Control and Economic Development in East African*

*History: The Case of Tanganyika, 1850–1950* (London: Heinemann, 1977), p. 69.
3 E. N. Barclay, *Big Game Shooting Records* (London: Witherby, 1932), pp. 18–20.
4 Cited by B. Grzimek, *No Room for Wild Animals* (London: Thames and Hudson, 1956), p. 59.
5 R. Tjader, *The Big Game of Africa* (New York: Appleton, 1910), pp. 299–303.
6 E.g. C. G. Schilling, *With Flashlight and Rifle* (London: Hutchinson, 1906); Col. Sir James Sleeman, *From Rifle to Camera: The Reformation of a Big Game Hunter* (London: Jarrolds, 1947), pp. 188–9.
7 Capt. C. H. Stigand, *The Game of British East Africa* (London: Cox, 1909), pp. 218 ff.
8 N. C. Pollock, *Animals, Environment and Man in Africa* (London: Saxon House, 1974), pp. 137 ff.
9 Republic of Kenya, *National Report on the Human Environment in Kenya* (Nairobi, 1971), p. 56.
10 Pollock, op. cit., pp. 71–2.
11 Sleeman, op. cit., pp. 192–3, quoting official statistics.
12 J. of the SPFE, I(1904), pp. 29–37; Hayden, op. cit., pp. 36–7.
13 *FO. Int. Conf. for the Preservation of the Fauna and Flora of Africa* (London, 1933), Doc. PFF 26.
14 *FO. 2nd Int. Conf. for the Preservation of the Fauna and Flora of Africa* (London, 1938).
15 L. M. Talbot, in *Proc. Jt. Mtg. ASRM/SAF/SCSA* (Logan, 1967), p. 5.
16 'Africa: Species of Mammals in Danger of Extinction', Doc. PFF 7 (1933).
17 *Lake Success Conf.*, pp. 65, 73, 113–23, 177 ff.
18 IUPN, *Proc. 2nd sess. Gen. Ass.* (1950), p. 51.
19 IUPN *Bull.*, II(6), 1953, p. 2.
20 IUCN *Bull.*, VI(6), 1957, p. 3.
21 IUCN, *Proc. 7th sess. Gen. Ass.* (1960), App. III, pp. 127 ff.
22 *Conservation of Nature and Natural Resources in Modern African States. Report of a Symposium ...* (Arusha, 1961), p. 9.
23 Ibid., p. 13.
24 IUCN, *Proc. 7th sess. Gen. Ass.* (1960), pp. 47–8.
25 *Tanzania. Coll. of African Wildlife Management* (FAO. FO: DP/URT/70/530, 1973), pp. 1–10; UNDP/FAO. FO: DP/URT/70/530, Aug. 1975).
26 IUCN, *Proc. 8th sess. Gen. Ass.* (1963), p. 65.
27 *Arusha Conf.*, pp. 69 ff.
28 IUCN, *Proc. 8th sess. Gen. Ass.* (1963), pp. 40, 129.
29 'Historical Note', in *OAU. African Convention on the Conservation of Nature and Natural Resources* (Addis Ababa: Gen. Sect., OAU, 1968).
30 K. Curry-Lindahl, 'The new African Conservation Convention', *Oryx*, X (2), 1969, 118.
31 Ibid., 119–20; OAU, *African Convention*.
32 Ibid. OAU.
33 Bogdanov, at IUCN, *Proc. 9th sess. Gen. Ass.* (1966), p. 45.
34 UNDP/FAO. *East African Livestock Survey*, I (FAO/SF, 1967), pp. 151, 155.
35 Col. and Prot. of Kenya, Game Dept., *Annual Report 1956–7*, p. 1.
36 Col. and Prot. of Kenya, Game Dept., *Annual Report 1960*, pp. 2–3.

37 Cited at Royal National Parks of Kenya, *Report 1959–60*, pp. 3–4.
38 Col. and Prot. of Kenya, Game Dept., *Annual Report 1961*, p. 1.
39 Cited by E. Robins, *Africa's Wild Life: Survival or Extinction?* (London: Odhams, 1963), pp. 40, 45–6.
40 Ibid., p. 50.
41 IUCN, *Proc. 8th sess. Gen. Ass.* (1963), p. 121.
42 From 'Chronological List of NYZS Conservation Achievements' (mimeo., 1974).
43 See further issues of *Jahresber. des Zoo. Gartens der Stadt Frankfurt a/M*.
44 *AWLF* (Nairobi, 1978, mimeo.); AWLF *News*, 8(1), 1973, and 9(1), 1974, pp. 16–18; statement by R. McIlvaine, *Daily Nation*, 9 February 1978.
45 L. Hoffmann and H. Jungius, 'Conservation in Tropical Africa', *Acta Tropica*, 29(4), 1972, 494–7; WWF, *Yearbook 1973–74*, p. 323.
46 See e.g. H. F. Heady, *Range Management in East Africa* (Kenya Dept. of Agr. and EAAFRO, 1960).
47 See n. 34 above.
48 Yuda Komora, *Daily Nation*, 11 February 1978.
49 IBRD, *The Economic Development of Kenya ...* (Baltimore: Johns Hopkins Press, 1963), pp. 171–2, 174; IBRD, *Kenya: Into the Second Decade* (Baltimore: Johns Hopkins Press, 1975), p. 500; Rep. of Kenya, *Development Plan 1970–74*, Ch. 16, pp. 427–8, 499; *Development Plan 1974–78*, Pt. 2, pp. 176 ff.
50 Clement Lubembe, Ass. Min. for Tourism and Wildlife, reported at *Daily Nation*, 24 February 1978. Cf. Perm. Sec. Komora; ibid., 11 February 1978; for a report on the trophy trade and Somali poaching, Gary Thatcher in *Christian Science Monitor*, 23 January 1979.
51 Comments by representatives of the Wildlife Clubs of Kenya, East African Wild Life Society, and Wild Life Society of Kenya, at *Daily Nation*, 25 February 1978, and *Sunday Nation*, 19 February 1978; Fibi Munene, 'What impact has the trophy ban?', *Daily Nation*, 17 February 1978.

*Chapter 9    Migratory bird protection*

1 Richard Mabey (ed.) (Harmondsworth: Penguin, 1977), pp. 62–3.
2 Foreword to J. Dorst, *The Migration of Birds* (Cambridge: Houghton Mifflin, 1962), p. vii.
3 R. E. Moreau, *The Palaearctic-African Bird Migration Systems* (New York: Academic Press, 1972), p. 44.
4 ICBP, *5th Bull.* (1939), pp. 54–5.
5 Herman, op. cit., pp. 126–37.
6 ICBP, *2nd Bull.* (1929), pp. 2–4.
7 ICBP *Bull.*, VI (1952), pp. 50–1.
8 Text ibid., pp. 56–9. There was no official English language version; this quasi-official one was prepared by Phyllis Barclay-Smith of ICBP.
9 Phyllis Barclay-Smith, 'Position of the International Convention for the Protection of Birds, Paris, 1950', ICBP *Bull.*, X (1967), pp. 118–20.
10 Ibid., pp. 120–4.

11  IUCN, *Proc. 9th sess. Gen. Ass.* (1966), p. 199.
12  Council of Europe, Parliamentary Assembly. *Report on the Protection of Birds and their Habitats in Europe*, Doc. 3798 (1976), pp. 8–9; *FAZ*, 17 March 1975.
13  See above, Ch. 3, n. 32.
14  For a brief summary see Sir Dudley Stamp, *Nature Conservation in Britain* (London: Collins, 1974), Chs 2, 5, 11.
15  ICBP *Bull.*, VI (1952), p. 50. ICBP meetings in Vienna and Rouen in 1937 and 1938, respectively, were major occasions for discussion of migratory wildfowl data gathered by the British.
16  IWRB *Newsl.*, 1 (November 1955), p. 8. On later IWRB correlation work see IWRB *Newsl.*, 4 (November 1957).
17  IWRB *Newsl.*, 7 (July 1959), p. 20.
18  ICBP *Bull.*, VIII (1962), pp. 17, 20–1; IWRB *Newsl.*, 7 (July 1959), p. 20.
19  IWRB *Newsl.*, 14 (December 1962), pp. 7–8.
20  *MAR Conf.*, pp. 26 ff.
21  *List of European and North African Wetlands of International Importance* (IUCN, 1965).
22  *Proc. 1st Euro. Mtg. on Wildfowl Conservation* (St. Andrews, 1963), pp. 273 ff.
23  ICBP *Bull.*, X (1967), p. 21; IWRB *Newsl.*, 17–18 (1964), p. 1; 19–20 (1965), p. 23.
24  IWRB *Newsl.*, 17–18 (1964), p. 11; *Proc. 2nd Euro. Mtg. on Wildfowl Conservation* (Noordwijk aan Zee, 1966), pp. 209 ff.
25  IWRB *Newsl.*, 23–24 (1967); 25–26 (1968).
26  *Proc. Tech. Mtg. on Wetland Conservation*, Ankara-Bursa-Istanbul, 1967, pp. 265 ff.
27  ICBP *Bull.*, X (1971), pp. 67–8; *Proc. Int. Regional Mtg. on Conservation of Wildfowl Resources* (Leningrad, 1968).
28  IWRB *Bull.* (1969), pp. 22 ff.
29  On the reasons for preferring 'waterfowl' over 'wildfowl' see IWRB *Bull.* (1971), p. 6.
30  *Final Act of the Int. Conf. on the Conservation of Wetlands and Waterfowl* (Ramsar, 1971).
31  *Rept. Int. Conf. on the Conservation of Wetlands and Waterfowl* (Heiligenhafen, 1974), Annex II.
32  IUCN, *Proc. 11th sess. Gen. Ass.* (1972), pp. 15–16.
33  *Int. Conf. on the Conservation of Wetlands and Waterfowl*, Final Act and Summary Record (Ramsar, 1971), pp. 5–6.
34  Gianfranco Bologna, 'La Migrazione degli uccelli', *Pro Avibus*, IX (6), 1974, pp. 3–6.
35  Aristide Meschia, 'Ancora dell'uccellagione?', *Pro Natura* (Milano), XXIV (85), 1975, pp. 2–3; Elizabeth David, *Italian Food* (Harmondsworth: Penguin, 1963), p. 247.
36  J. Vincent, 'List of Bird Species appearing in the Red Data Book ...' (ICBP, mimeo., 1968), pp. 1–3.
37  ICBP *Bull.*, X (1967), pp. 21, 37; on the 1952 Bologna meeting, ibid., VII (1958), p. 11.
38  Council of Europe, Co. of Mins., Res. (67)24, and (67)25.
39  *Study of Birds in Need of Special Protection in Europe* (Strasbourg: Council of Europe, 1974).

40 Council of Europe, Co. of Mins., Res. (73)31; the report cited in n. 12 above, pp. ii–iii, 4, 7, 13–14.
41 ICBP *Bull.*, xi (1971), pp. 43–4, 50, 53, 223–4; on the 1972 Romania meeting, ibid., xii (1975), p. 33.
42 *Jahresber. des Zoo. Gartens der Stadt Frankfurt a/M*, 115 (1973), p. 36.
43 LIPU, *La Posizione della LIPU sulla Caccia in Italia* (Doc. della Lega, N. 1, n.d.), pp. 2, 7, 8.
44 EEC, OJ No. C 112 (Dec. 20, 1973), p. 40.
45 *Agence Europe Bull.*, 2111 (10 December 1976), p. 4; 2121 (24 December 1976), p. 5.
46 'Modifications of a Proposal for a Council Directive on Bird Conservation', COM (77) 379 (29 July 1977). For the original proposal see Commission of the European Communities, 'Proposition de Directive du Conseil concernant la Conservation des Oiseaux', COM (76) 676 (20 December 1976).
47 *Agence Europe Bull.*, 2347 (12 December 1977), p. 4; 2348 (14 December 1977), p. 8.
48 IUCN *Bull.*, 9 (7–8), 1978, p. 46.

*Chapter 10    Wildlife conservation and world politics*

1 Iona and Peter Opie, *The Lore and Language of Schoolchildren* (Oxford University Press, 1959), p. 240.
2 K. Deutsch (ed.), *Ecosocial Systems and Ecopolitics* (UNESCO, 1977), p. 359.
3 V. Kożak *et al.*, *The Héta Indians: Fish in a Dry Pond* (New York: Am. Mus. Nat. Hist., 1979), p. 391.
4 M. F. D'Souza, M. S. Abdel Salam and D. C. Murphy, 'The Epidemiology of Allergy in Kuwait: A Pilot Random Survey', (Sabah, mimeo., n.d.), pp. 7–8.
5 Lettre au Commissaire de Région, No. 245/044/Rte/74, 2 October 1974, in Archives, Dept. Polit. Affs., Mongala Subregion, Lisala.
6 Harroy, op. cit., p. 2.
7 Fred Bergsten, 'Interdependence and the reform of international institutions', *International Organisation*, 30(2), 1976, 370.
8 D. H. Henning, *Environmental Policy and Administration* (New York: Elsevier, 1974), pp. 48–50, citing research by M. Grodzins on recreation systems. The second phrase is Burton Klein's.

# Index